BLACK AMERICA SERIES

BLACKS AT BRADLEY

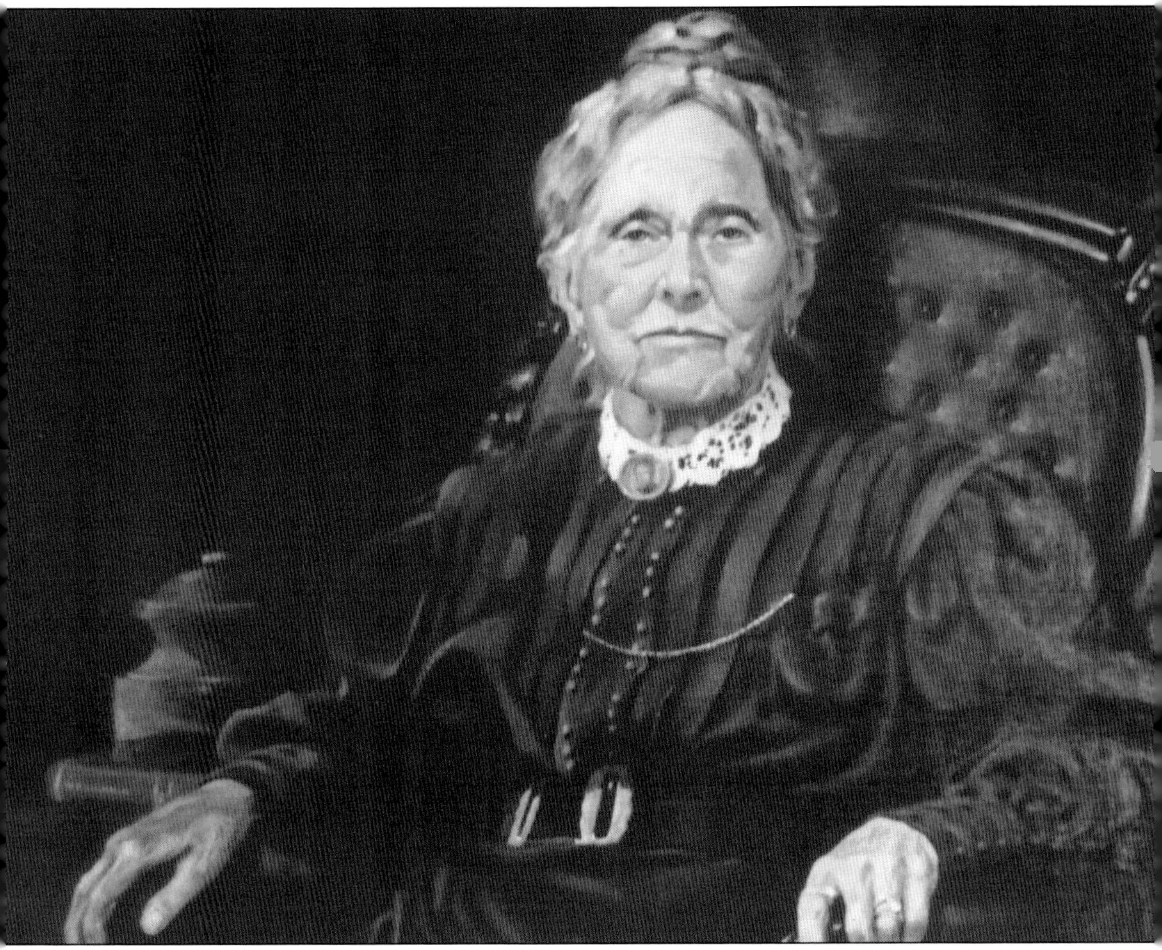

In this picture from the early 1900s, Mrs. Lydia Moss Bradley, founder of Bradley University (1897), is seated at her home in Peoria. Mrs. Bradley was born in Vevay, Indiana on July 30, 1816, and was the owner of several properties and profitable businesses in Peoria. At the time of her death she was one of the wealthiest women in the United States. Although her life was filled with tragedy, including the death of her husband and all six of her children before the age of 14, Mrs. Bradley supported numerous causes and groups—including African-American churches and providing scholarships for African-American students. For the African Americans who attended the institution, her philosophy of providing a quality education for anyone regardless of sex, class, or race would have a long-lasting impact, even after her death at the age of 91 on January 16, 1908.

Cover design Shanon Hymbaugh.
Photographic credits Duane R. Zehr.

BLACK AMERICA SERIES

BLACKS AT BRADLEY

1897–2000

Arwin D. Smallwood, Ph.D
Assistant Professor of History and Director of African-American Studies
Bradley University

ARCADIA
PUBLISHING

ISBN 978-0-7385-0824-5

Published by Arcadia Publishing
Charleston, South Carolina

Printed in the United States of America

Library of Congress Catalog Card Number: 2001086880

For all general information contact Arcadia Publishing at:
Telephone 843-853-2070
Fax 843-853-0044
E-Mail sales@arcadiapublishing.com
For customer service and orders:
Toll-Free 1-888-313-2665

Visit us on the Internet at www.arcadiapublishing.com

Contents

ACKNOWLEDGMENTS

This book would not have been possible without the assistance and support of the following:

First, and most importantly, I would like to thank God and my loving wife, Alisa Mayfield Smallwood. Since I was a graduate student, she has taken her time to read and critique my work. She has always been honest and supportive, and I have always loved her for it. Again as always she has proven to be invaluable in completing this work; her suggestions, comments, and support were much needed and greatly appreciated. I am blessed to have her as my wife, mother of my children, and best friend.

I must also thank the students in my History of Bradley class, which I taught in the fall of 1996, as part of Bradley's centennial celebration. In teaching the course, I thought it might interest students to read early newspaper articles and review old annuals in order to give them a feel for early life at the university. They were required to photocopy articles and images that struck them as being significant. The students involved in this initial project were as follows: Glen E. Birnbaum, Eva Braxton, Jamal R. Buchanan, Michelle Caffarello, Jason M. Feiner, Ira Finn, Latoya I. Grady, Charles J. Hammer, Emily M. Harter, Kristen M. Kargus, Jami Michelle Krogmeier, Ryan Ladage, Deborah A. Mast, Allison Renae McDonald, Kristine E. Miyata, Jeremy I. Moy, Gretchen L. Petrakis, Shane D. Pitzer, Nancy A. Ridgeway, Nesby Rodriguez, Angela M. Schwiers, Holly J. Wasserman, and Lacretia T. Young.

Due to the success of this class, I assigned the same topic for my AAS 300 courses in the spring of 1997 and the spring of 1998, on contemporary issues in African-American History with the requirement that students identify and reproduce materials only pertaining to African Americans. The students involved in the spring 1997 class included: Butch Acena, Jamal Buchanan, Dakia Hargrett, Arletha Johnson, and Brenda McFadden. The students involved in the spring 1998 class included: Kendrick Bailey, Sherman Fernandes, Leonardo Linval, Juan Martinez, Melissa Williams, Layla Willingham, and Robert Joynt. I also worked with a number of these students as a research mentor. Student involvement in this project was invaluable and highlights Bradley University's commitment to teaching students inside as well as outside the classroom.

Special thanks also goes to staff of the Special Collections Department of the Cullom-Davis Library, especially Mr. Charles Frey, Mrs. Karen Deller, and Mrs. Sherri Schneider, who assisted my students and research assistants in navigating the collection and allowing materials from special collections to be photographed for inclusion in this work. I would also like to thank Duane Zehr, University Photographer, who completed the photography and assisted in the scanning of images for inclusion in this book as well as Shanon Hymbaugh for her extraordinary cover design.

Finally, I would like to thank several administrators, including: David Broski, President, for giving permission to use his photo; Gary Anna, Vice President for Business Affairs, for approving the use of certain images in the book; and Kent Huntsman, for helping to identify, contact, and gather photos of African-American alumni of note for inclusion in this work. Most importantly, I would like to thank the hundreds of African-American students who have passed this way and have left a lasting legacy of which all past, present, and future students of Bradley can be proud.

INTRODUCTION

The founder of Bradley University, Mrs. Lydia Moss Bradley, was an extraordinary woman. Not only did she run a successful business, which made her a millionaire by 1897 when she founded Bradley University, but she also carried on philanthropic work all over the city of Peoria. Today there is scarcely an institution, from churches and hospitals to parks, that has not benefited from her early efforts. For African Americans who lived and worked in the community, she was just as generous. From providing money for Black churches to funding Black scholarships for education, Mrs. Bradley recognized the needs in the Black community and assisted where and when she could. Her family had owned slaves in Kentucky, and by her adulthood in Indiana she had grown to loathe the institution of slavery and has been rumored to have assisted the Underground Railroad in smuggling slaves out of the South. Therefore, it is not surprising that when she founded Bradley, she founded an open institution where women and men, rich and poor, Black and White could obtain an education that would improve their quality of life, their community, and their nation. Although her other numerous accomplishments and legacies have been documented, little has been mentioned about her relationship with African Americans and the impact her decision in founding this institution had on them. No one has discussed in depth the impact that her scholarships and open admissions policy had on determining whether there would be an African-American presence at Bradley.

By 1963, hundreds of African Americans had passed through Bradley amidst circumstances that were less than ideal. However, they had been given an opportunity for an education at a majority-White institution that would have been denied them in the South and in many state and private schools in the state of Illinois. African Americans like Nathaniel Horn, class of 1977; Henry Thomas, class of 1974; Edwin Ukpaby, class of 1980; Willie Scott, class of 1983; D. Lyneir Richardson, class of 1987; Jean Miller; Garry Moore; Pam Adams; Leo Harman; Rita Ali; John Stenson, class of 1975; the first African-American police chief in the history of Peoria; Laraine Bryson, president of the Tri-County Urban League, class of 1977; Nathan Martin, class of 1984; the first African-American student body president; Mitchell "J.J." Anderson (he played basketball in the NBA and overseas in Europe, where he was known as the Michael Jordan of the sport; his jersey was retired), class of 1982. Therefore, it is important that this story be told as honestly and accurately as possible. This is a task that has been made both more important and more difficult due to the loss of sources.

In January of 1963, Bradley Hall, one of the four original buildings on Bradley's campus, was gutted and virtually destroyed by a fire that was nearly impossible to extinguish due to the sub-zero temperatures which caused the hoses to freeze. With the loss of thc original Bradley Hall in this fire, and the student records it contained, no effort was made until now to reconstruct or document the African-American presence and contributions to the institution. Using annuals, student newspapers, and photos provided by African-American alumni, this nearly lost history is being documented for the first time. This book is not intended to be the definitive history of Blacks at Bradley. The intention is to uniquely document a history that was virtually untraceable in any other way.

One

An Open Door
The First Students of Color at Bradley
1897–1943

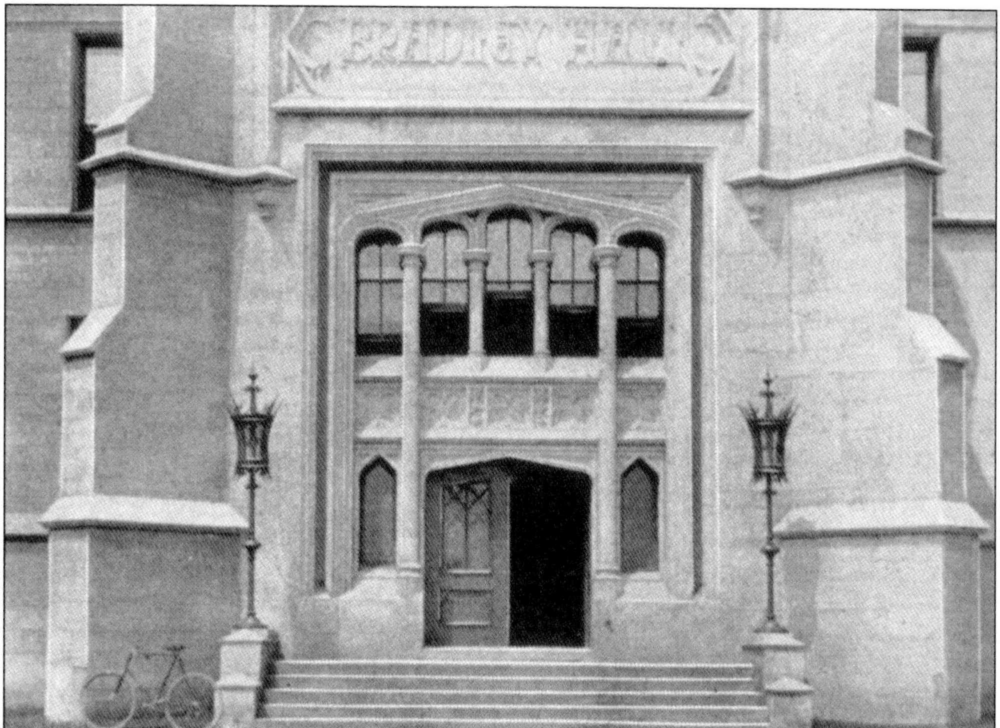

This photo, taken around 1897, shows Bradley Hall with one of its doors open. The photo is symbolic in that it shows the intent of the university—that all students, regardless of their race, class, or sex were free to attend. In fact, not only was Mrs. Bradley known to provide scholarships for some of the first African-American students, but all students (at her request) were only responsible for the cost of books and supplies, in effect attending the institution at no cost. The absence of any students in this picture captures the spirit of many of the early African-American students. Nameless and faceless, but present as part of Bradley University from its beginning.

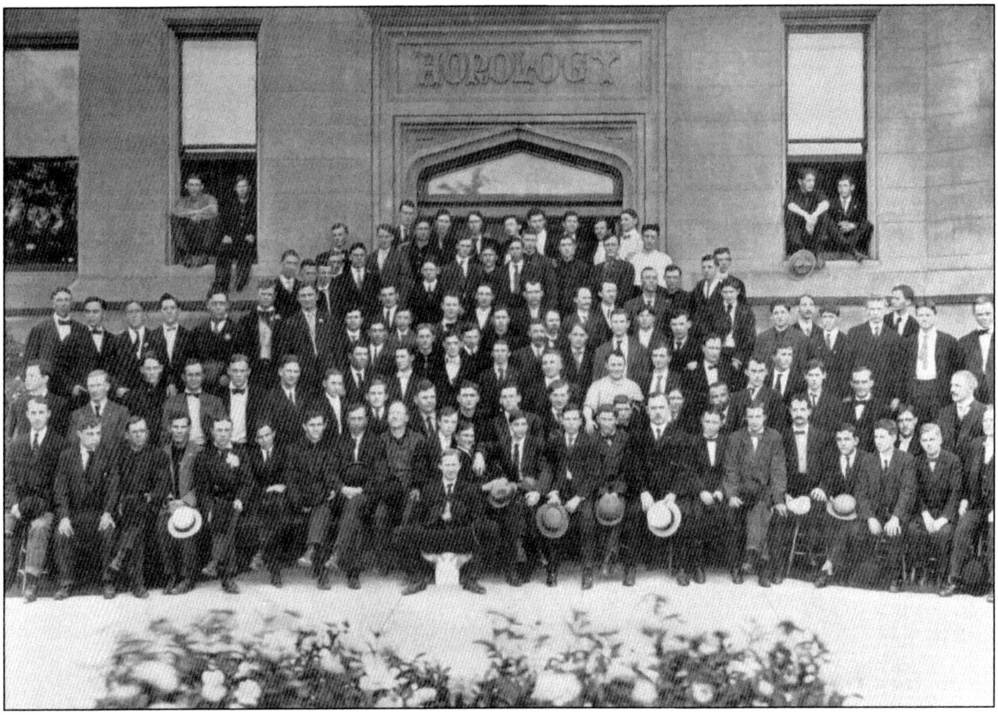

Names are not recorded in this photo, but the image shows students in front of the Horology Building in 1908. There appears to be an African-American student among them in the second row, fifth from the right.

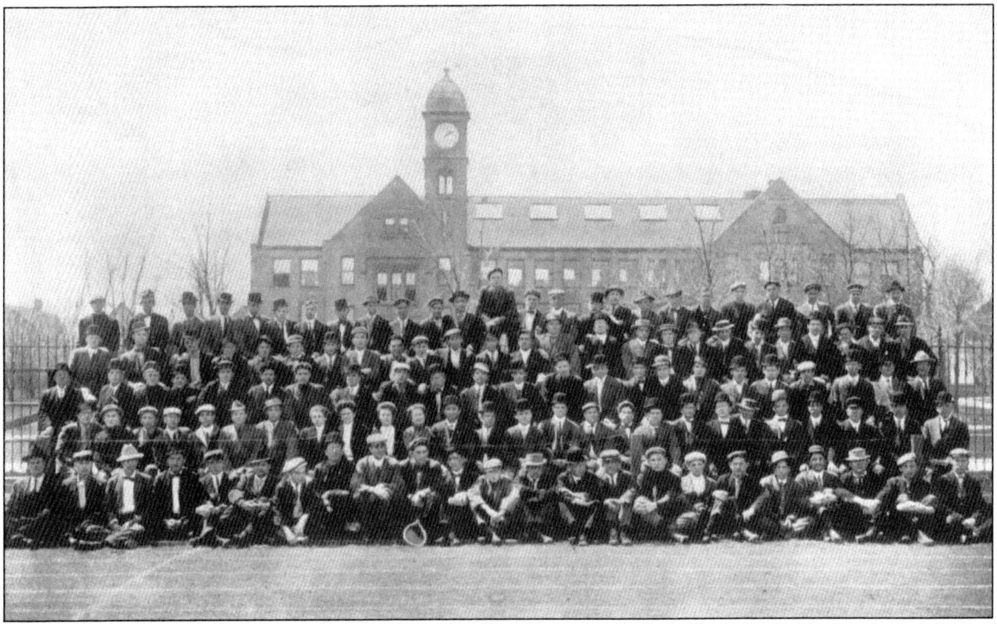

Several African Americans can be seen in this 1914 photo of the senior class, captured in front of Westlake Hall.

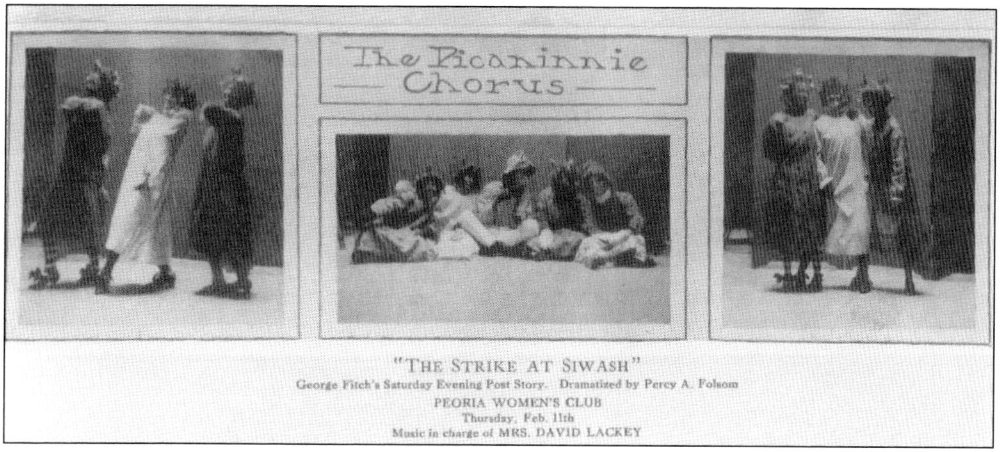

This 1914 photo of the *Picaninnie Chorus*, a play put on with the support of the Peoria Women's Club, shows that although African-American students attended Bradley, the university and the Peoria community were not always sensitive to the racism that confronted them daily.

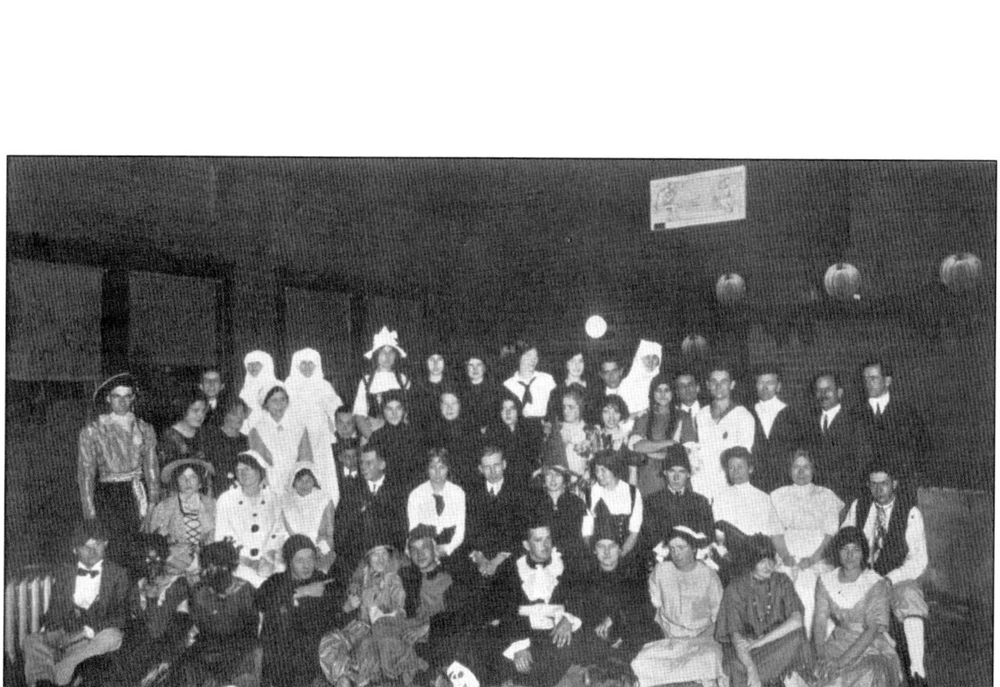

Even the drama department at Bradley routinely performed plays in which students were painted in black face, as this 1914 image of the cast of a play demonstrates.

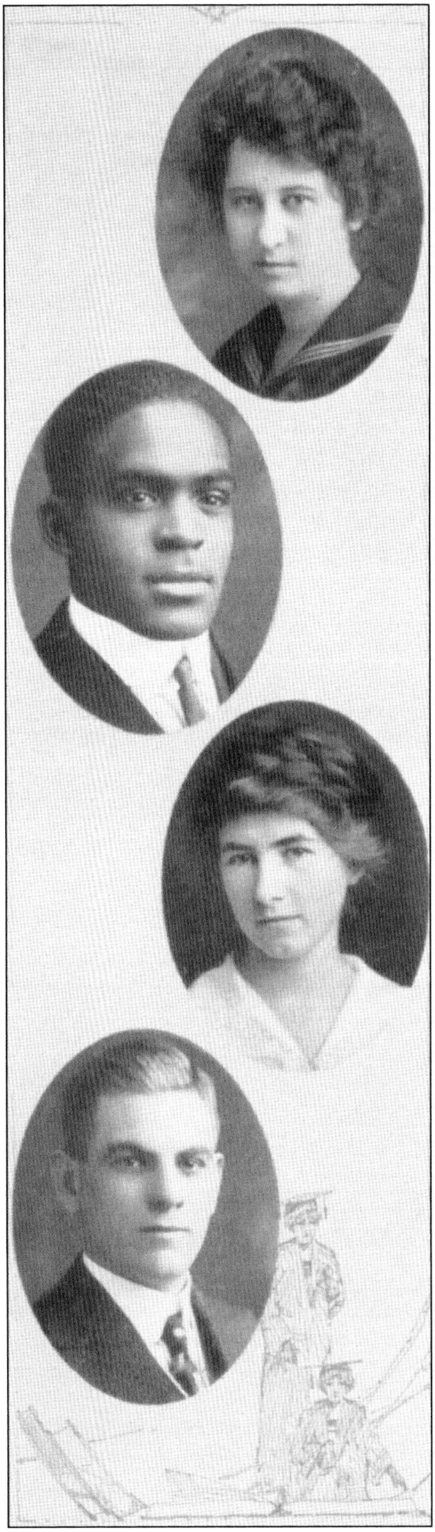

This photo is of Marimon Hansbery, a 1917 graduate with a degree in Manual Training. Hansbery was from Indianapolis, Indiana.

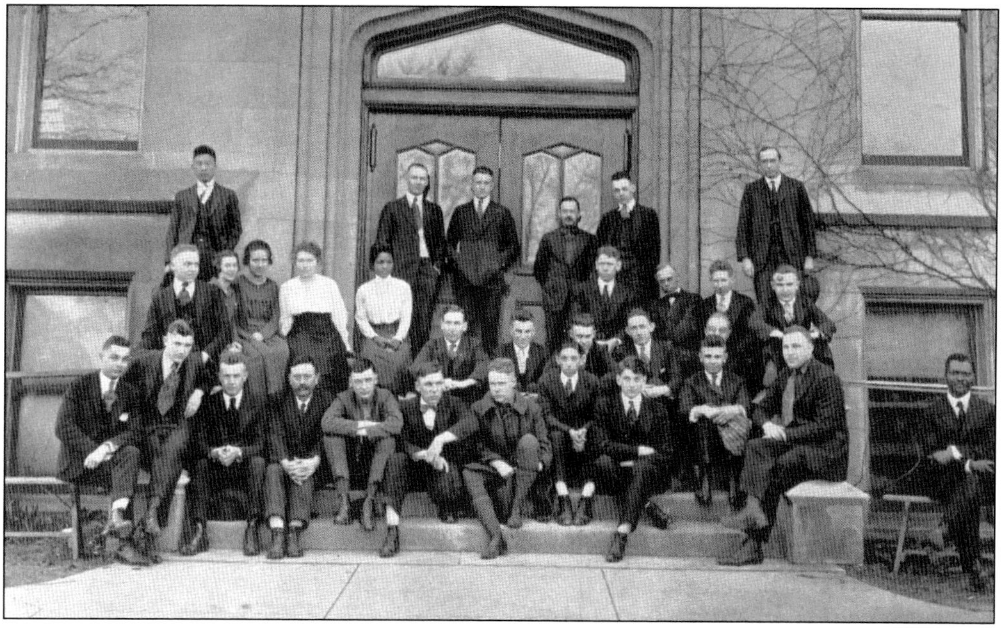

This photo, taken in 1919 in front of Bradley Hall, depicts an African-American male sitting alone to the far right and an African-American female sitting in the midst of the group but obviously not feeling a part of the group. There is also what appears to be an individual who appears to be of Native American descent standing alone. This picture demonstrates that while people of color were allowed to attend Bradley, they did not always feel welcomed or respected by their fellow White students or the faculty and staff.

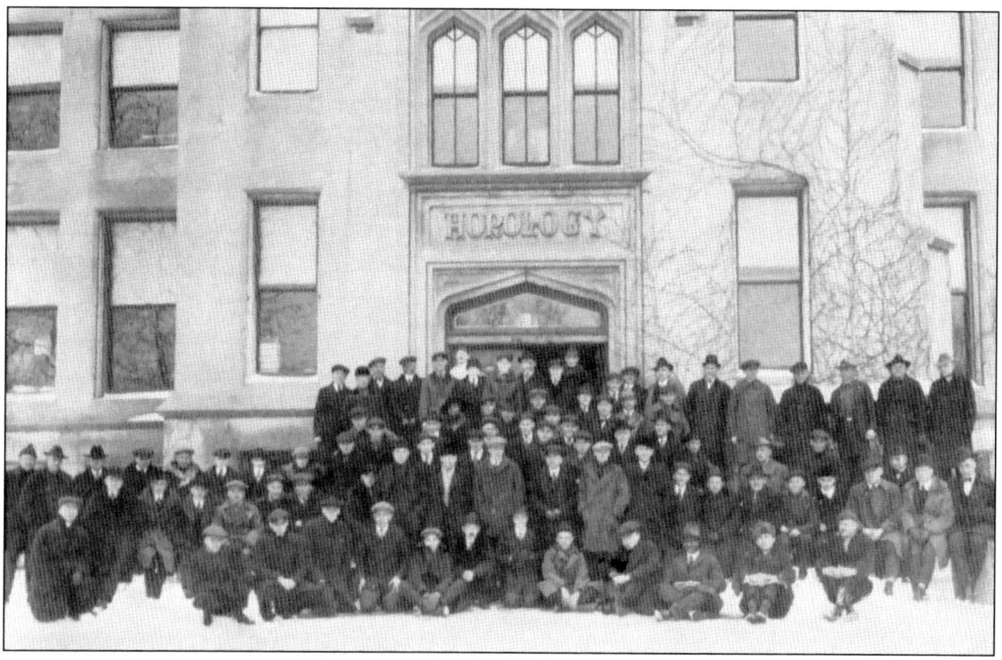

In this photo from 1920 are two African Americans, one male in the front row and another person in the third row from the back. They are pictured in front of Westlake Hall.

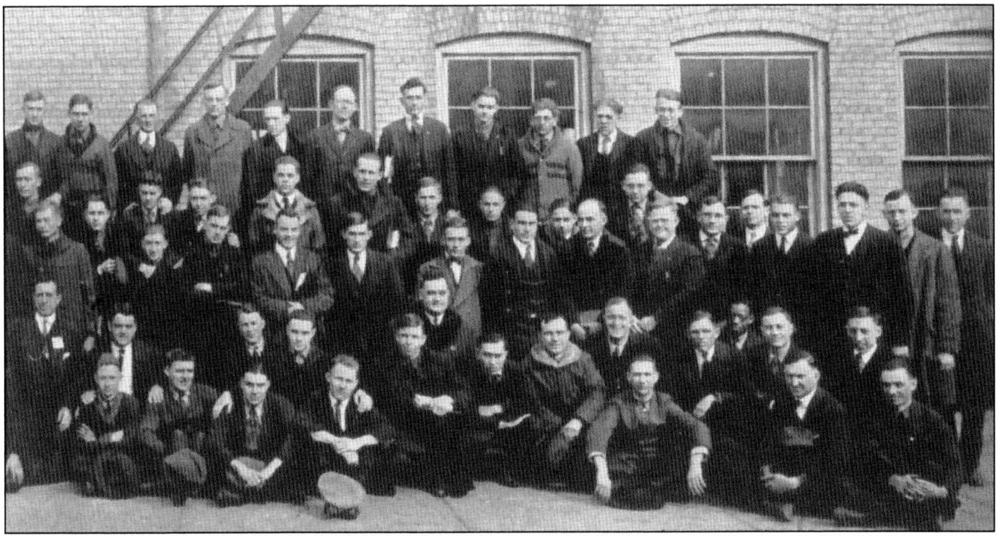

This departmental photo of the Vocational and Tractor Department was taken from the 1921 *Polyscope*. An unidentified man, second row, third from the right, was a member of the department.

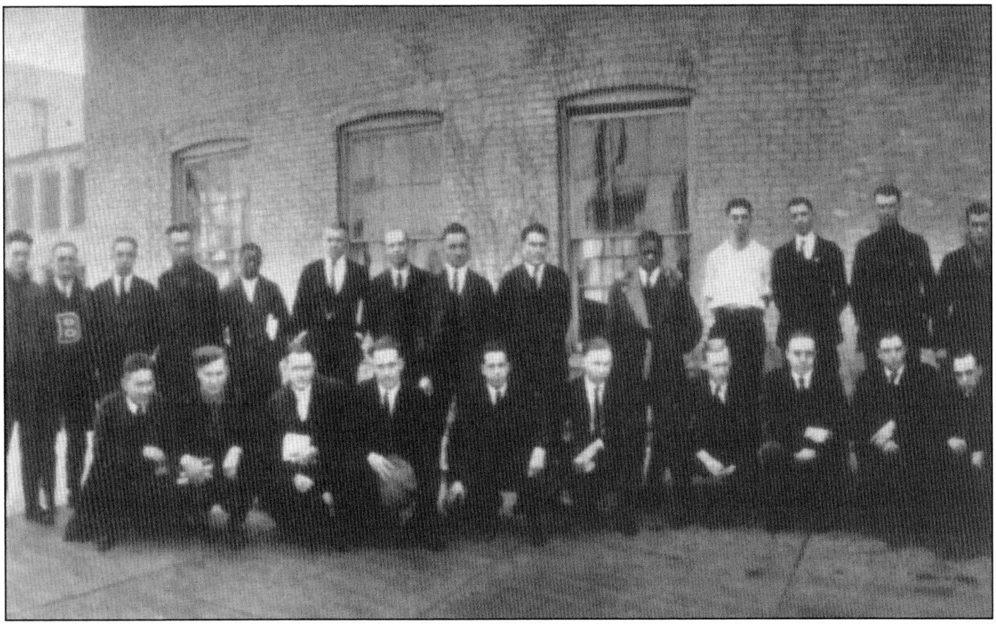

In this 1922 photo of the Vocational Department, two African Americans can be easily identified.

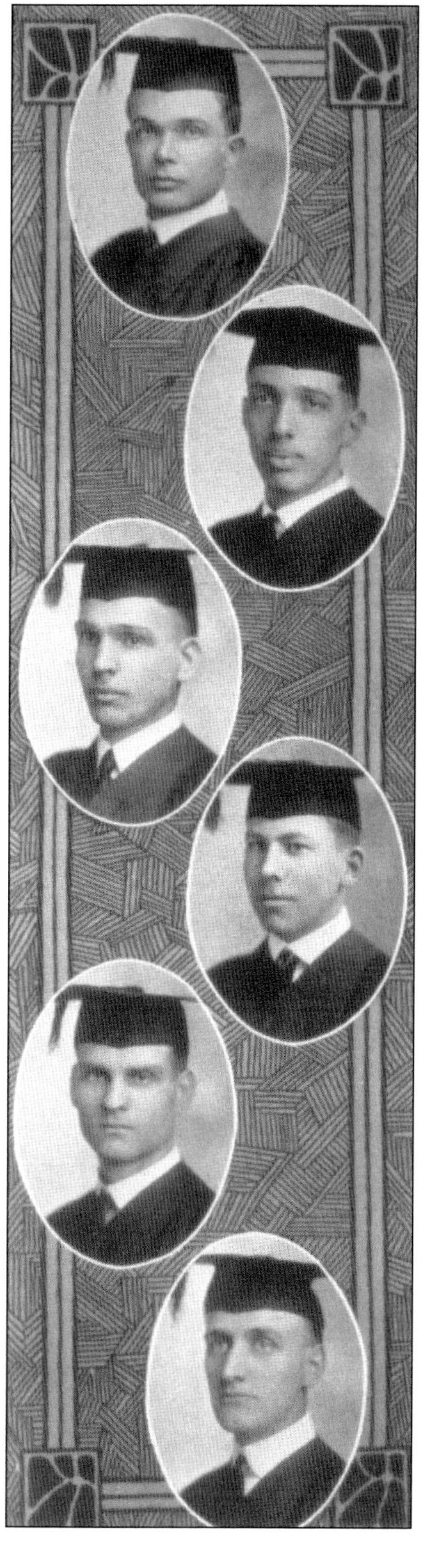

This photo depicts W.F. Greathouse of Moundville, Alabama, who graduated in the class of 1922. No major was listed.

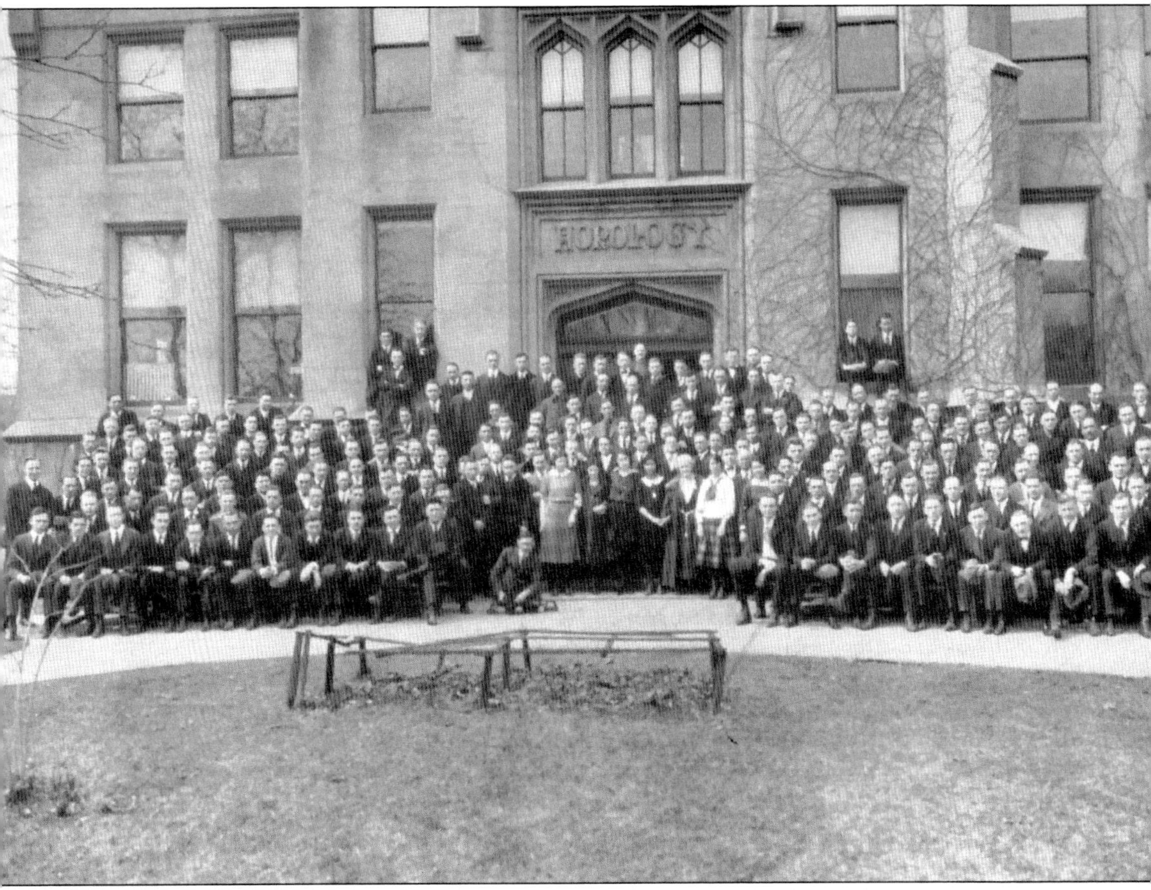

This is a group photo of the 1922 members of the School of Horology.

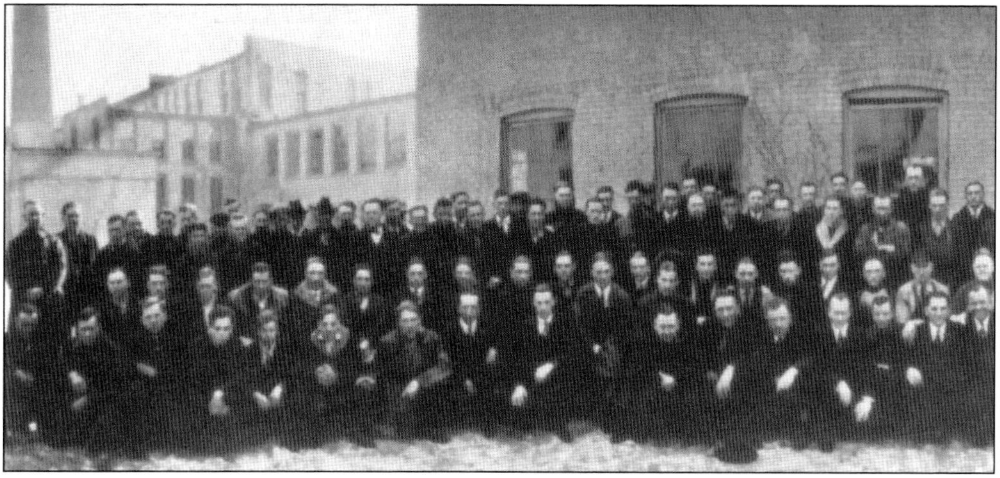

Members of the Manual Arts Department from 1922 are pictured above. Two African Americans appear in this photo.

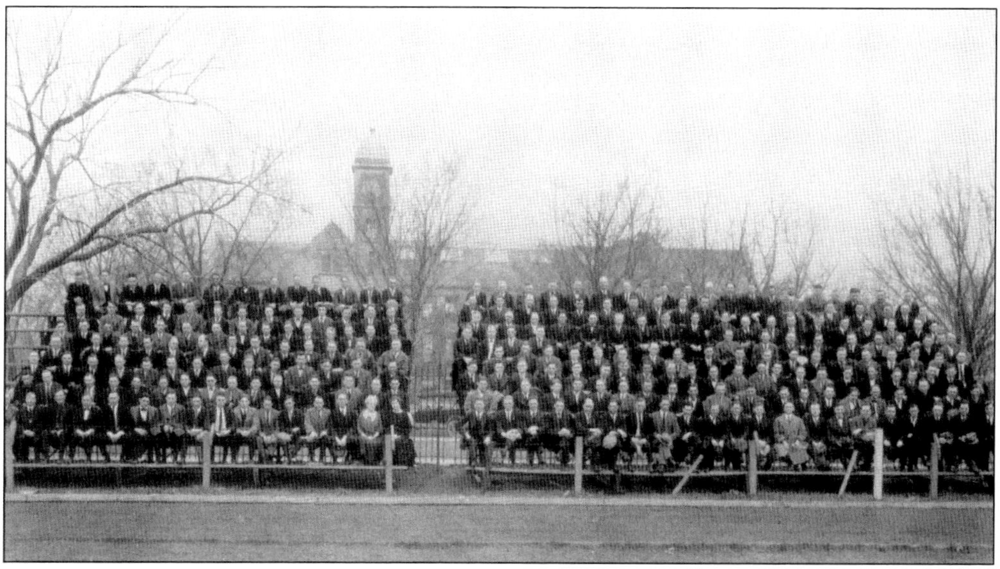

Students are seated on bleachers by the football field in this photo taken in 1923.

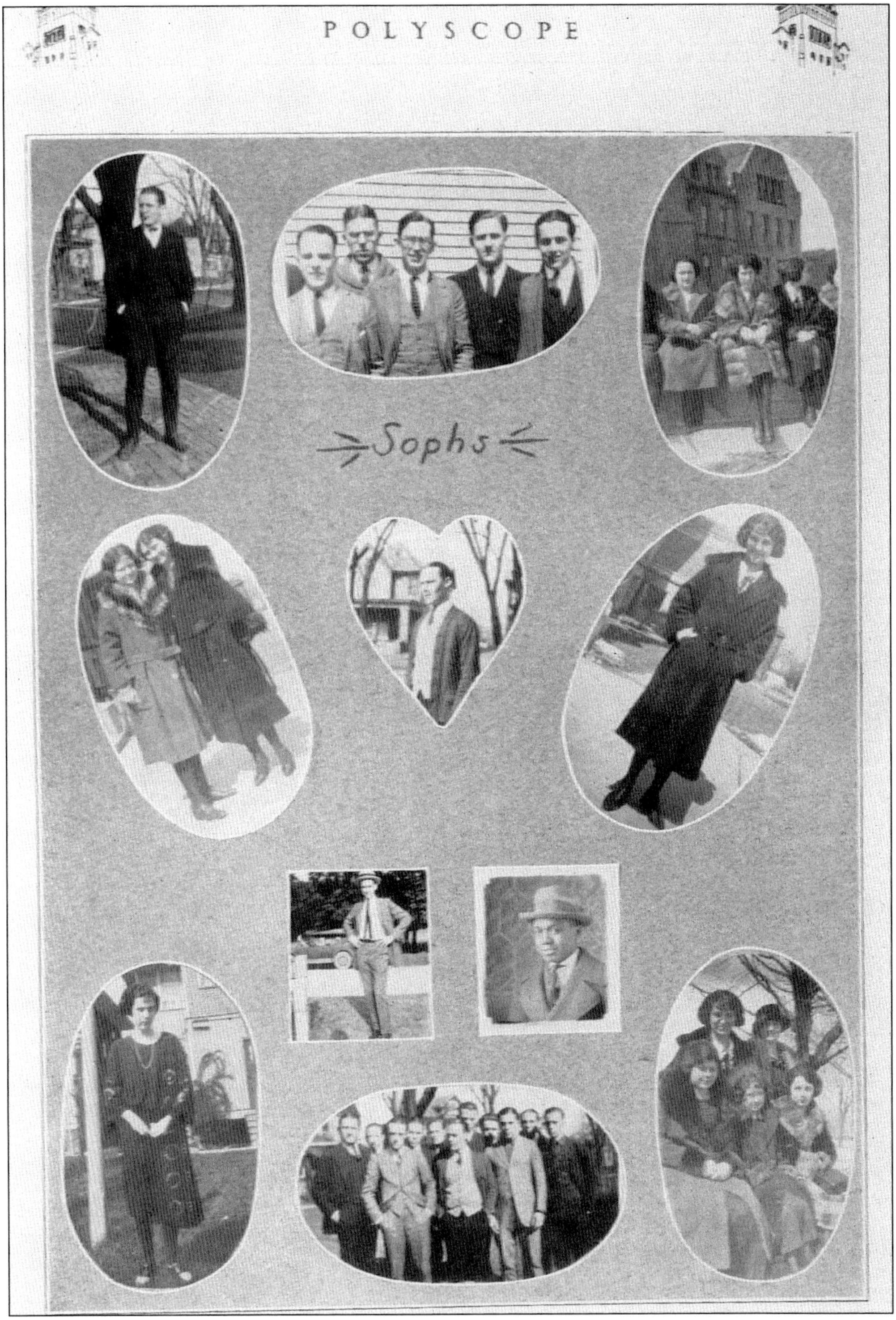

This is a collage of pictures taken in 1923, depicting members of the sophomore class. Near the bottom is a photo of an unnamed African-American student.

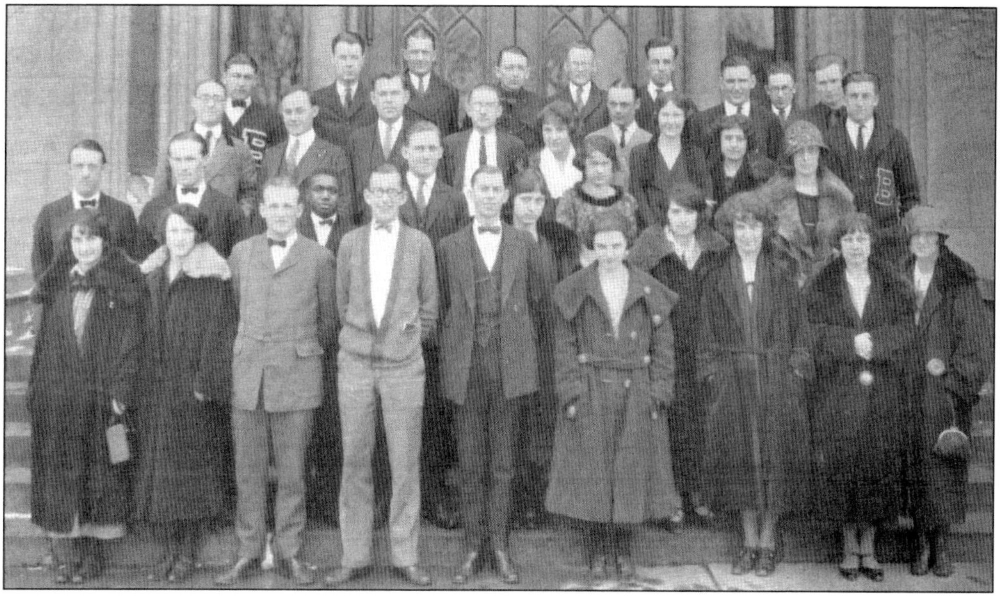

This group photo was taken in 1924. An African-American male is visible on the second row.

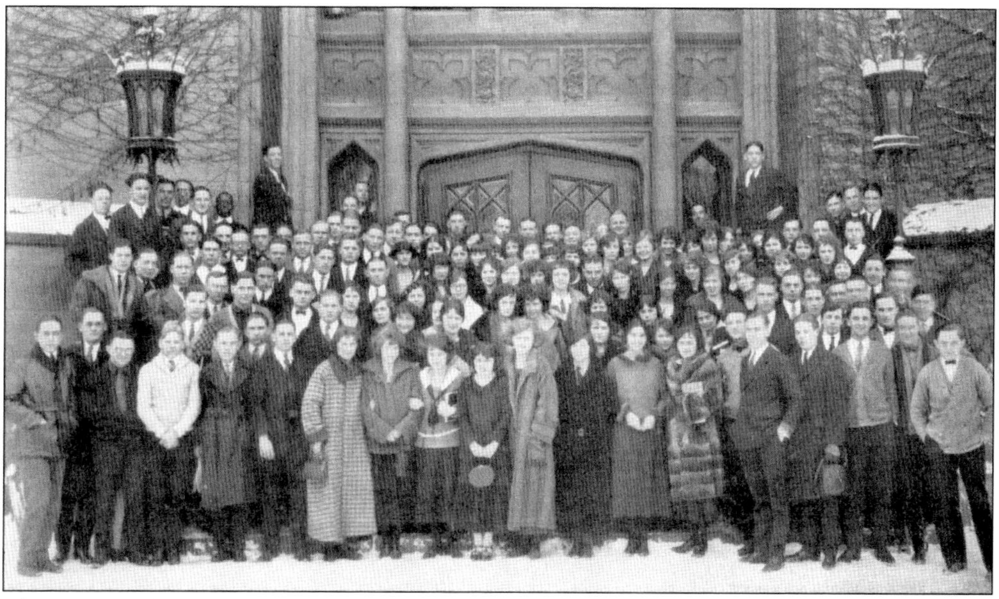

This group photo was taken in front of Bradley Hall in 1924. An African-American male is visible in the top left-hand corner in the back row.

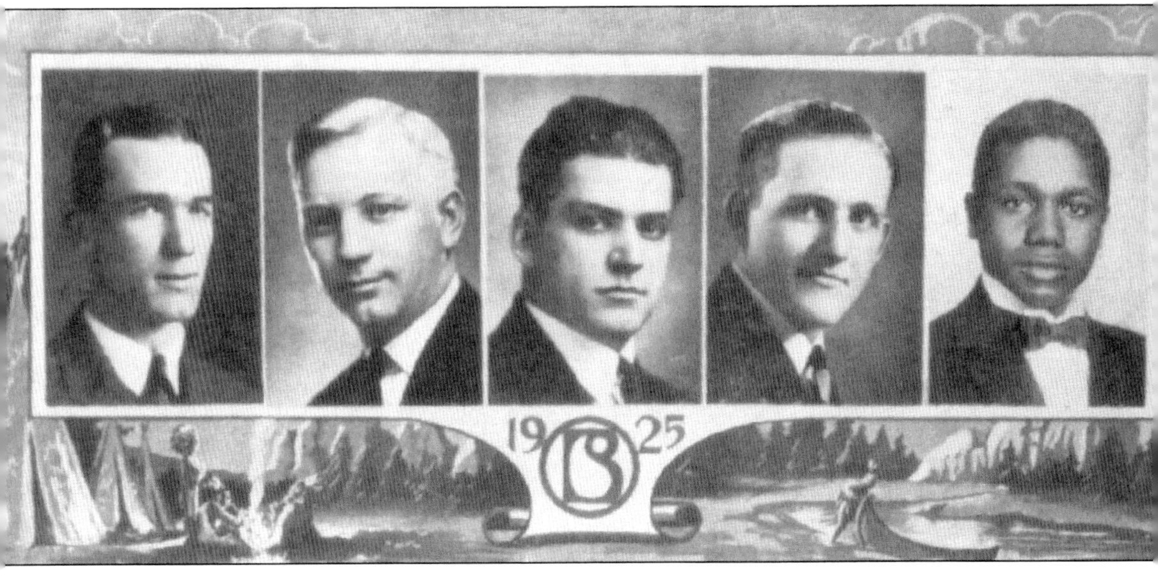

Like James M. Harris Jr., who graduated with an A.B. in Sociology in 1925, most of Bradley's early African-American students were academic standouts. Harris, who was from Peoria and is on the far right, was a member of the French Club, YMCA Discussion Group, and was an honor course student in Sociology.

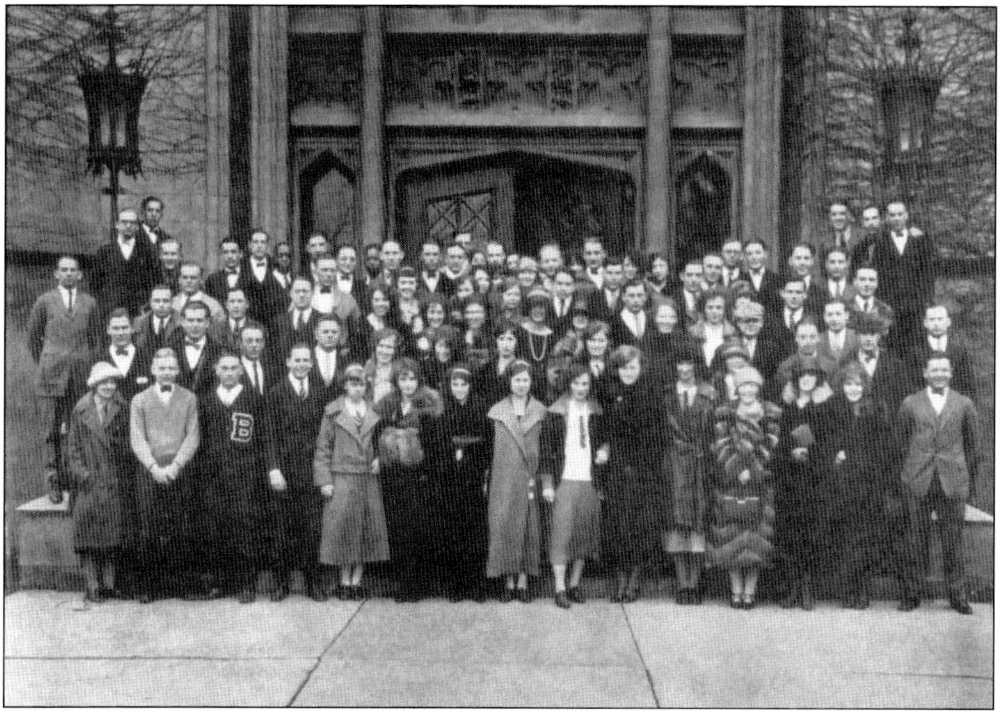

In the back row of this photo taken in front of Bradley Hall in 1925, an African-American male student is clearly visible.

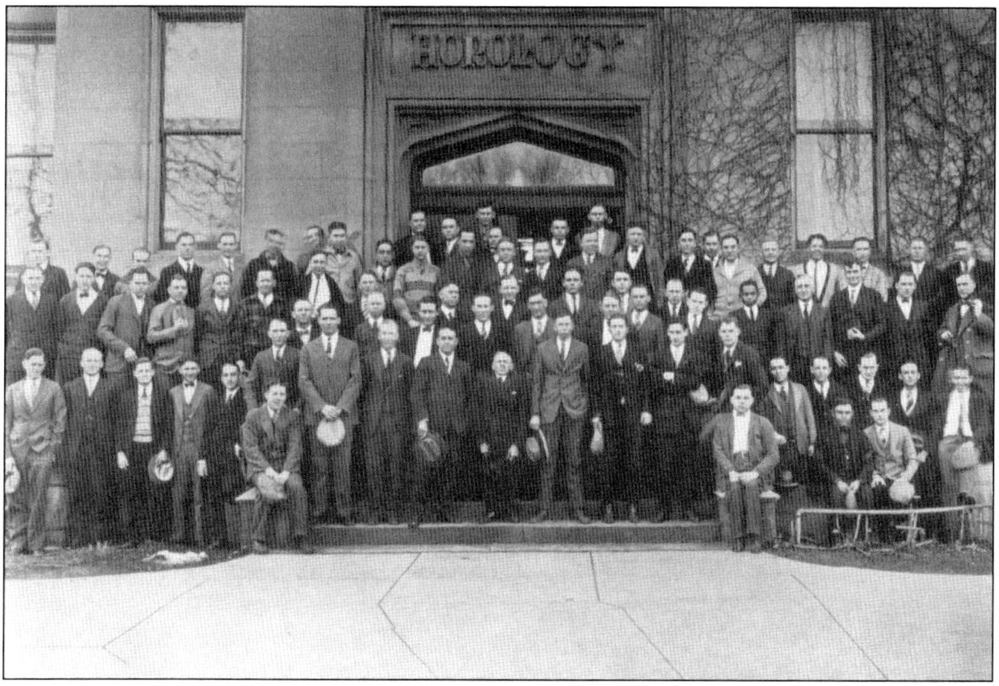

Members of the School of Horology are depicted in a photo taken in 1926 in front of Westlake Hall. An African American is located in the third row on the right.

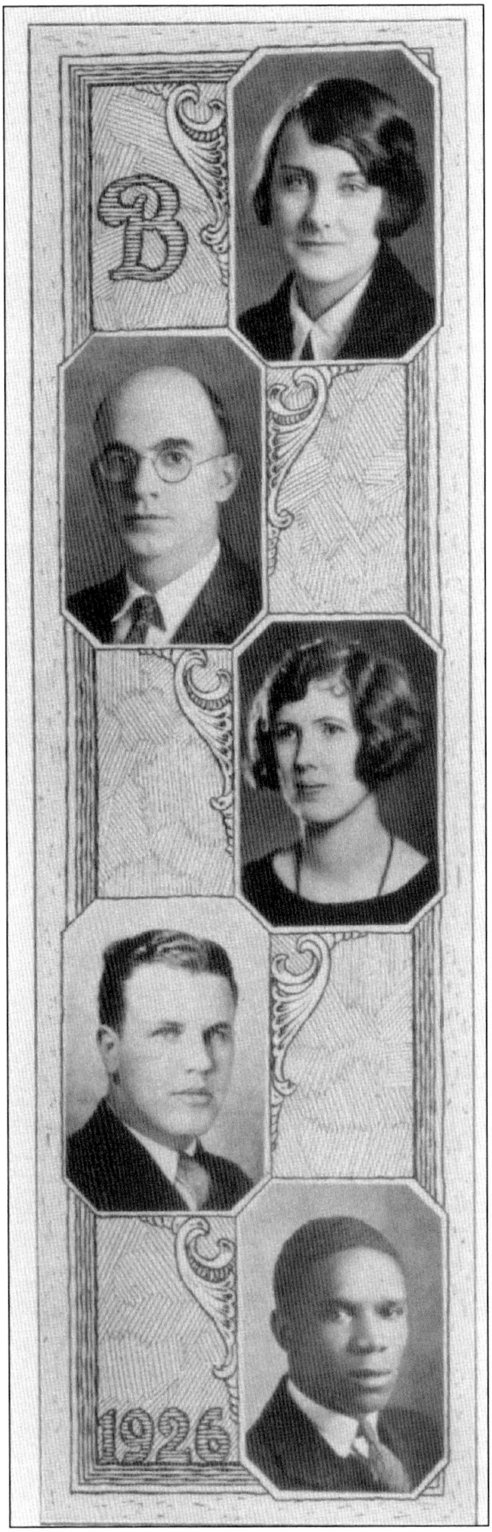

This photograph shows Joseph E. Fuller, who graduated with an A.B. in 1926. Neither his major nor hometown was listed.

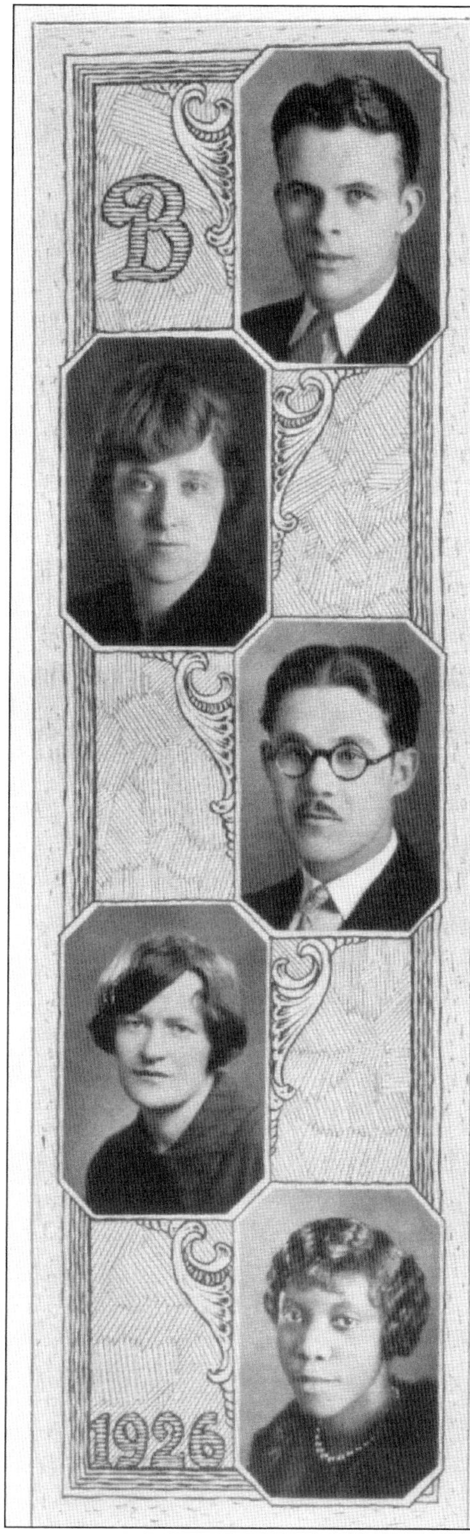

This is a photograph of Anna Campbell, who graduated with an A.B. in 1926. While at Bradley, Campbell was a member of YWCA, Y. Commission, W.A.A., and the women's basketball and varsity hockey teams.

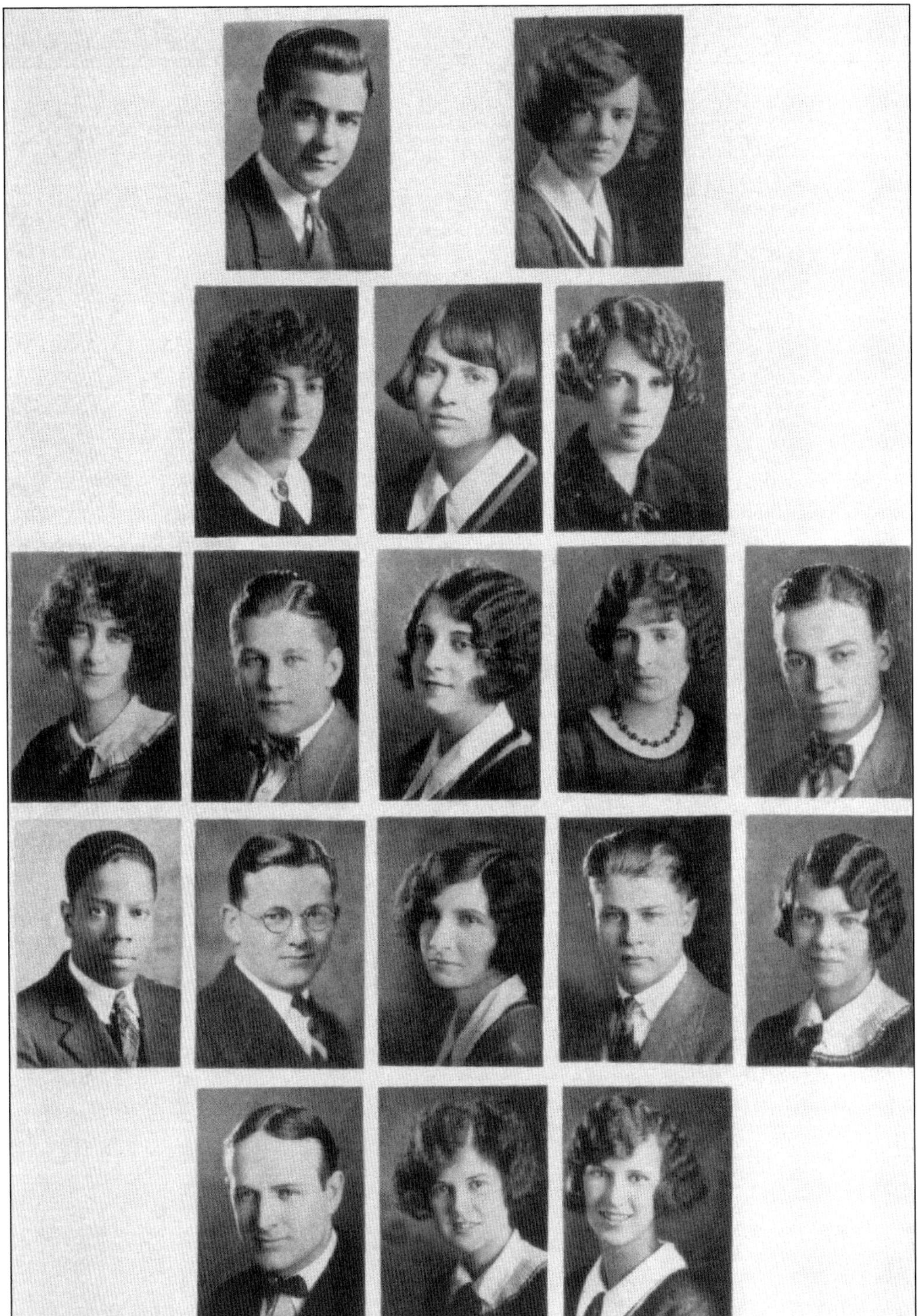

Shown above is an African-American member of the class of 1926.

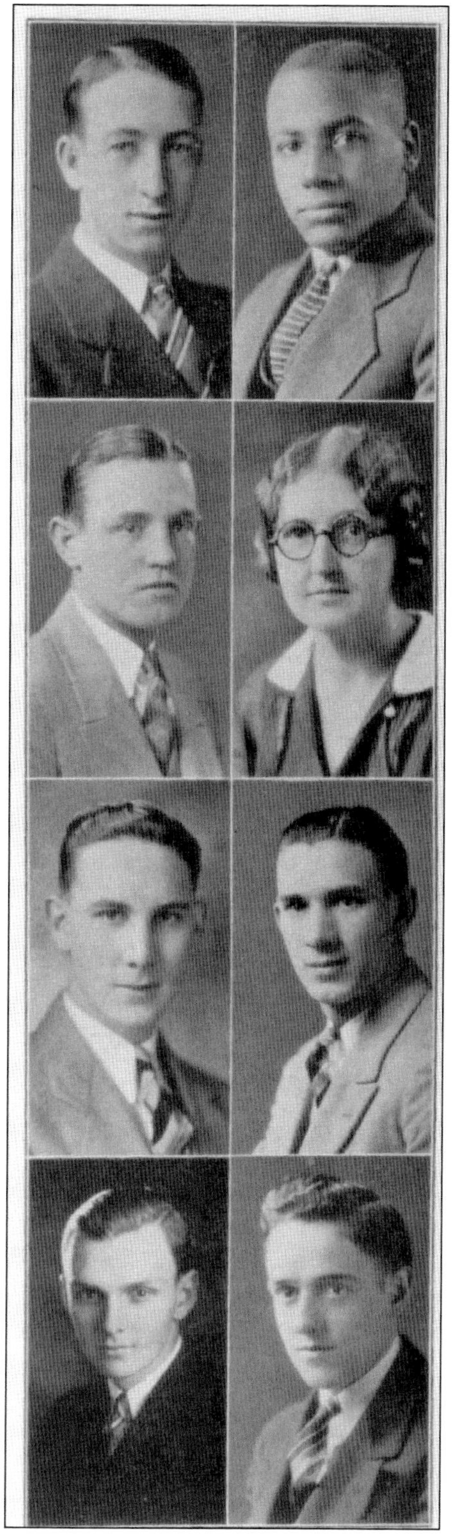

This is a photograph of Edgar Allen Hawley, a member of the graduating class of 1928, with a B.S. in Business Administration. Hawley was from Dallas, Texas.

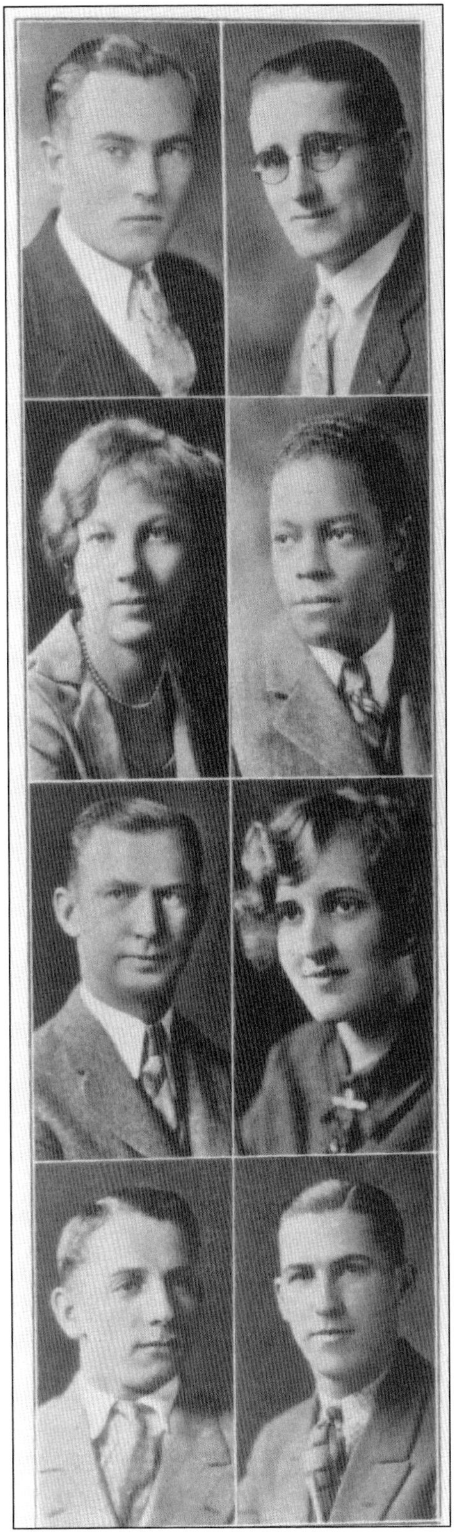

Shown here is a photograph of James D. Parks, a member of the graduating class of 1928, with a B.S. in Art. Hawley was a member of the *Polyscope* art staff, the half-mile relay team, inter-class track, varsity cross-country, and intramural basketball. Parks was from St. Louis, Missouri.

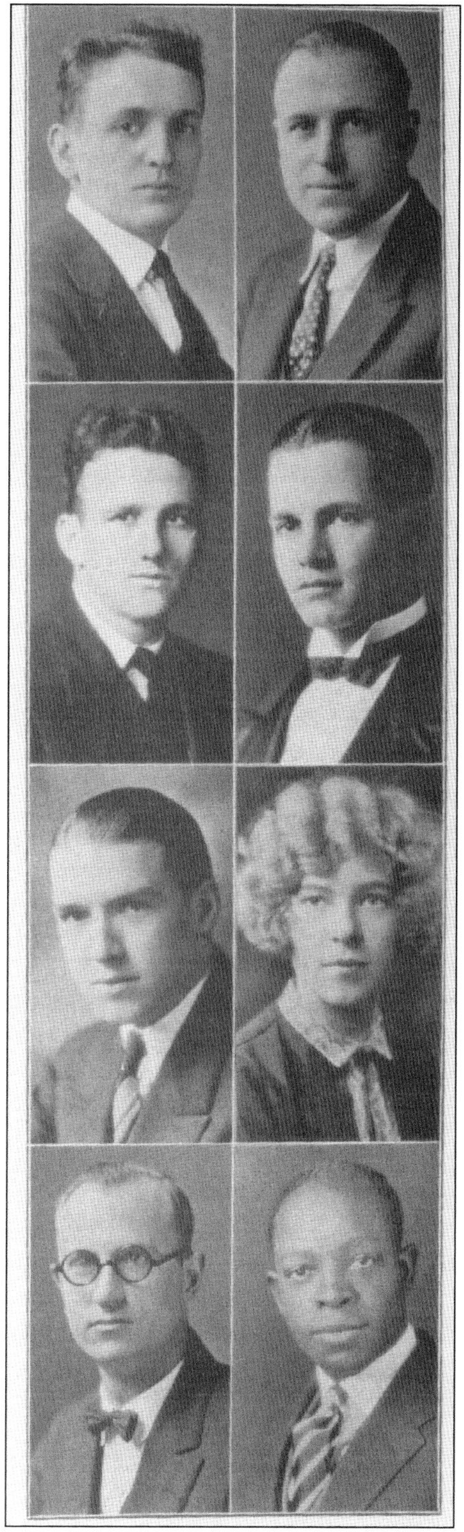

This photograph depicts George Lee Johnson of the graduating class of 1928, with an A.B. in Language and English. Johnson was from Dallas, Texas.

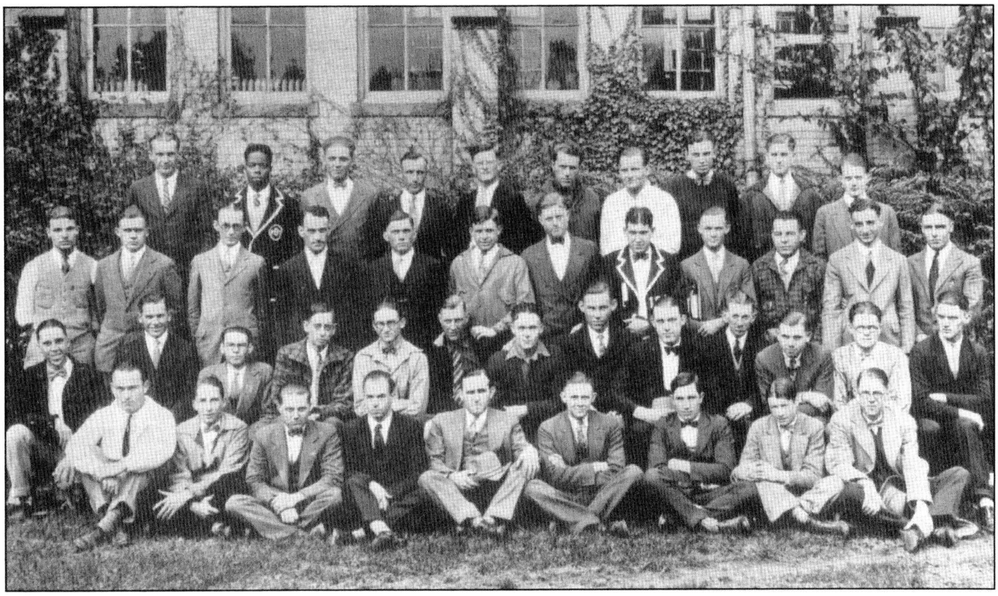

James D. Parks is shown in this 1928 group photo.

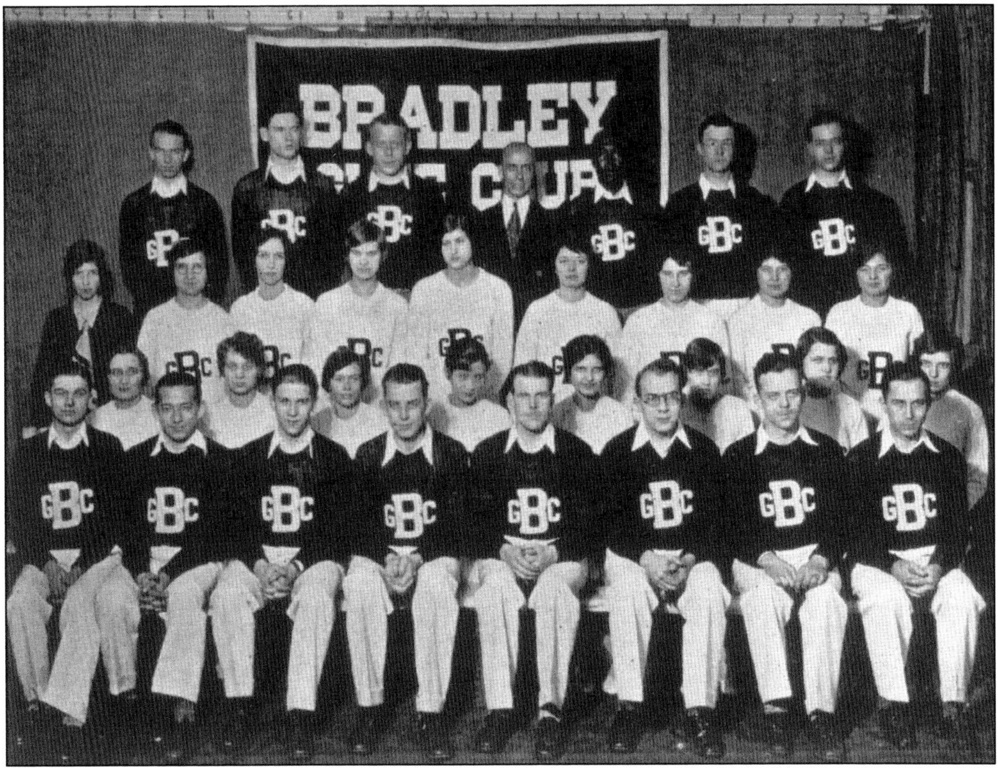

This 1931 photo depicts the first Bradley mixed chorus. Prior to 1931, Bradley had the Women's Glee Club and the Men's Glee Club. In this photo, the only African-American member of the club can be seen in the back row.

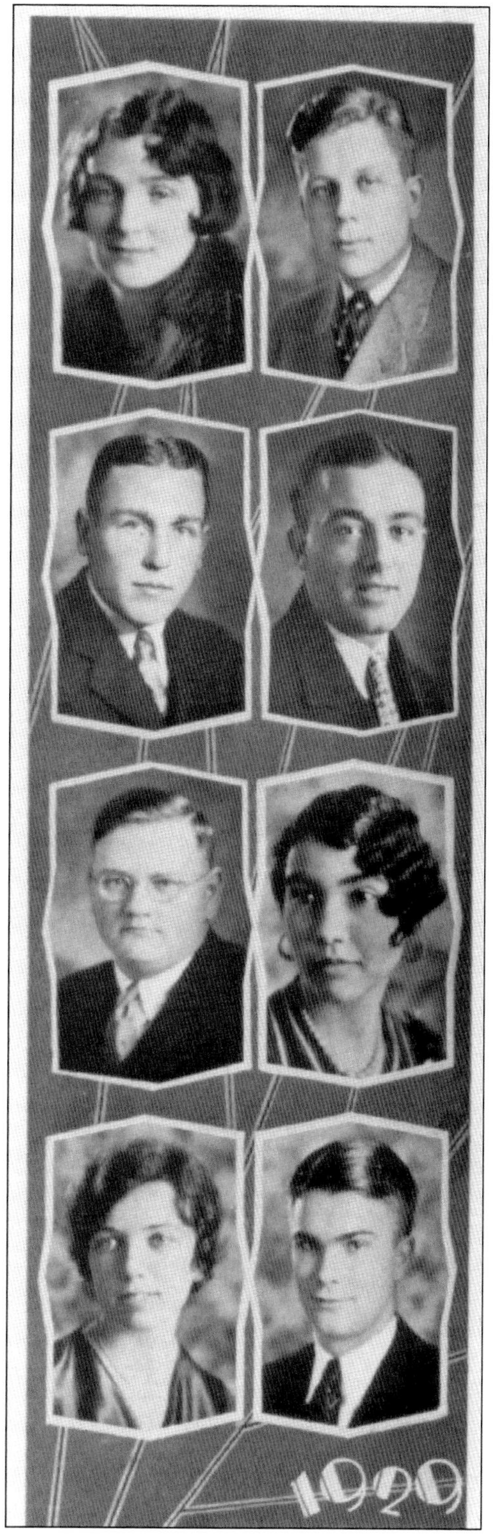

This photograph depicts Phyllis Honesty in the graduating class of 1930. Honesty graduated with an A.B. degree, and her major was not listed. However, it most be noted that shc completed her first two years of training at Wilberforce University in Ohio, which was one of the first historically Black universities established in 1853. It is noteworthy that Bradley University accepted transfer credits from a Black college, allowing her to finish on time when hundreds of universities around the country were still barring Blacks from even being admitted.

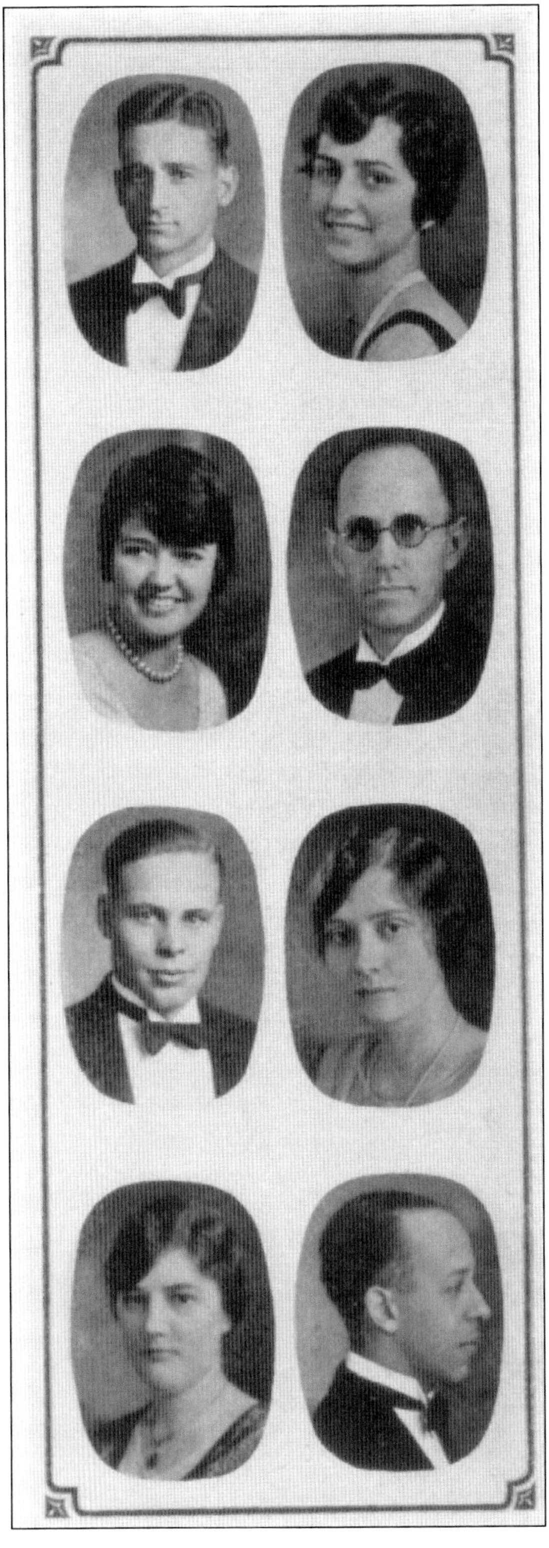

Ernest J. Hooper, a member of the graduating class of 1931, is pictured here. Hooper was a member of Omega Psi Phi and a transfer student from Cheyney Training School for Teachers, another early historically Black university in Cheyney, Pennsylvania, where he must have joined the fraternity since there were no Black fraternities at Bradley at that time. Hooper finished with a B.S. degree. Neither his major nor his hometown was mentioned.

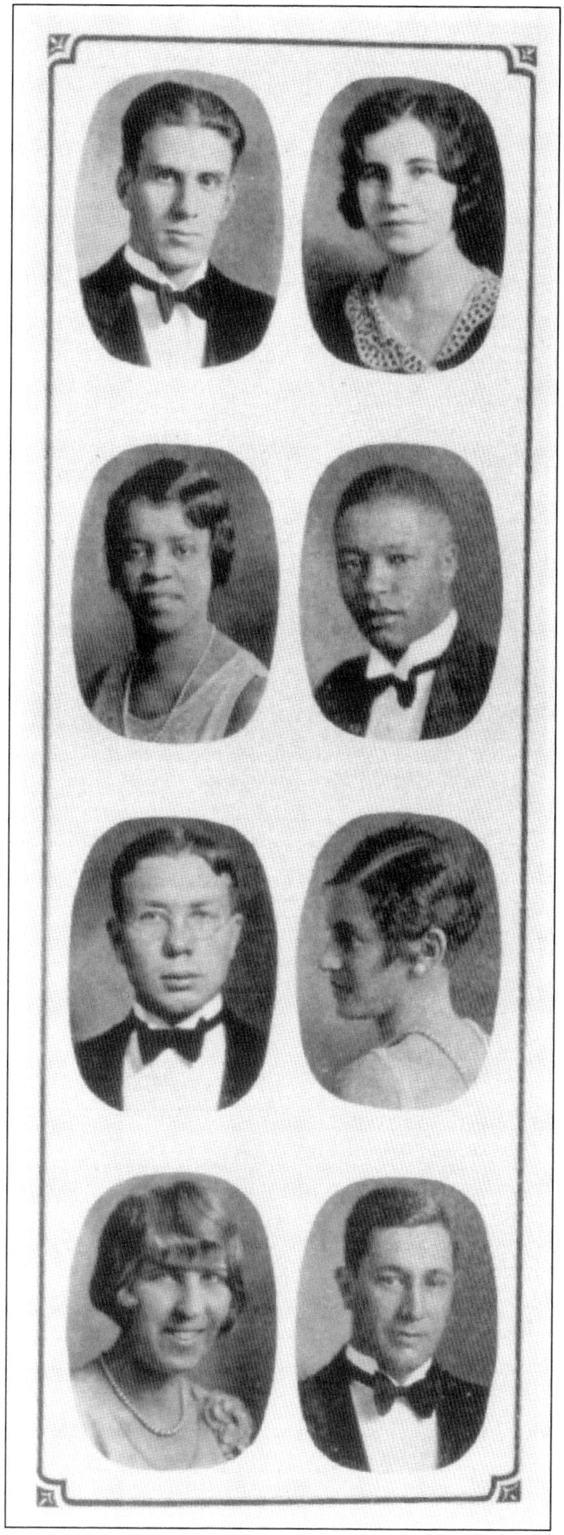

This is a photograph of Katherine Anthony, who graduated with a B.S., and Bruce R. Irving, who graduated with an A.B. in 1931. Neither their major areas of study nor their home towns were listed.

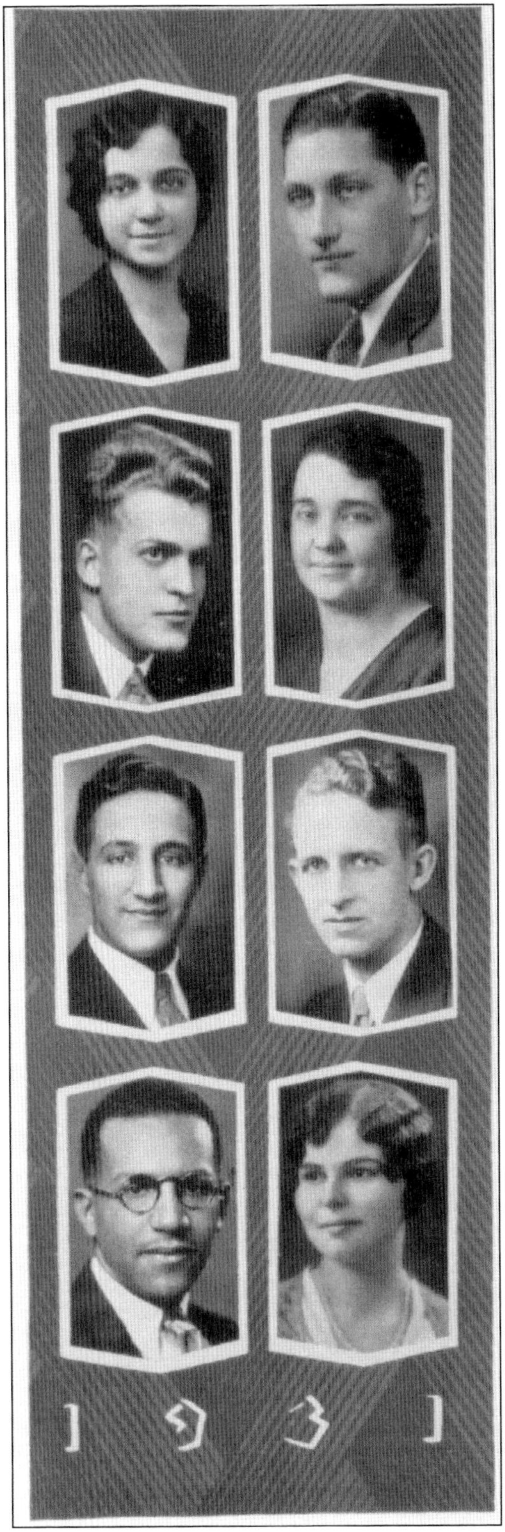

This photograph shows Leon DeVaul, who finished Bradley in 1931 with a B.S. degree. Neither his area of study nor his hometown was listed.

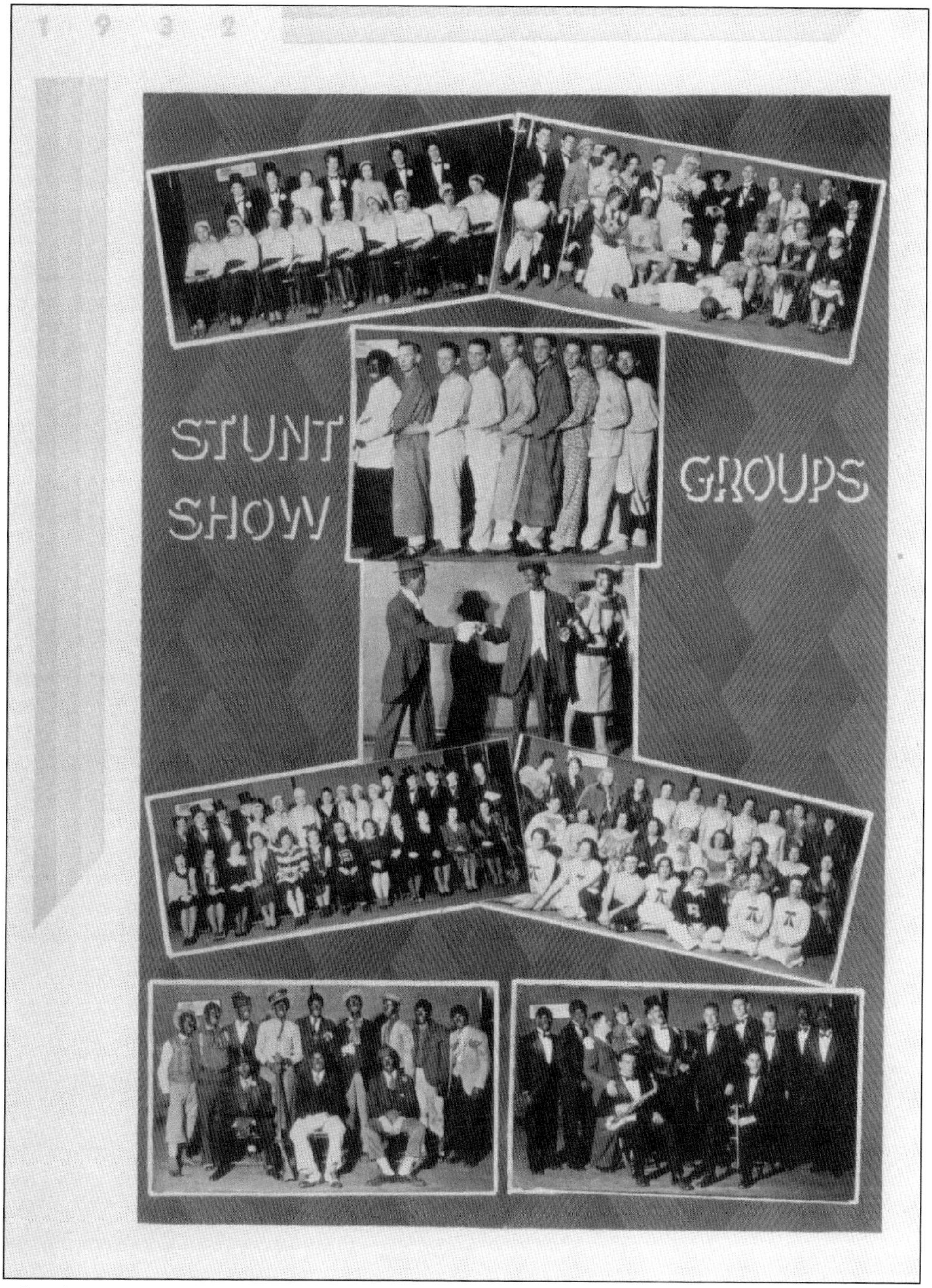

Like the early years, African-American students continued to struggle with racism and racial stereotypes, which were common around the country during this time. In this 1932 collage of photos, stunt shows, which were usually put on during homecoming by White fraternities and sororities, are depicted. Several of the most popular shows included portrayals of students in blackface.

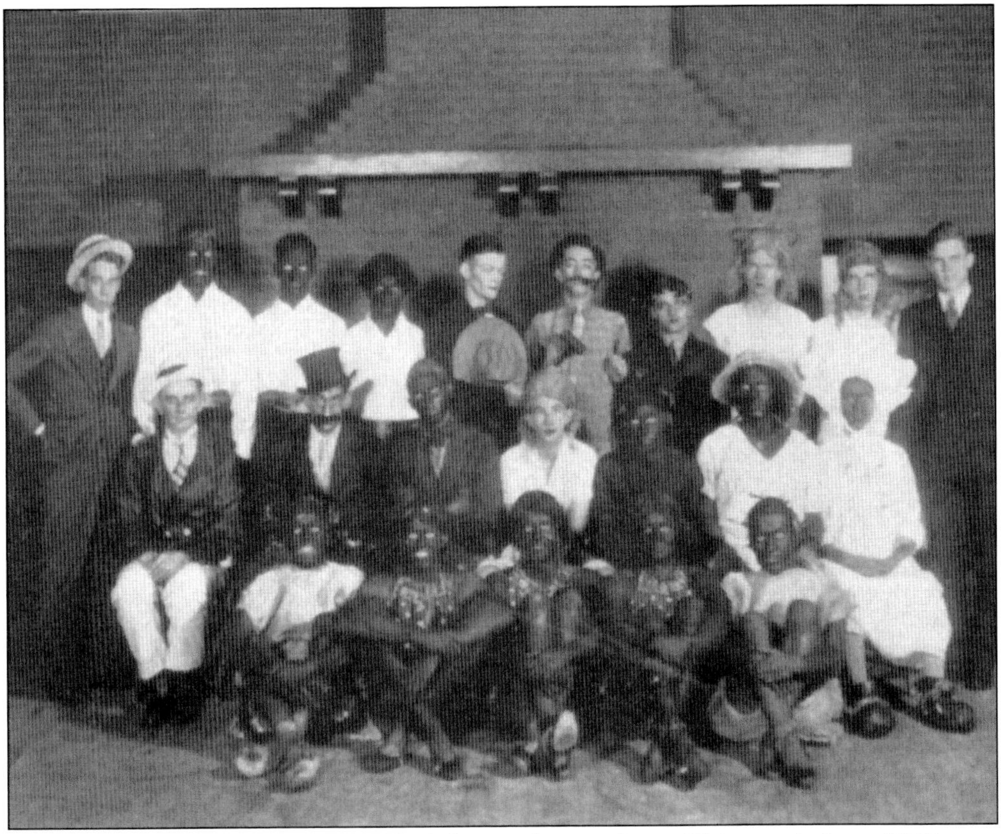

Another portrayal of students in black face is shown above. This one is from 1935.

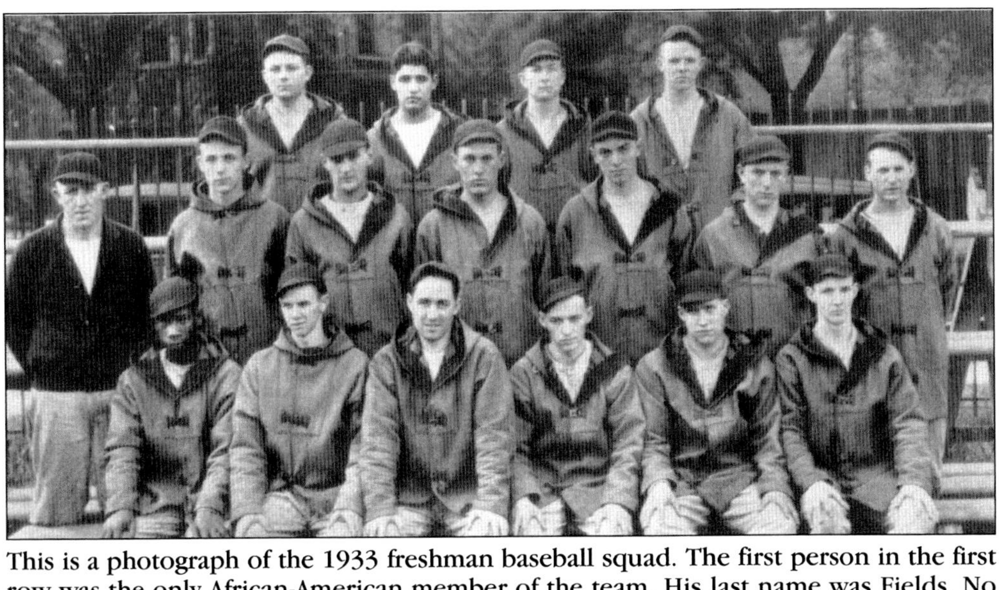

This is a photograph of the 1933 freshman baseball squad. The first person in the first row was the only African-American member of the team. His last name was Fields. No first name or hometown was listed.

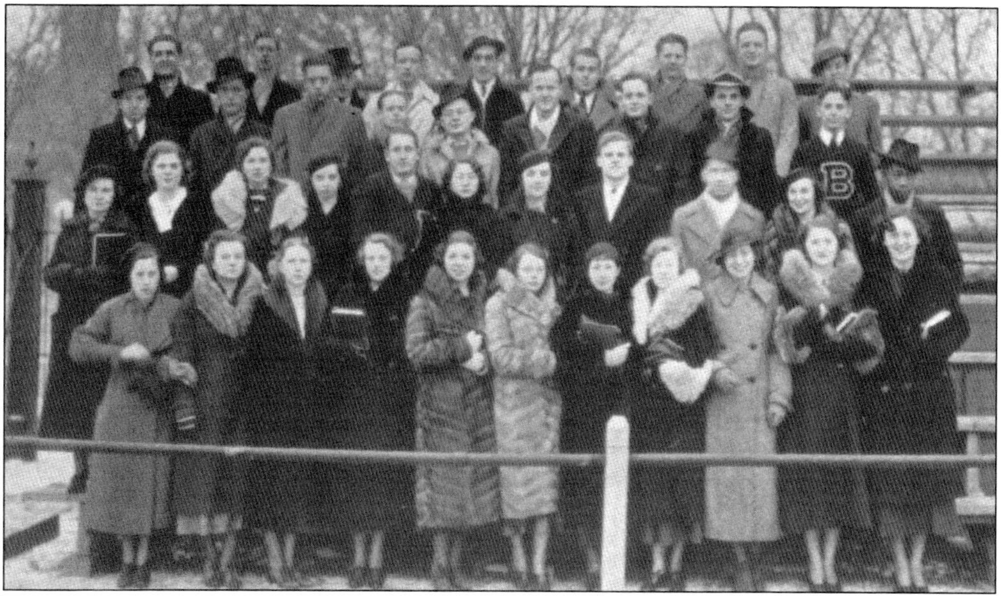

Fields was also a member of this club. He is depicted in this 1936 group photo.

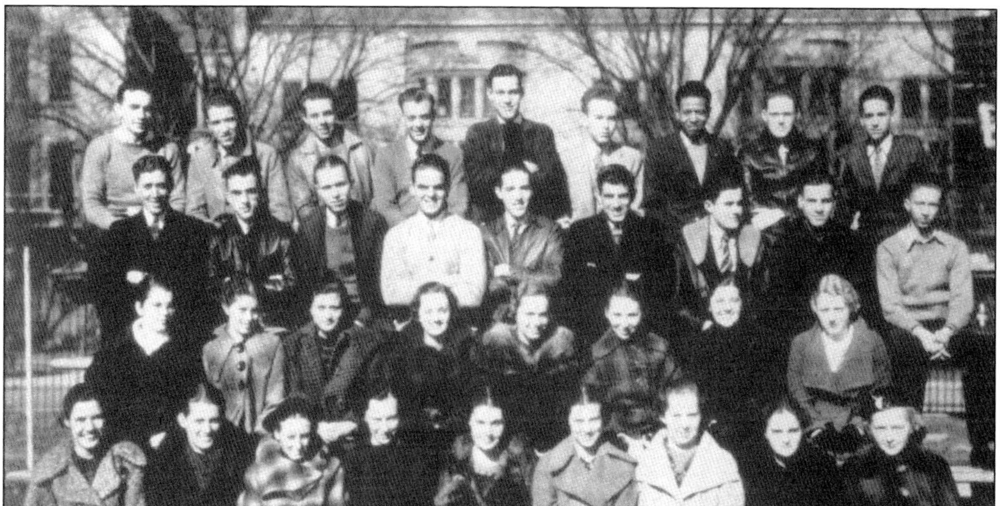

This group photo is of the 1938 freshman class. An African-American student by the name of A. Jackson is shown in the top row, third from right. No hometown, major, or complete name is given.

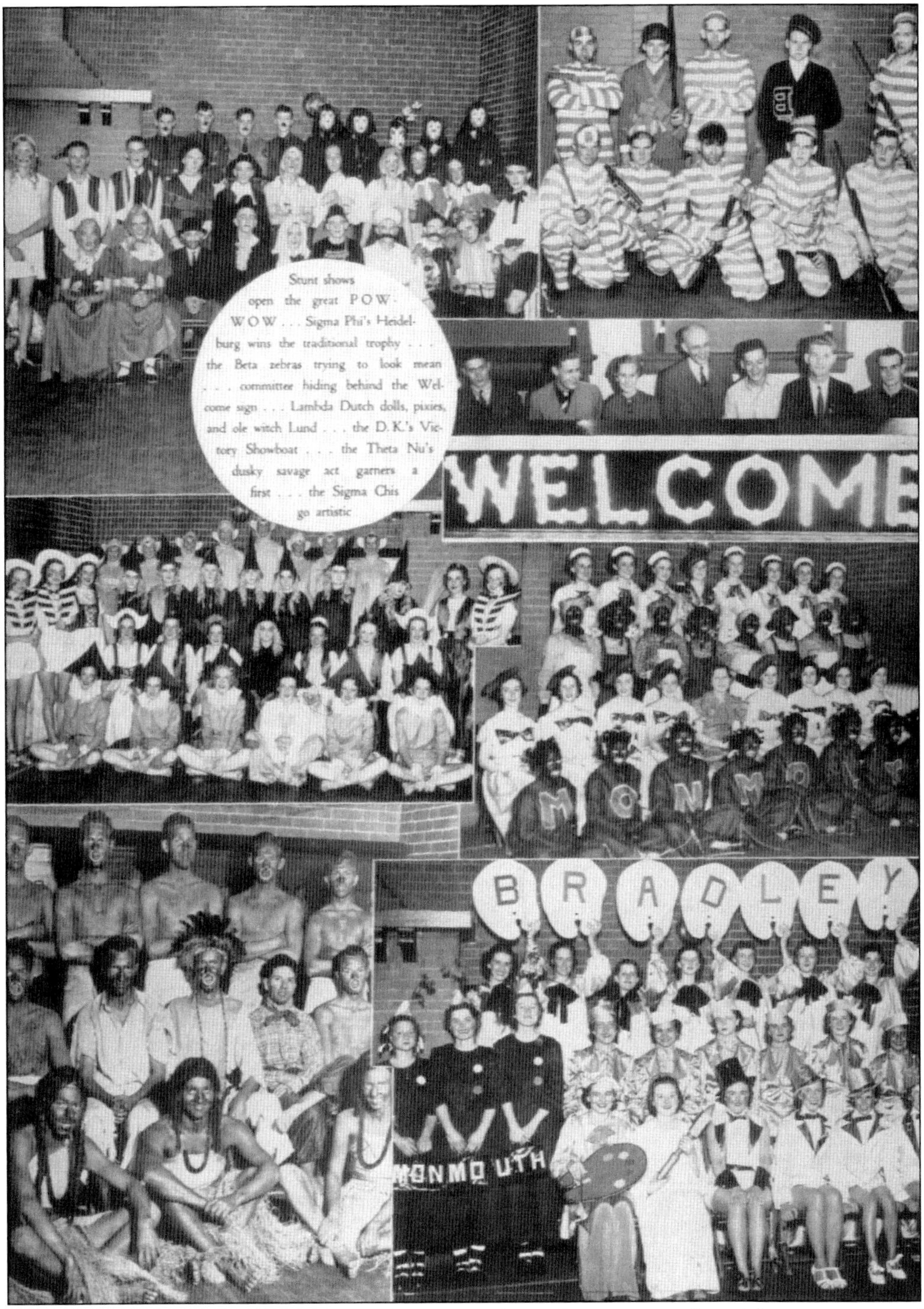

African-American students continued to struggle with racism and racial stereotypes of Blacks common around the country during this time. Another collage of stunt shows is depicted here, this one from 1938.

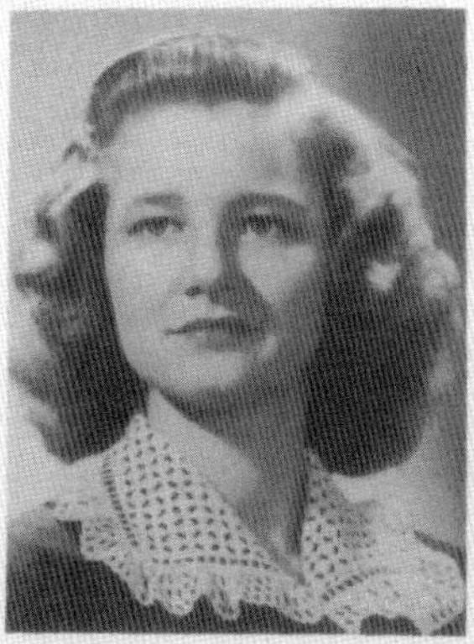

JUNE EILEEN SHALKHAUSER, B.S. Washington, Ill.
Sigma Chi Gamma, Social Chairman, 2, President, 4; Federation of Scholars, 2-4; Vice-President, Freshman Class, 1; Inter-sorority Council, President, 4; Women's Self Governing Board, 4; Maid to Homecoming Queen, 2; Board of Control, 4; Y.W.C.A., 1-4; A Cappella Choir, 4; Girls' Chorus, 4; Commerce Club, 1; Polyscope, Assistant Editor, 2, Snap-shot Editor, 4; Union Building Committee, 4; Co-Chairman of Homecoming Dance, 2.

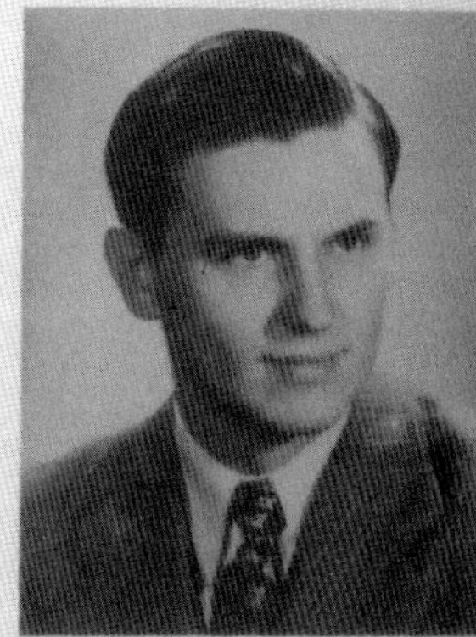

ROBERT SHARP, B.S. Green Valley, Ill.
Lambda Chi Alpha; Phi Sigma Pi, 3-4, President, 3; Beta Tau Epsilon, 2-4, Secretary, 3; Band, 2-3; A Capella Choir, 3.

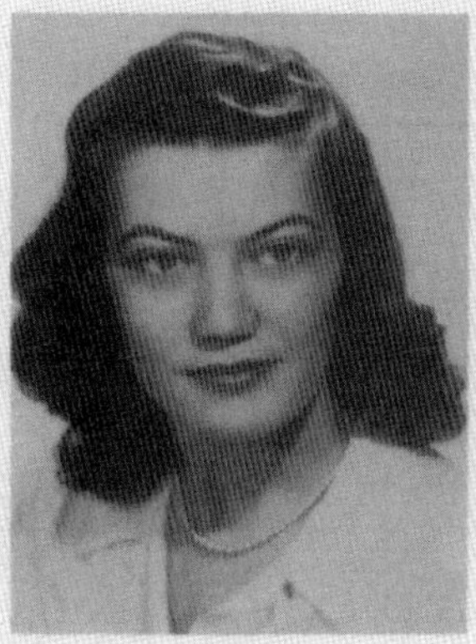

MARJORIE SIMON, B.S. Peoria, Ill.
Lambda Phi, President, 4; Federation of Scholars, 4; Inter-Sorority Council, Treasurer, 4; English Club, 3-4; W.A.A. Board, 2; Chairman of Inter-Sorority Spring Dance, 3; Tech, 'Shootin' the Breeze", 4; Polyscope, 4.

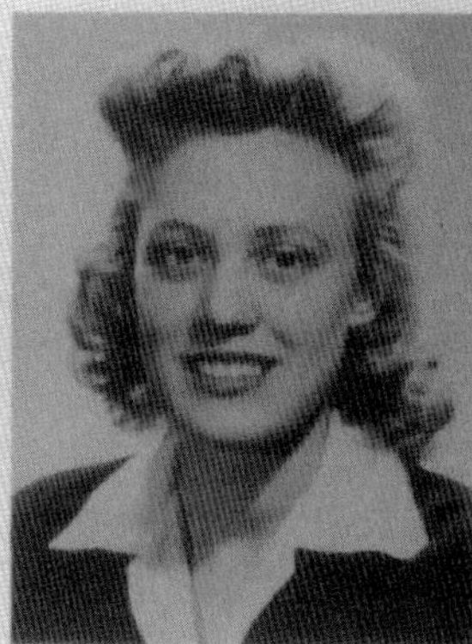

HELEN LOUISE SMITH, B.S. Peoria, Ill.

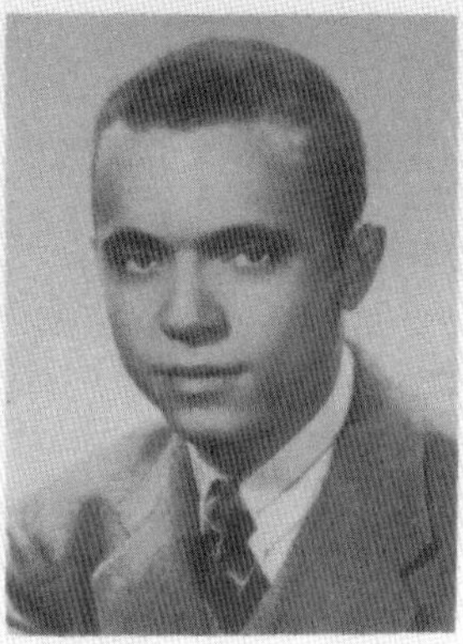

WILLIS SPRATTLING, B.S. Peoria, Ill.
U. S. Army Air Corps Reserve, Called to Active Duty, January 13, 1944; Federation of Scholars, 1-3; Epsilon Phi Alpha, 2-3.

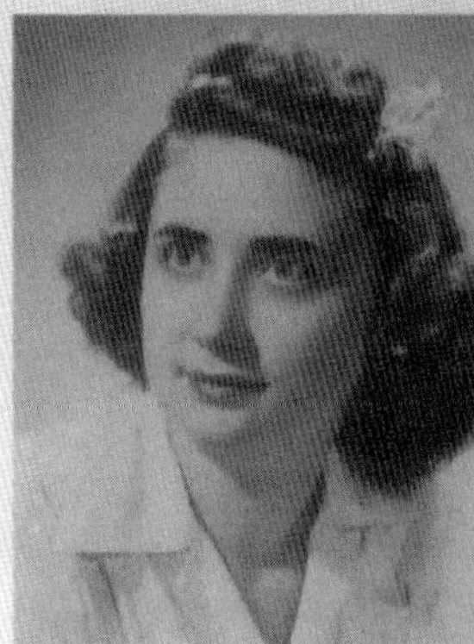

MEDIA STUBBLEFIELD, B.S. Peoria, Ill.
Lambda Phi, Secretary, 4; Mask and Gavel, 1-4; Spanish Club, 4; English Club, 4; Commerce Club, 3, Secretary, 3; Y.W.C.A., 1-3; Tech and Polyscope, Business Staff, 3.

This photograph shows Willis Sprattling, who received his B.S. in 1943. Sprattling was from Peoria, and while attending Bradley he was a member of Epsilon Phi Alpha, Federation of Scholars, and the U.S. Army Air Corps Reserve. He was called to active duty along with many other Bradley students in 1944.

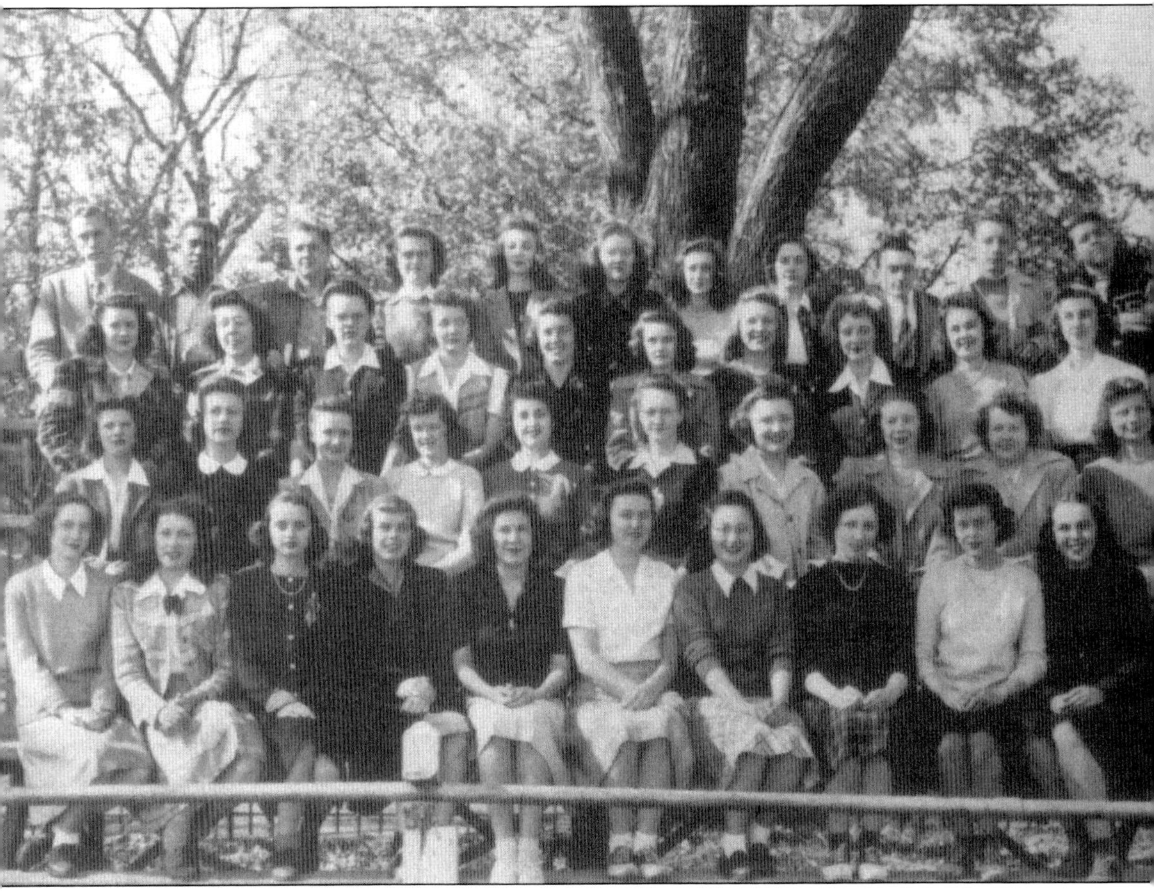

This photograph of members of the sophomore class is in the 1943-44 *Polyscope*. Second from the left in the back row is Tyrie Booker.

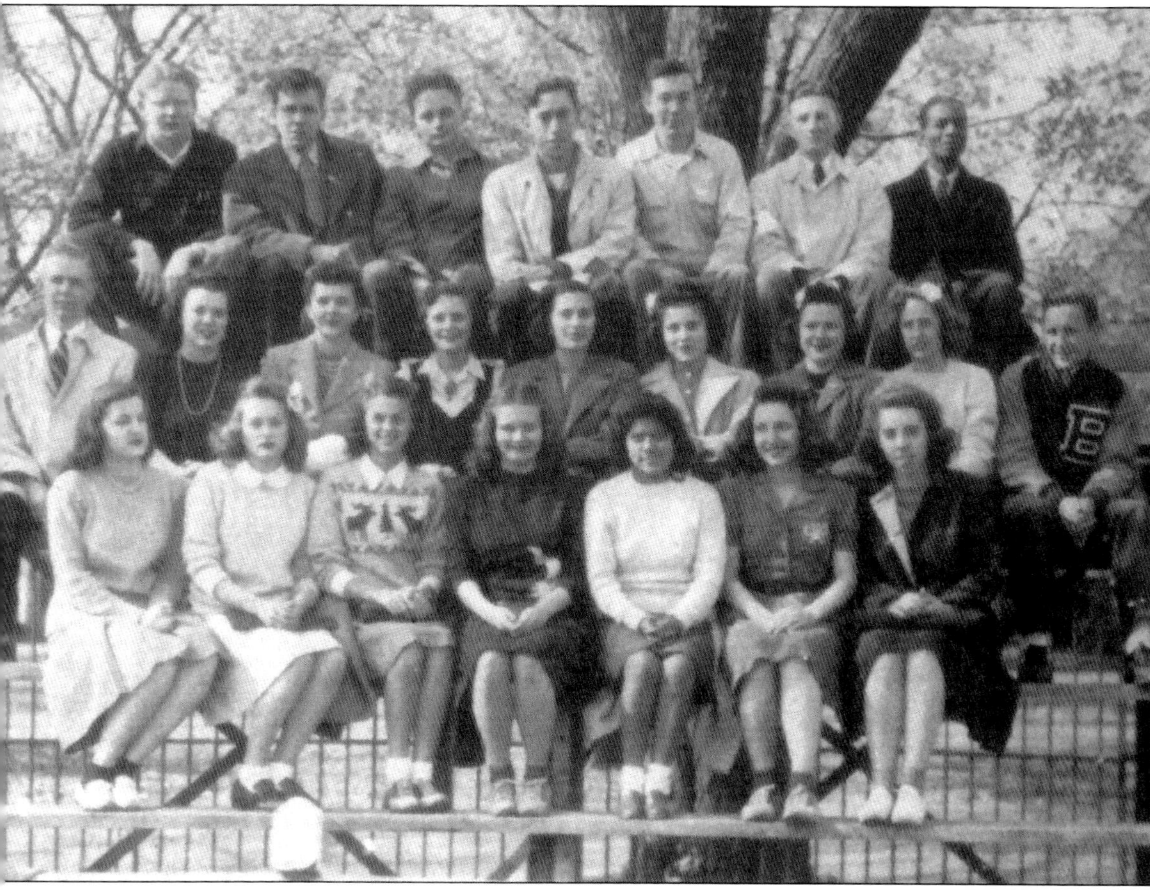

This is another photograph of members of the sophomore class in the 1943-44 *Polyscope*. Wymon Huckaby is the last person in the top row to the right.

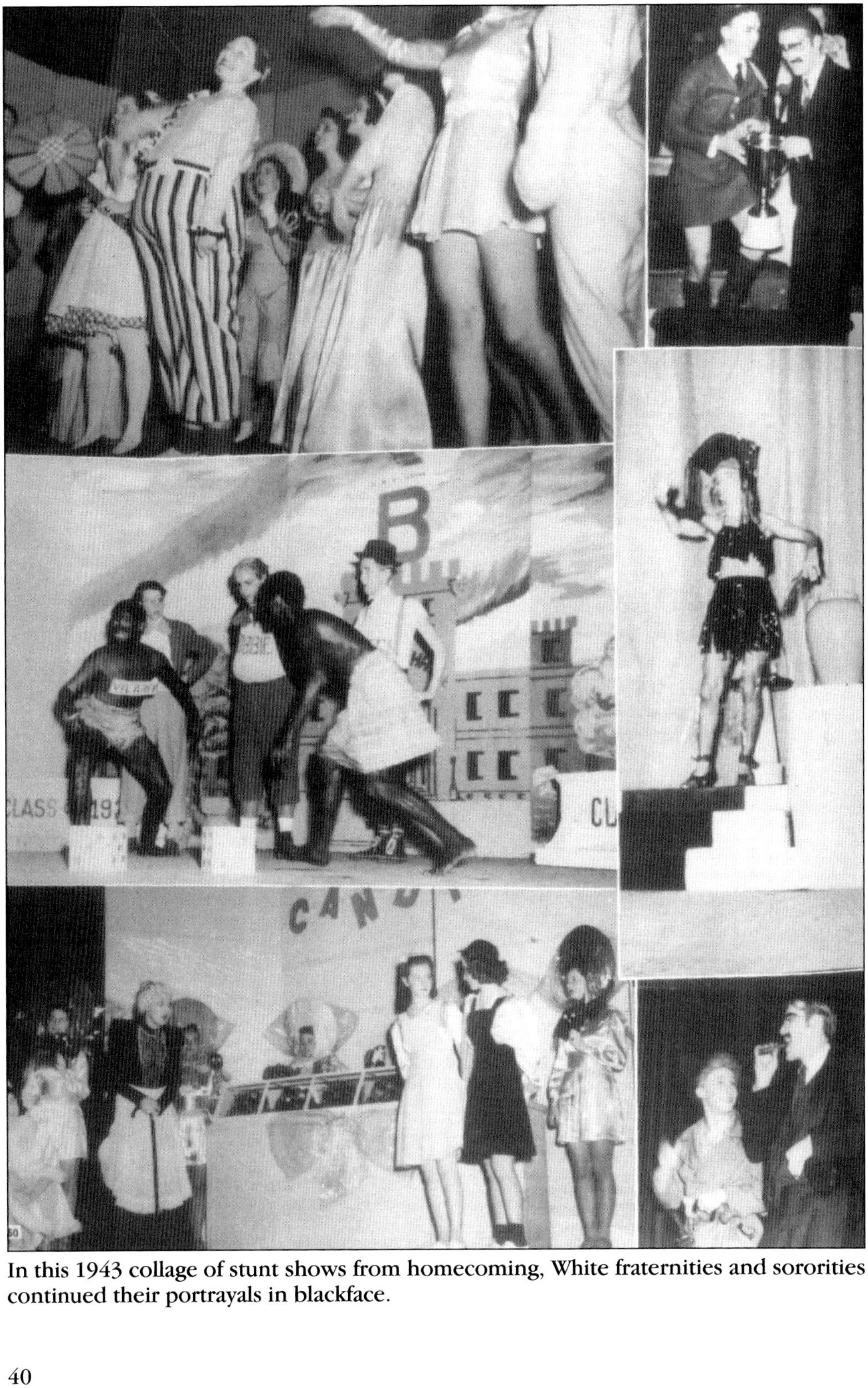

In this 1943 collage of stunt shows from homecoming, White fraternities and sororities continued their portrayals in blackface.

Two

Strangers in a Strange Land
Bradley's Invisible Students and Faculty 1944–1956

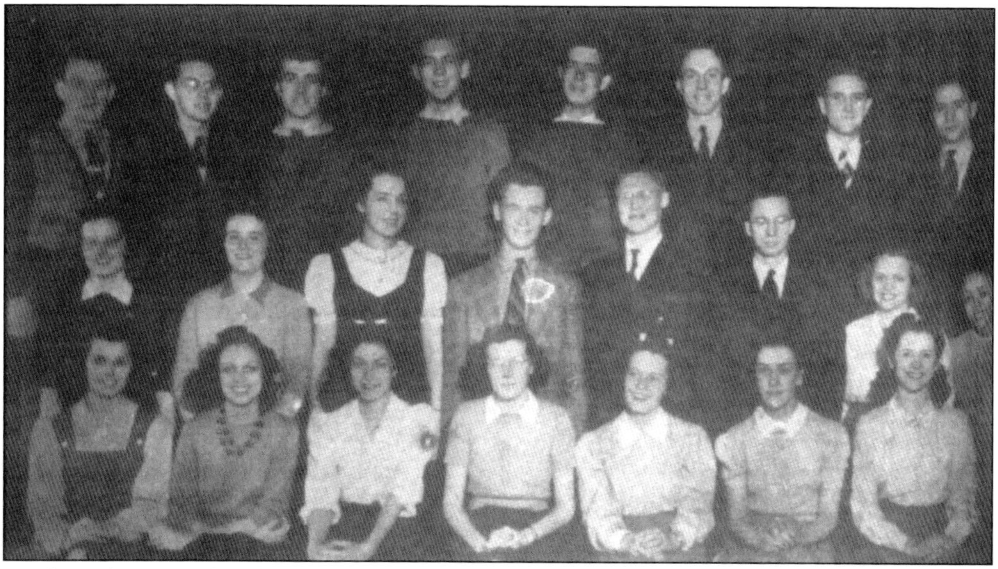

In this photograph of members of the 1944 freshman class, E. Norton, an African-American female, is visible at the right end of the second row. No information is given on her major or hometown. In the same annual, Marguerite Wallace of Monmouth, Illinois, who was a transfer student from Western State Teachers College, graduated in the class of 1944 with a B.S.

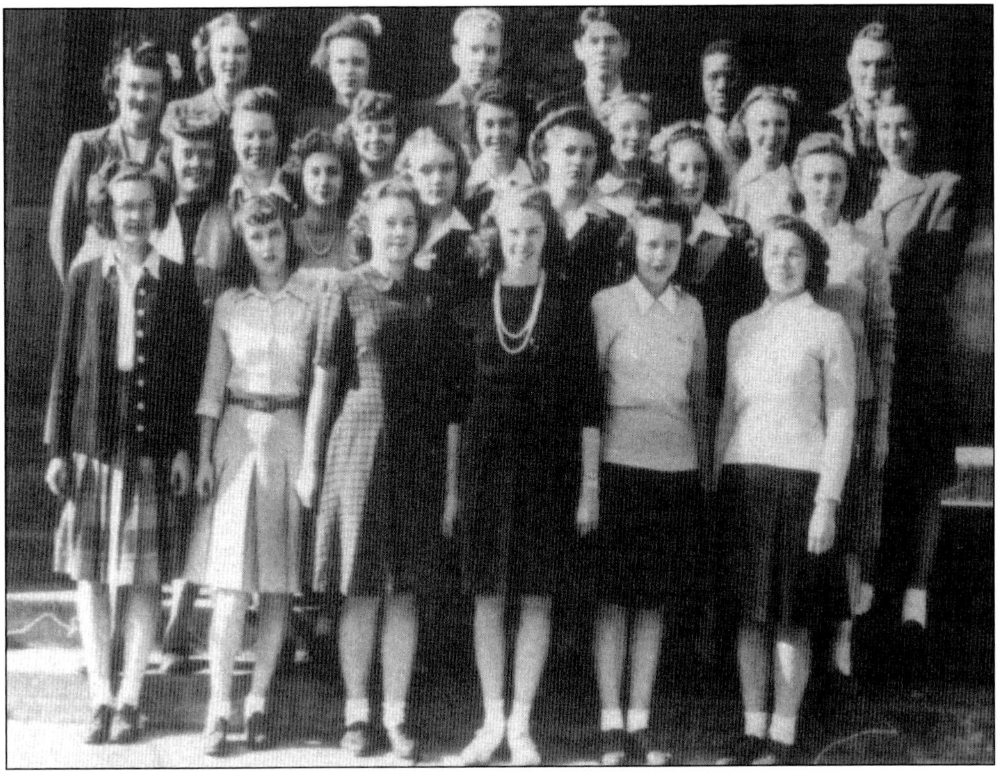

Shown above is a photograph of members of the 1945 sophomore class. Second on the end of the fourth row is Tyrie Booker.

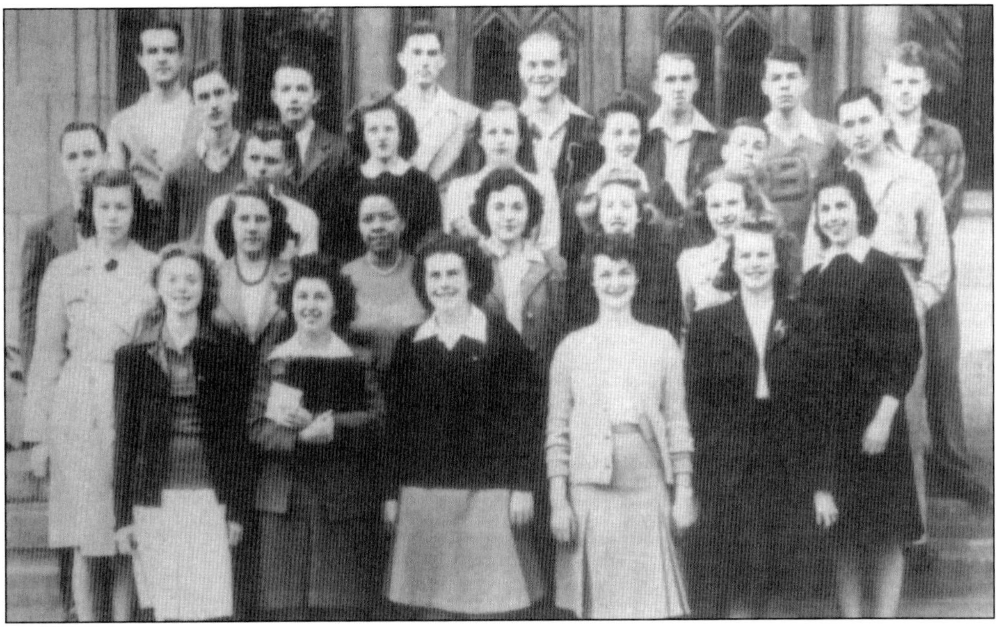

This is a photograph of members of the 1945 freshman class. In the middle of the second row is Hazel Fitcher.

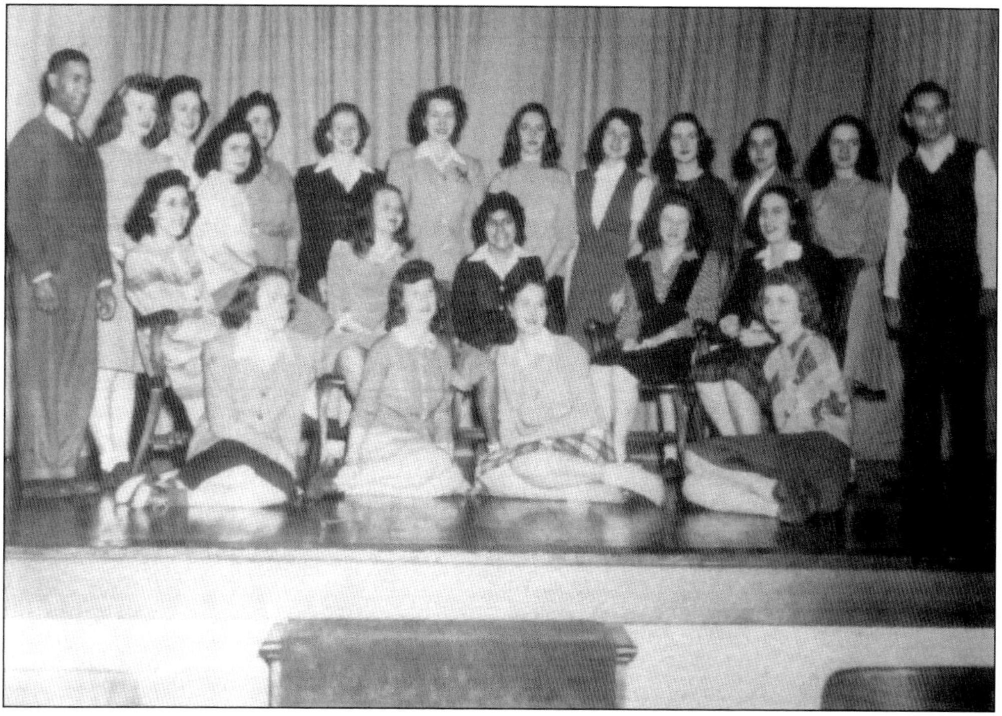

This is a picture of Tyrie Booker, a member of the 1945 Spanish Club. Booker is the first person in the third row, shown along with other students, some of whom appear to be of Latin descent.

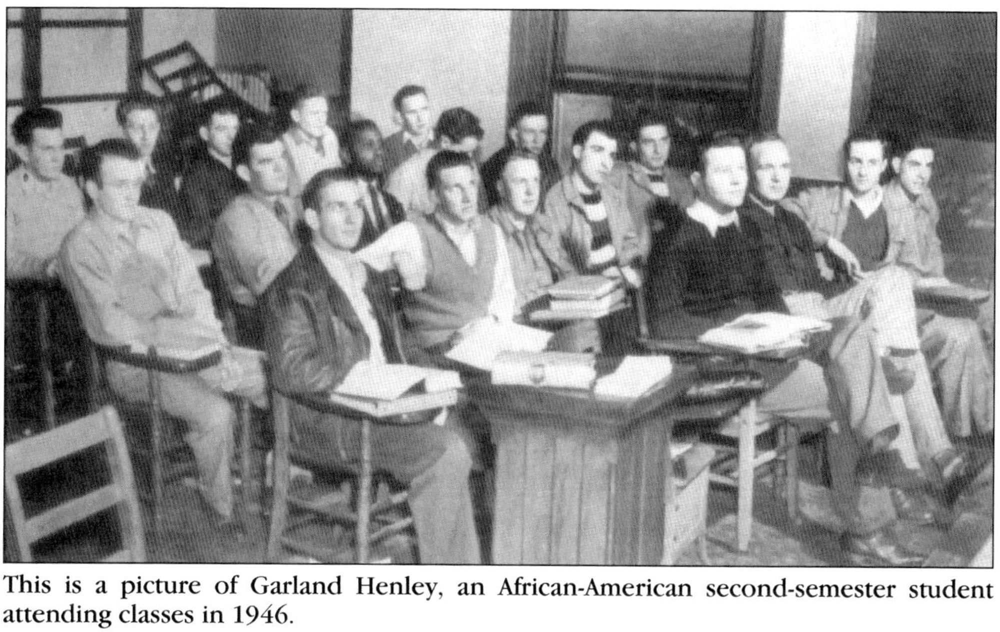

This is a picture of Garland Henley, an African-American second-semester student attending classes in 1946.

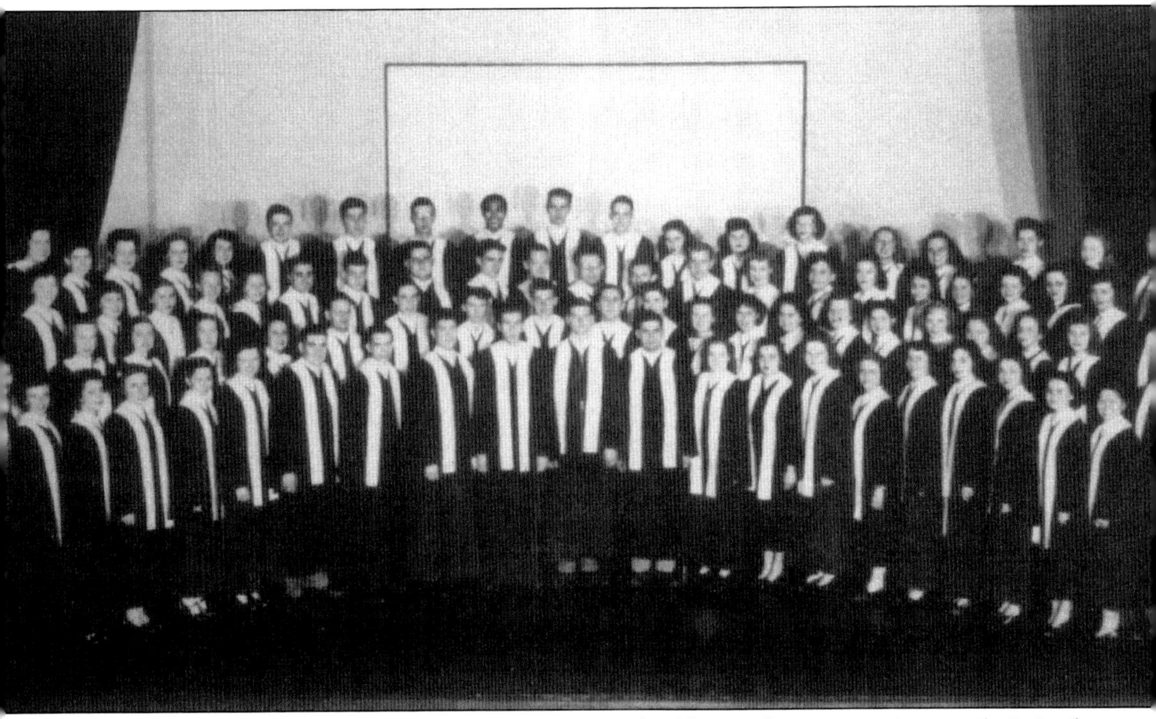

In this photo of the A Cappella Choir from 1945-46, an African-American male is in the center of the top row.

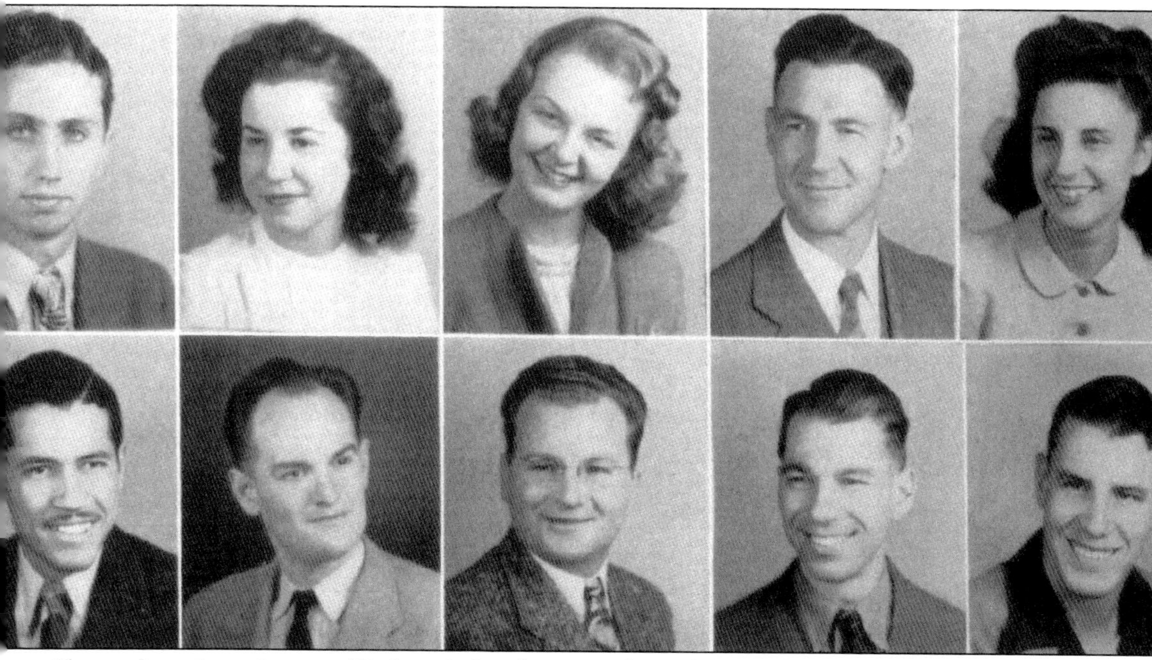

Shown here is a picture of Robert J. Smith, a member of the 1947 junior class.

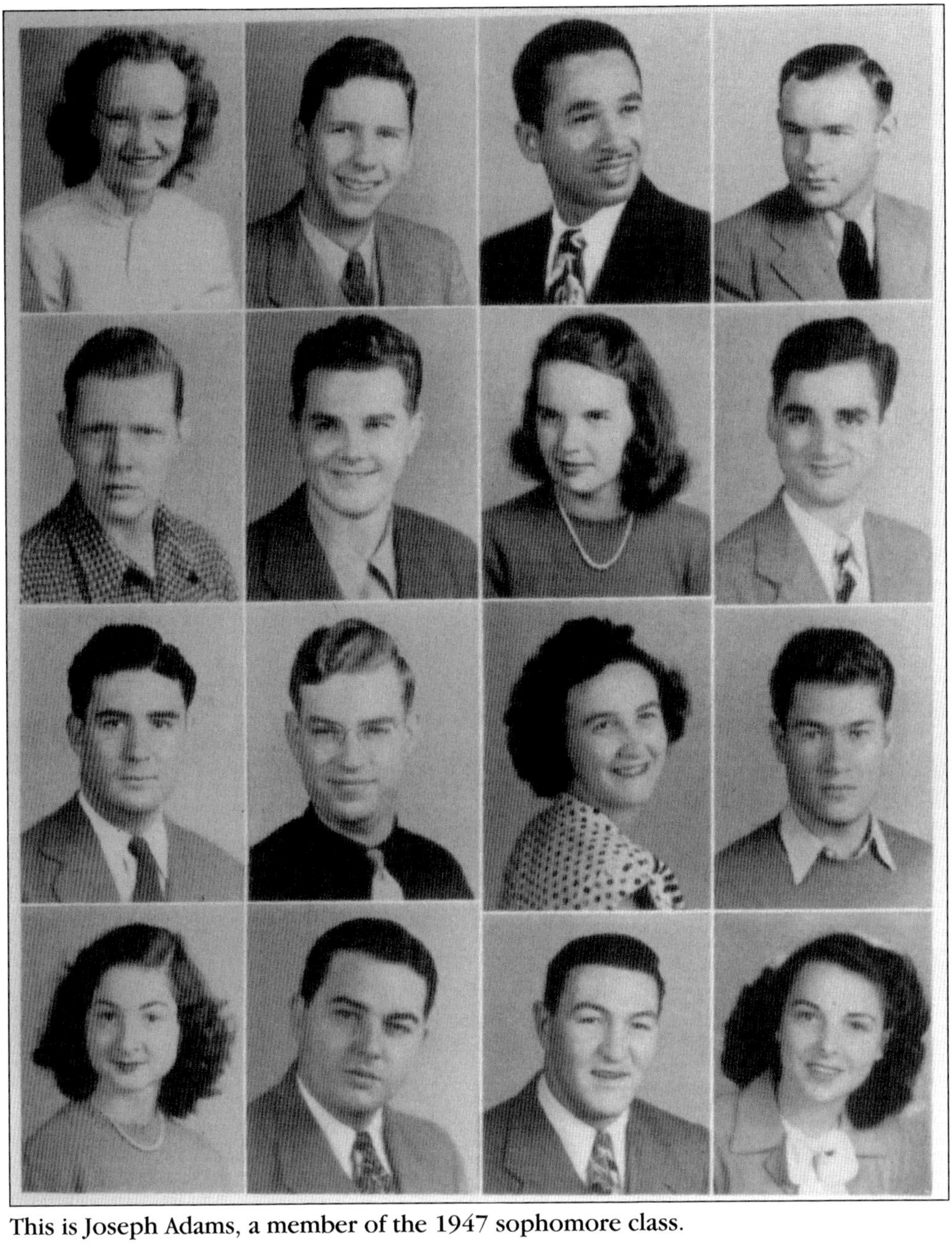

This is Joseph Adams, a member of the 1947 sophomore class.

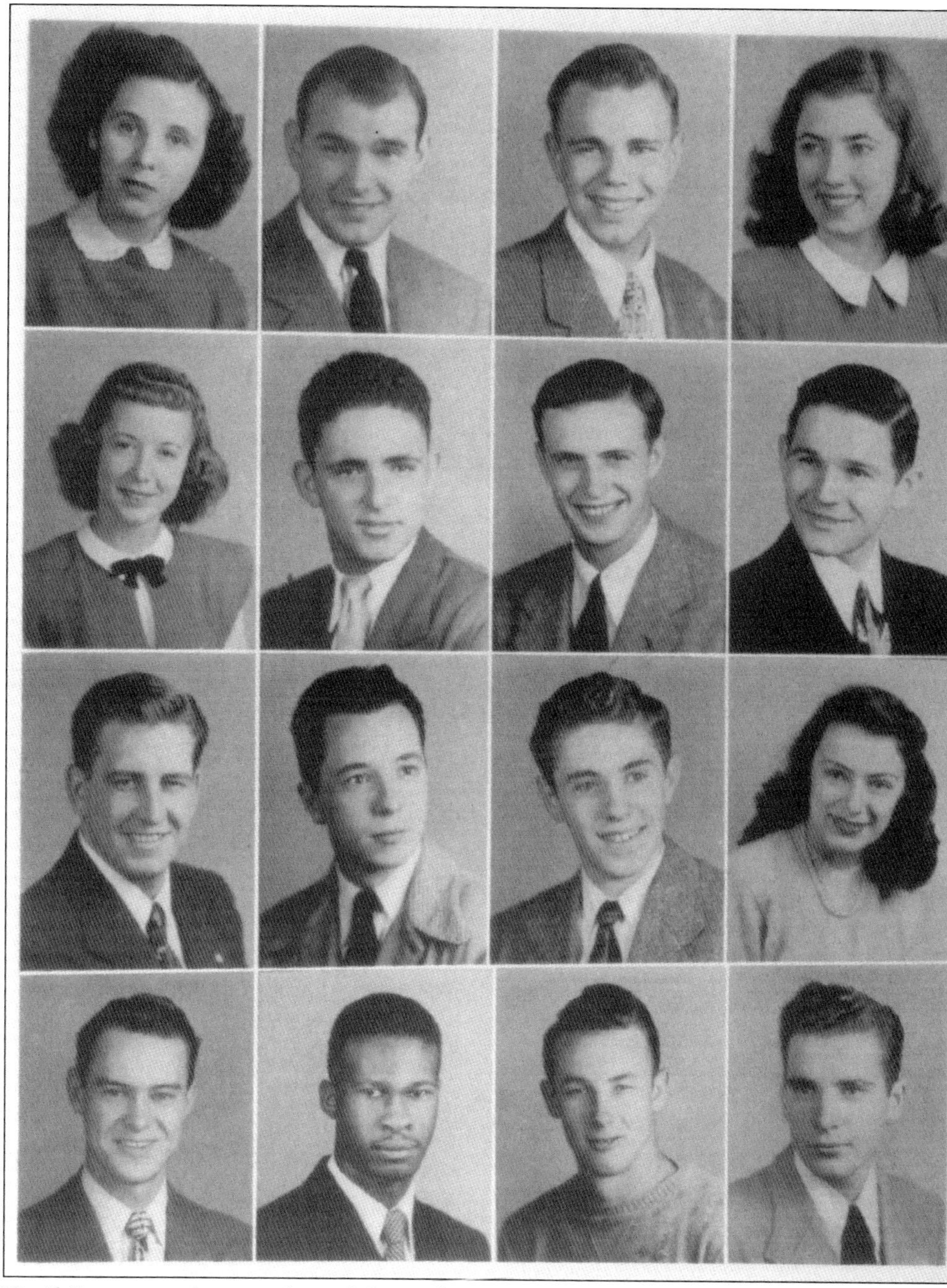

Virgil Greenwood, a member of the 1947 freshman class, can be seen in this photo. He and George C. Conner, Walter Ezzell, Lewis Flint, George Hickman, Crawford Hodges, Frank Owens, Edward Robinson, and John White were a part of the freshman class of 1947. This was the largest class of African-American students with pictures in the annuals at any one time in the university's history to that point.

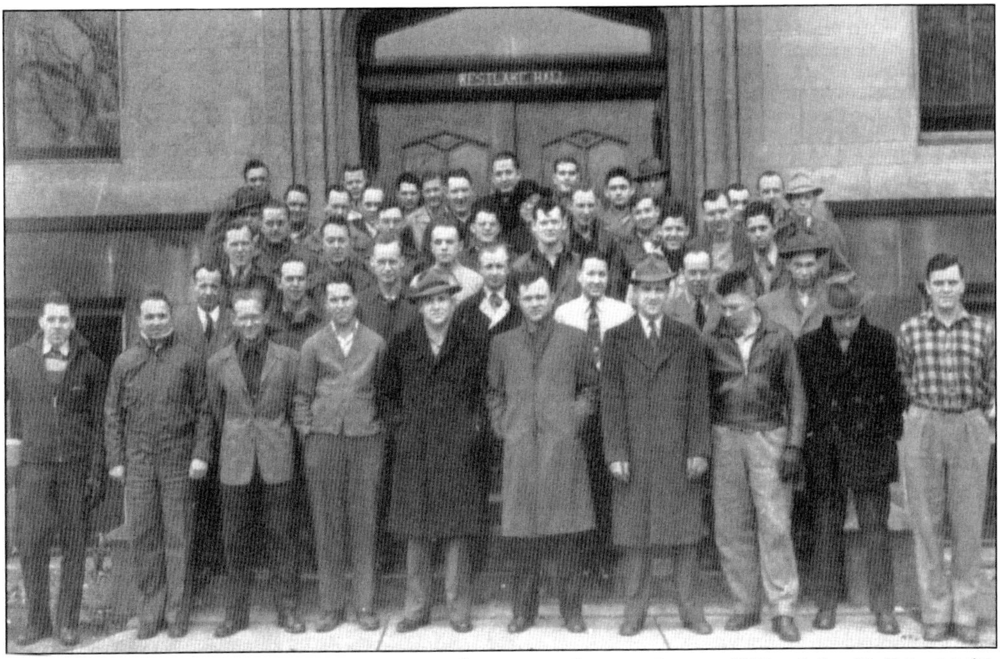

This is a group shot of the Horology students standing in front of Westlake Hall in 1947. There is an African-American male student one row from the top on the end wearing a hat, and an African American standing in the back row at the far left.

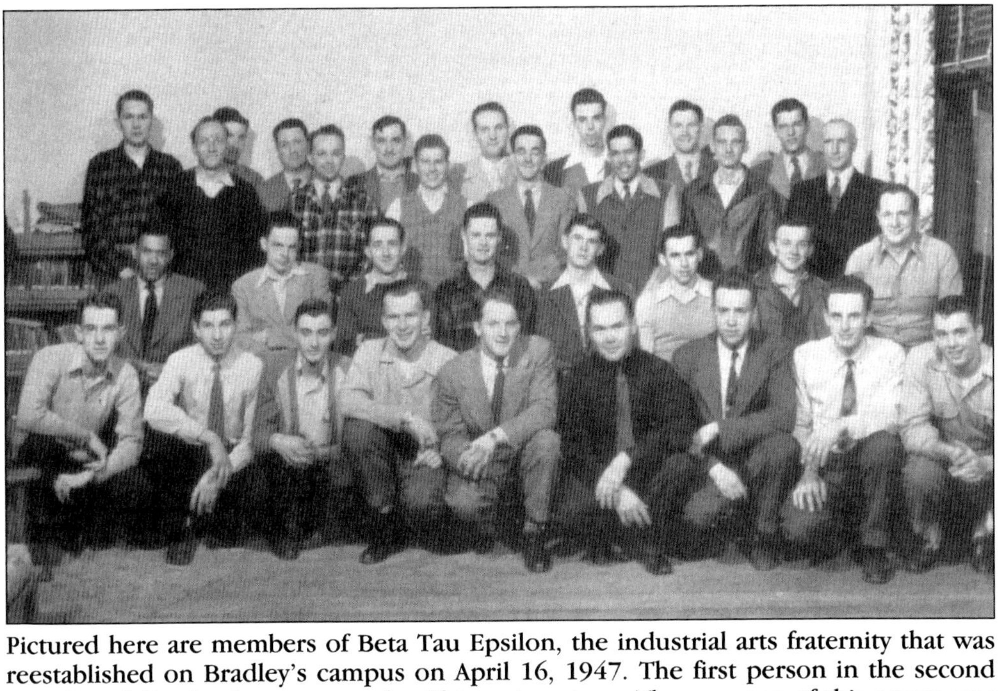

Pictured here are members of Beta Tau Epsilon, the industrial arts fraternity that was reestablished on Bradley's campus on April 16, 1947. The first person in the second row, David Gambuti, appears to be African American. The purpose of this group was to expose industrial arts students to the various industrial plants in the area including Caterpillar, Keystone, and the Northern Regional Research Laboratory.

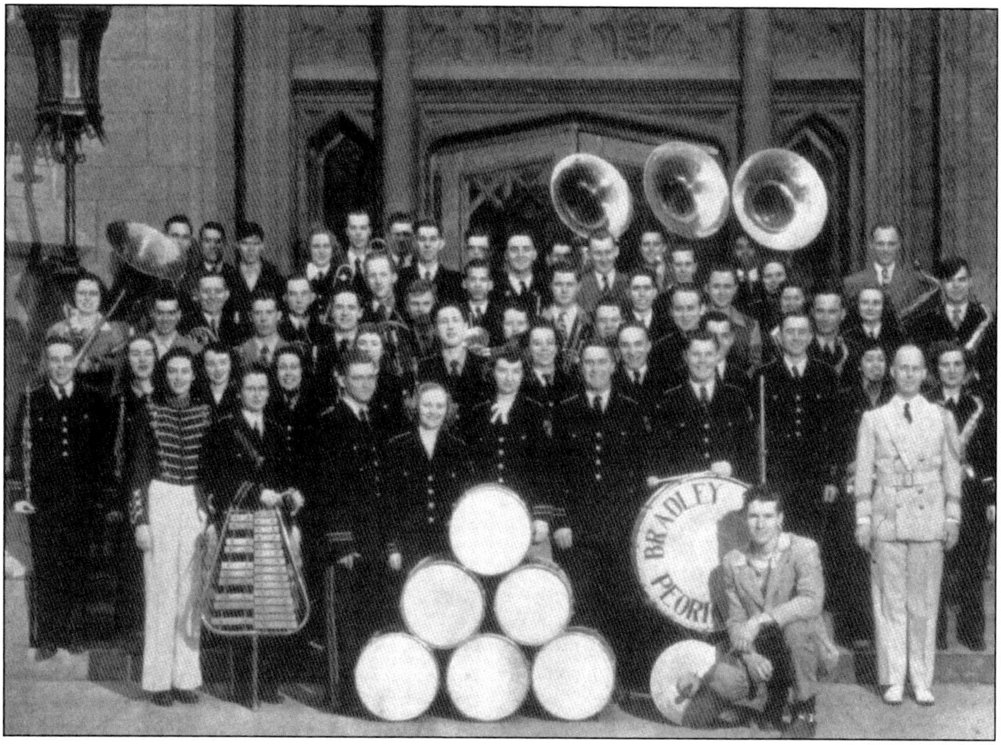

Members of the 1947 Bradley Band are pictured here. The last person in the last row to the right, Elbert Hardeman, was a tuba player in the band.

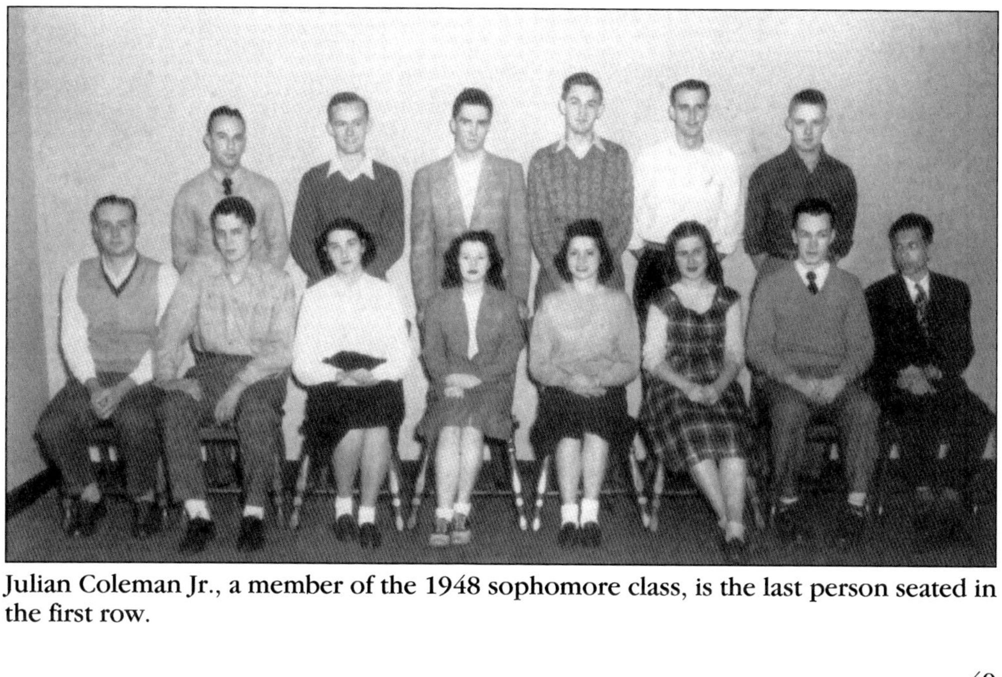

Julian Coleman Jr., a member of the 1948 sophomore class, is the last person seated in the first row.

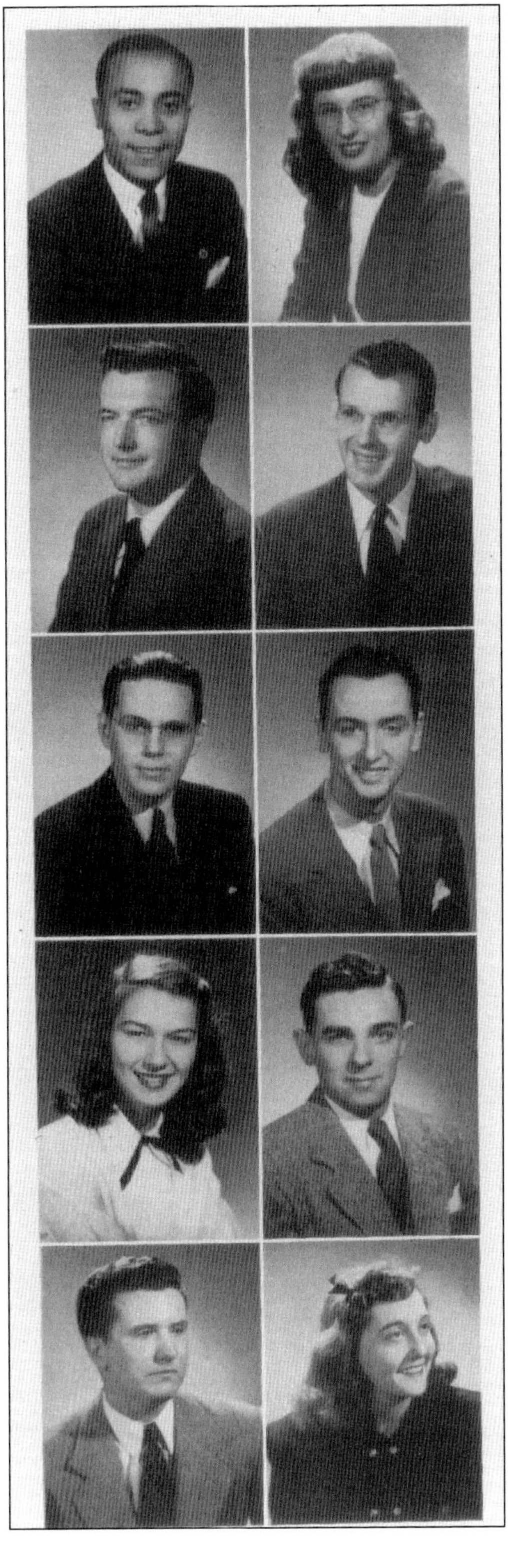

Troy D. Norton was a graduating senior in the class of 1948, with a B.S. in History and Political Science. Norton, from Peoria, Illinois, was a Student Federalist, a member of the Commerce Club, and involved with Inter-Varsity Christian Fellowship.

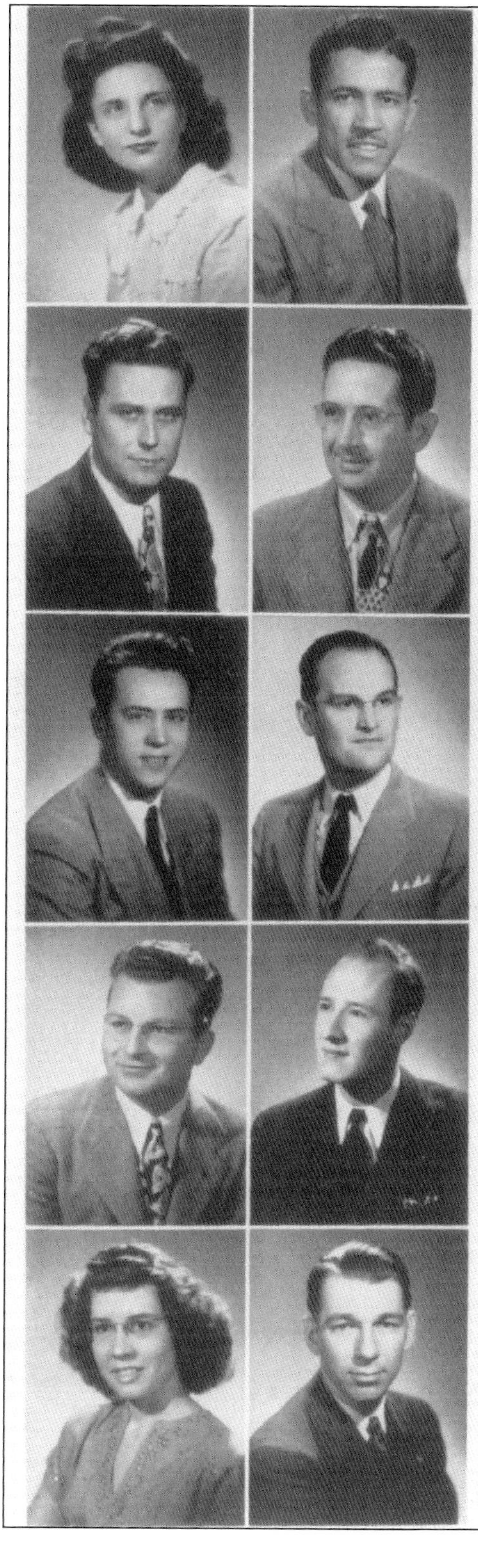

Robert J. Smith was a graduating senior in the class of 1947, with a B.S. in Industrial Arts. While at Bradley, Smith was a member of Beta Tau Epsilon, Federation Scholars, and the winner of the Phi Sigma Pi Scholarship Medal. Smith was from Springfield, Illinois, and was a transfer student from Howard University in Washington D.C.

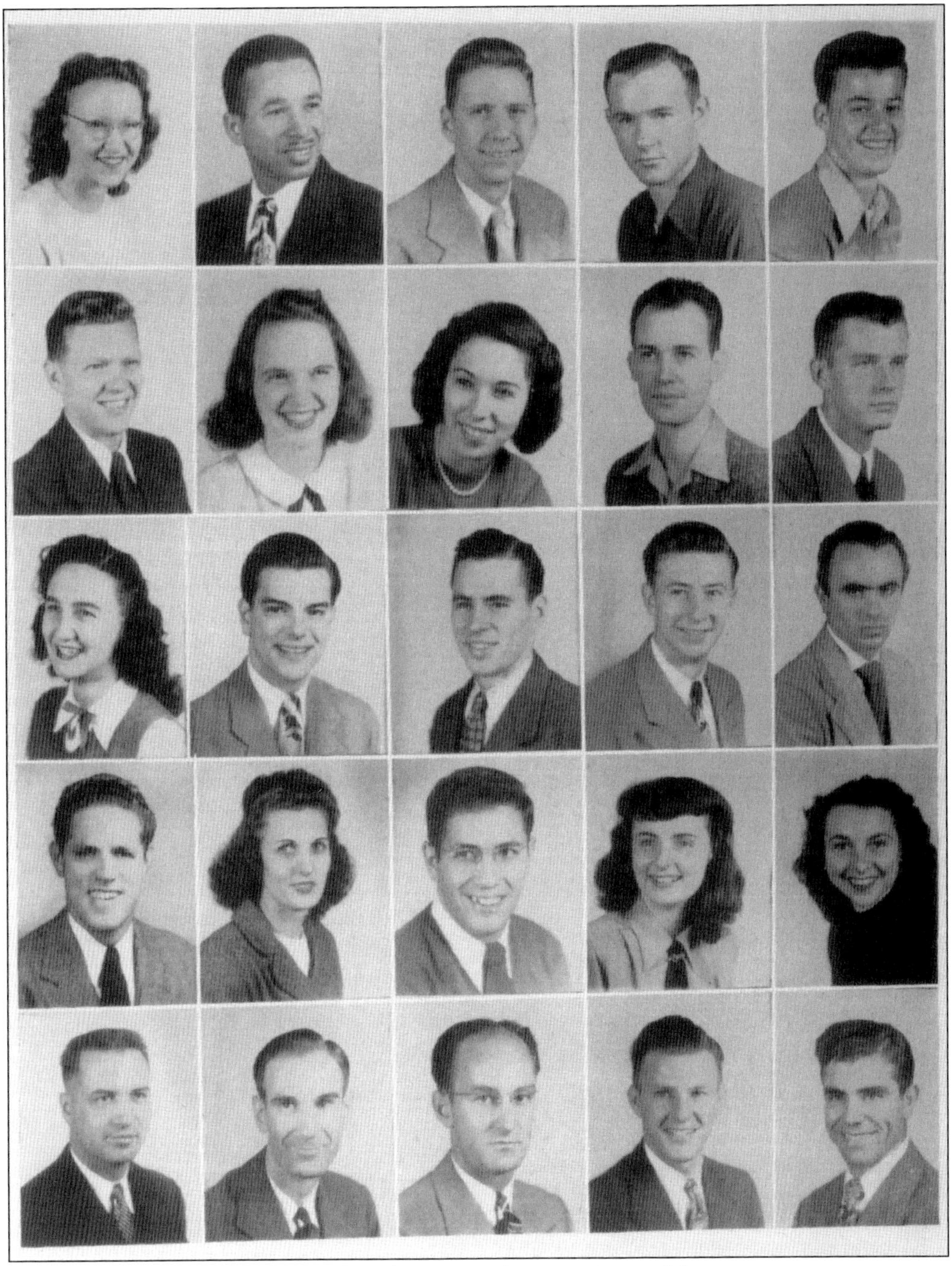

Joseph Adams, a member of the 1948 junior class, is pictured here.

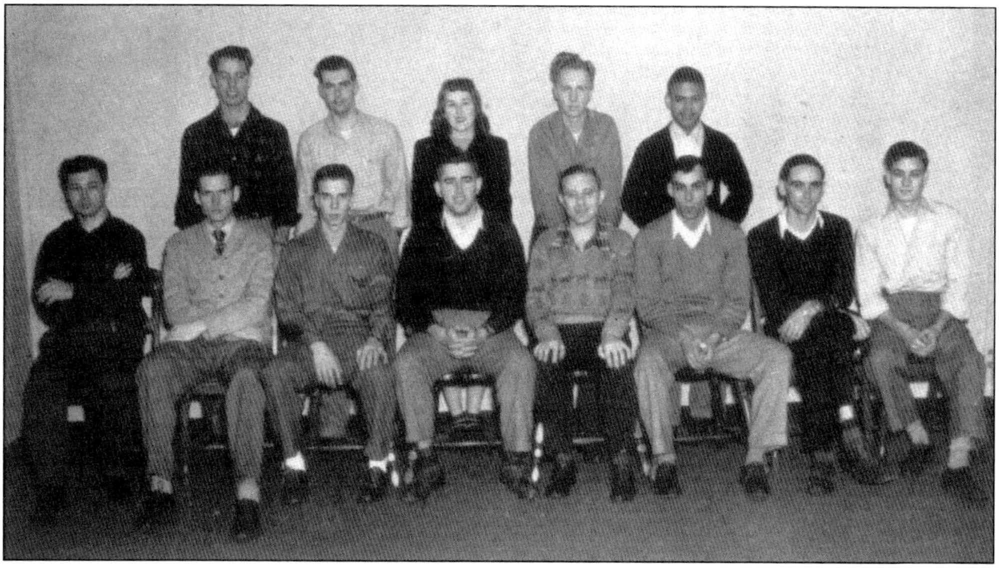

Lewis Flint, the last person standing in the top row, was also a member of the 1948 sophomore class.

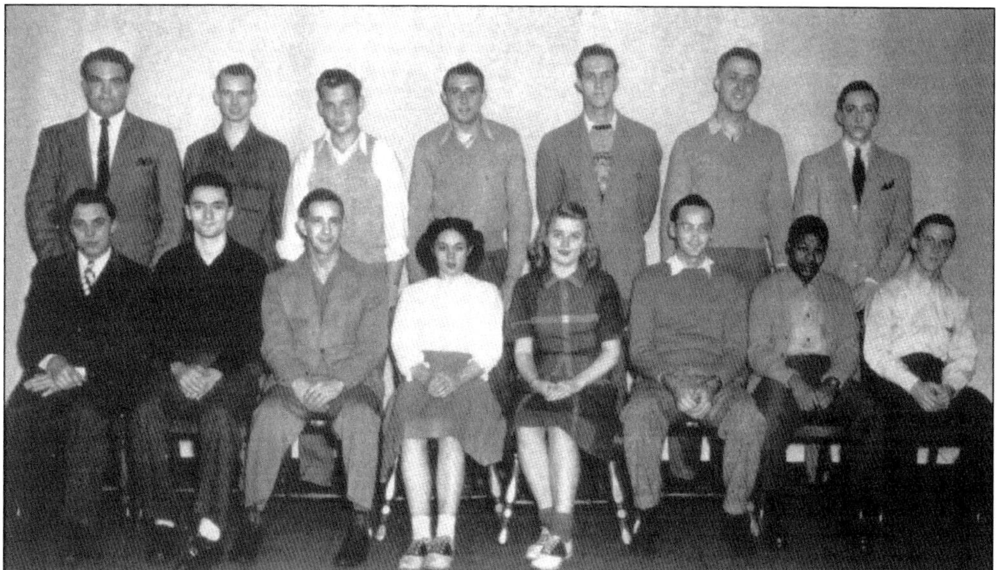

George W. Hickman Jr., seated in the first row, second from the right, was also a member of the 1948 sophomore class.

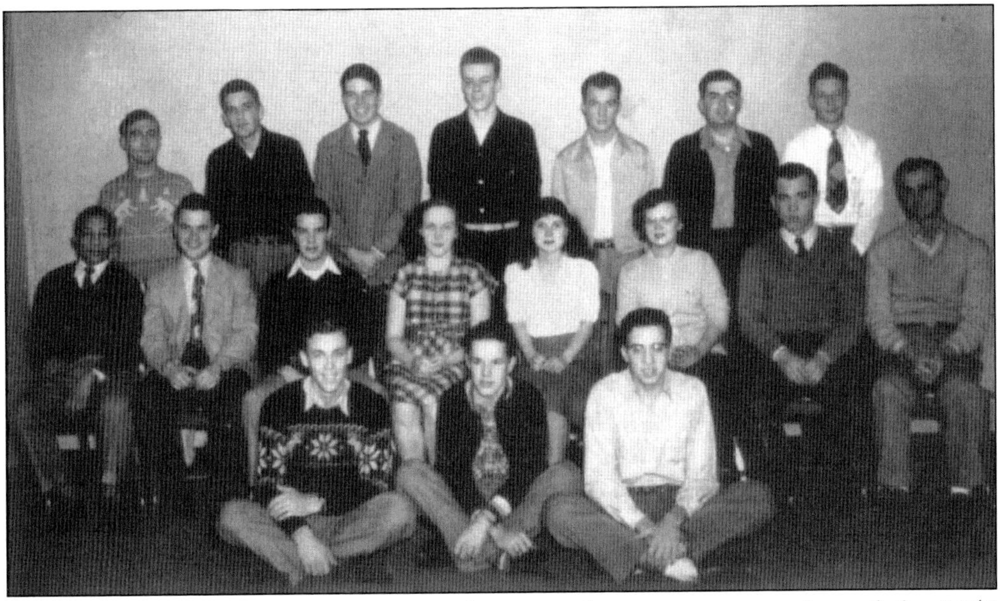

Wilmer M. White, the first person in the second row, was a member of the 1948 sophomore class.

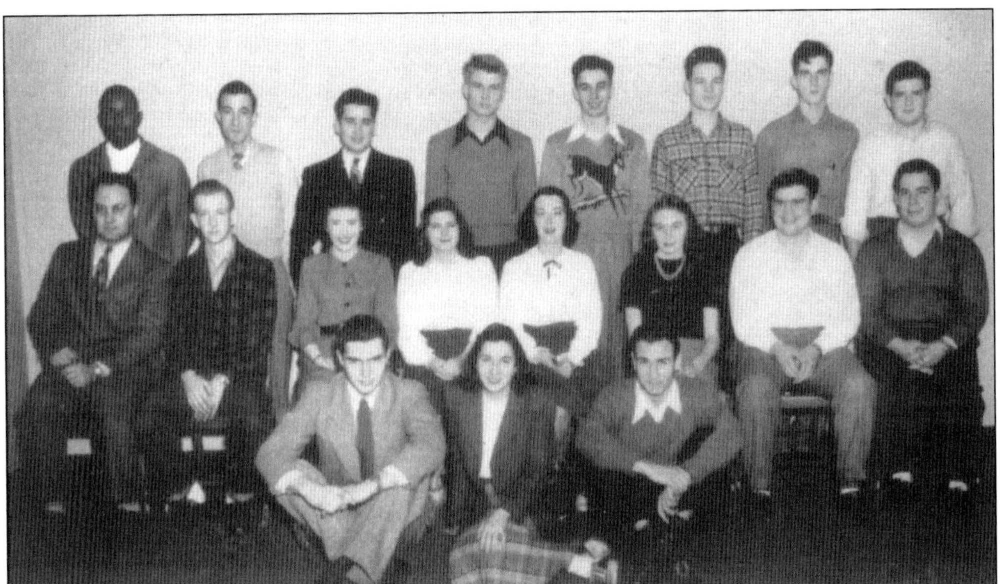

Richard C. Hands, the first person standing in the back row, was a member of the 1948 freshman class.

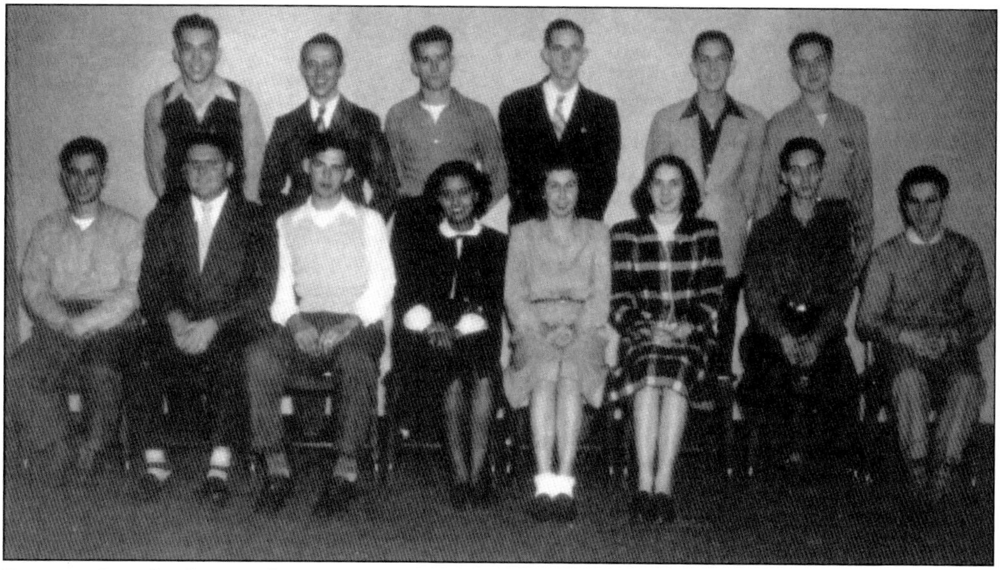

Frances Spurlock was also a member of the 1948 freshman class.

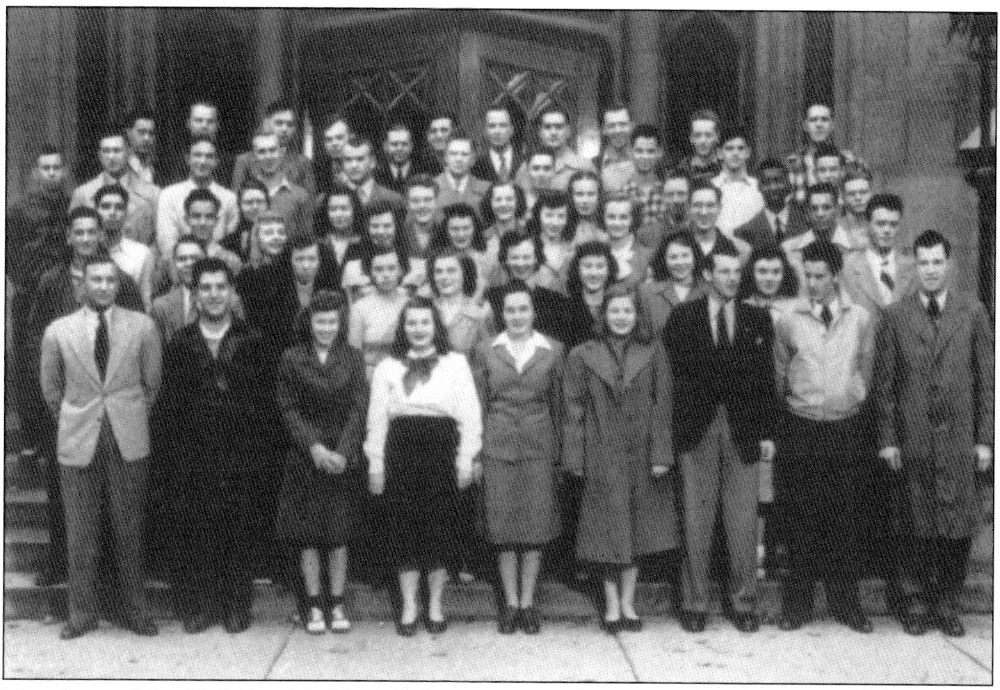

Members of the 1948 Pre-Medical Club are pictured here. Two African Americans appear in this photo. The next-to-last person in the third row is Harrison Smith, and just above him at the end of the fourth row is George Blick.

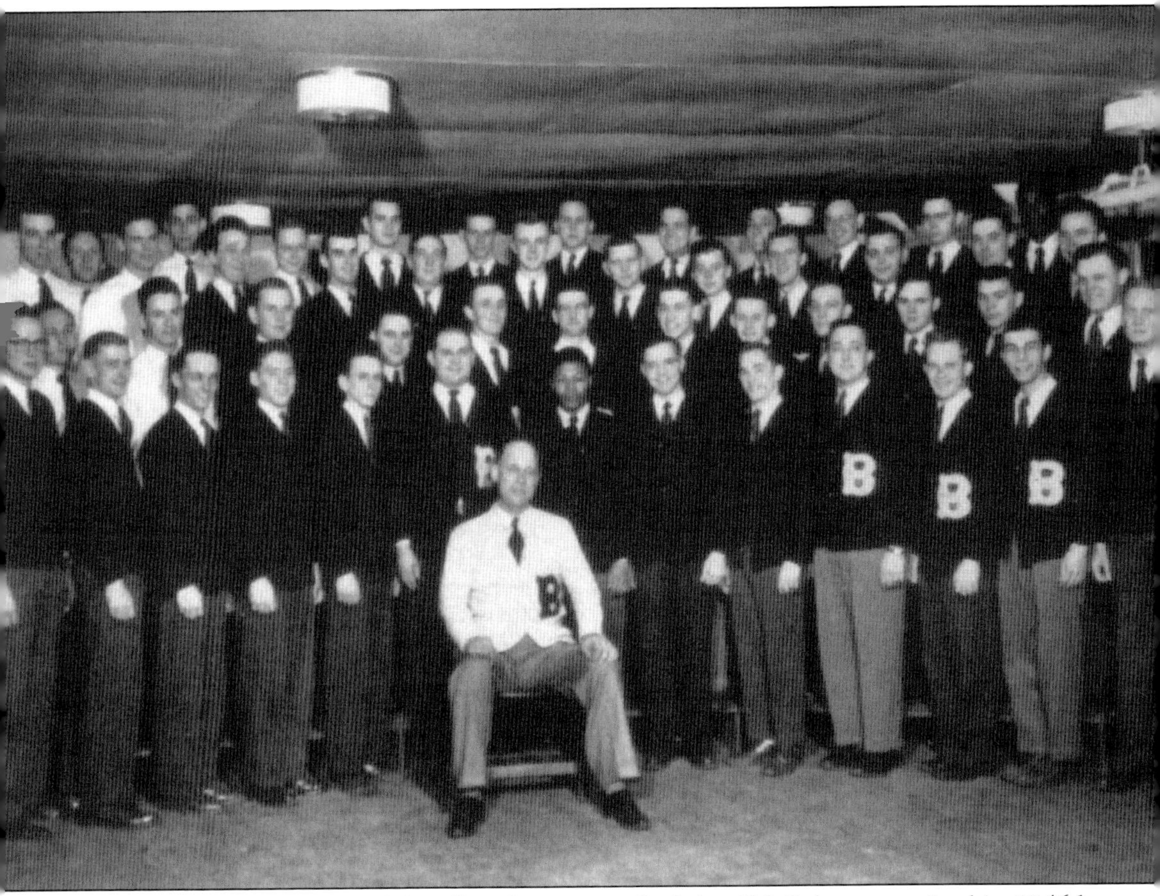

This is a group photo of the all-male group called the Chieftains, organized in 1946 by Cardon V. Burnham. This group was originally composed of only veterans, but by 1948 had expanded to include any male student who was interested. The group sang a wide repertoire including light opera and spirituals. In the center of the first row is George W. Hickman Jr., standing behind Cardon V. Burnham, who is seated in the center.

Shown here is a group photo of the members of the Bradley chapter of the Inter-Varsity Christian Fellowship. This organization was open to all Bradley students and was affiliated with the international office in Chicago. The group met twice a week to study the bible and to hear prominent religious speakers. They also held a yearly banquet to which local high school seniors were invited. The first person in the second row is Roy Norton, and the fourth person in the fifth row is Troy Norton.

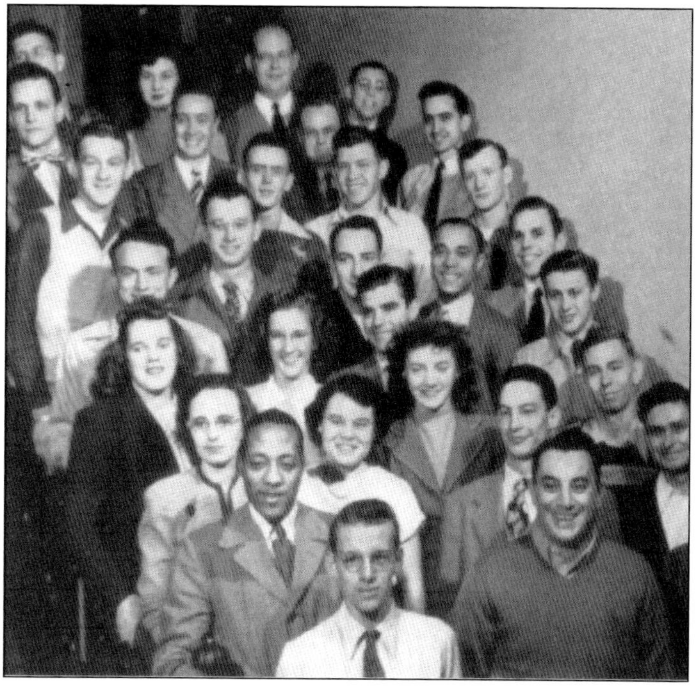

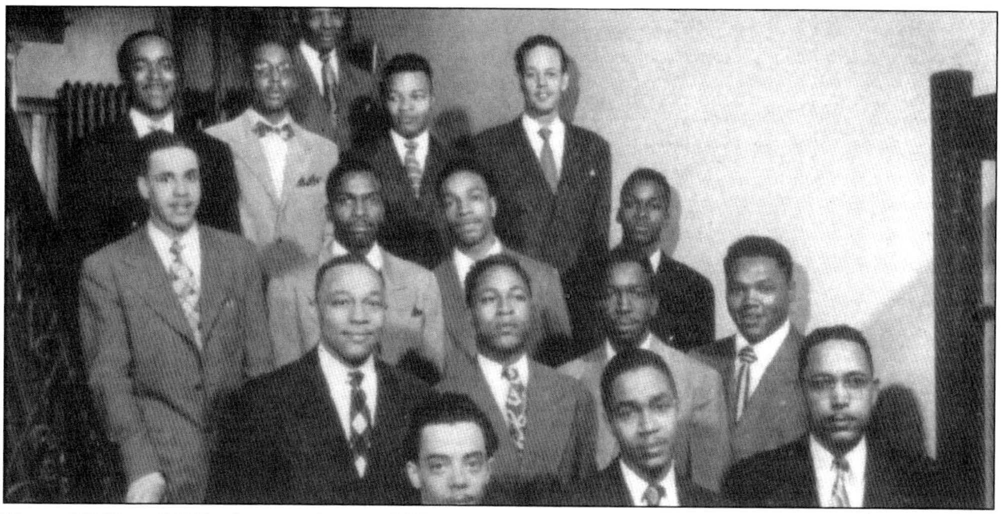

From 1945 to 1950, the numbers of African Americans attending Bradley began to increase significantly. As a result of this increase, more and more African Americans became involved in various social and academic organizations and sports. Many Blacks also felt the need for fraternal and sororital groups. On March 5, 1948, several African-American male students established Xi Epsilon, the Bradley chapter of Omega Psi Phi, an all-Black Greek fraternity. This photo contains pioneer members from 1948. They are, from left to right: (first row) Jean Flowers; Lafayette T. Jackson, president; Tony S. Rudd, vice president; (second row) Wilmer M. White; Henry Seward Jr.; Edward Robinson; Walter Maddox; (third row) Samuel J. Gibson Jr.; Alonzo Robinson; John H. Smith; Thomas Johnson; (fourth row) Hayman C. Bell; Walter Richard; Willie Adams; James H. Stubblefield; (fifth row) Clifford A Thomas.

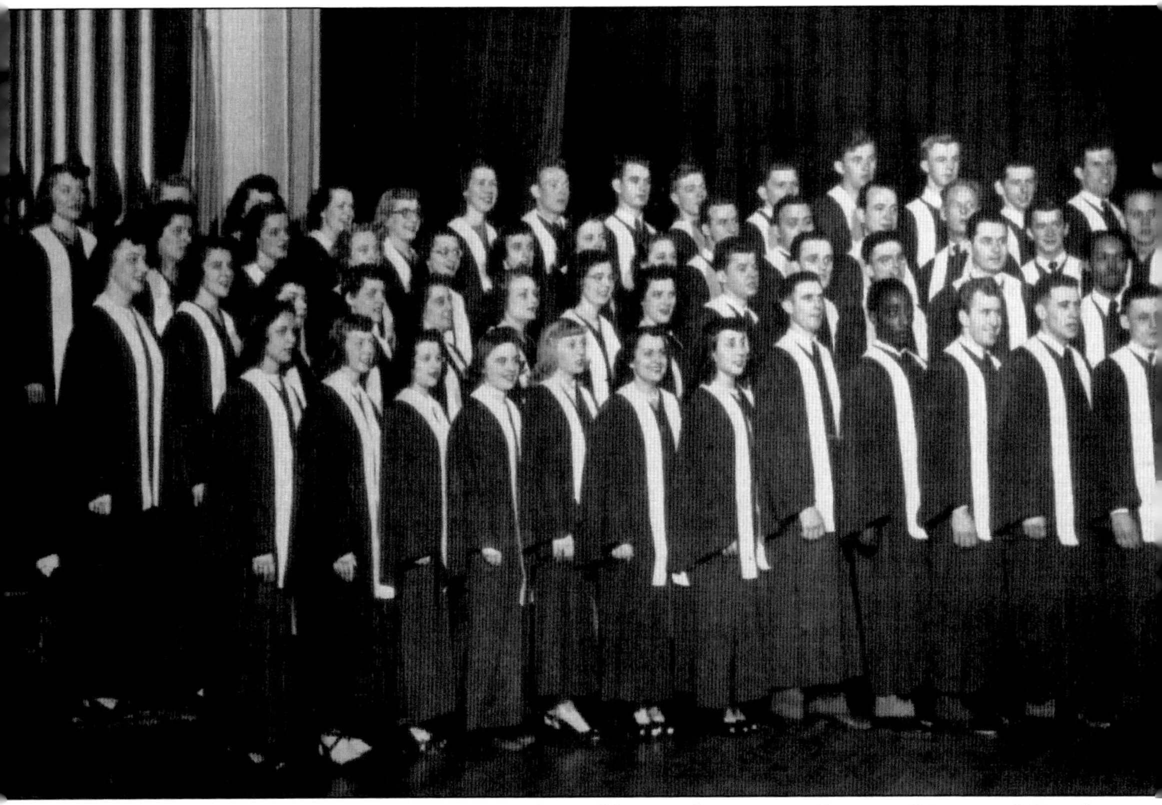

The 1947-48 A Capella Choir was conducted by Cardon V. Burnham and Leonard Crook. The choir was mixed with male and female students, and they performed at campus events such as Founder's Day.

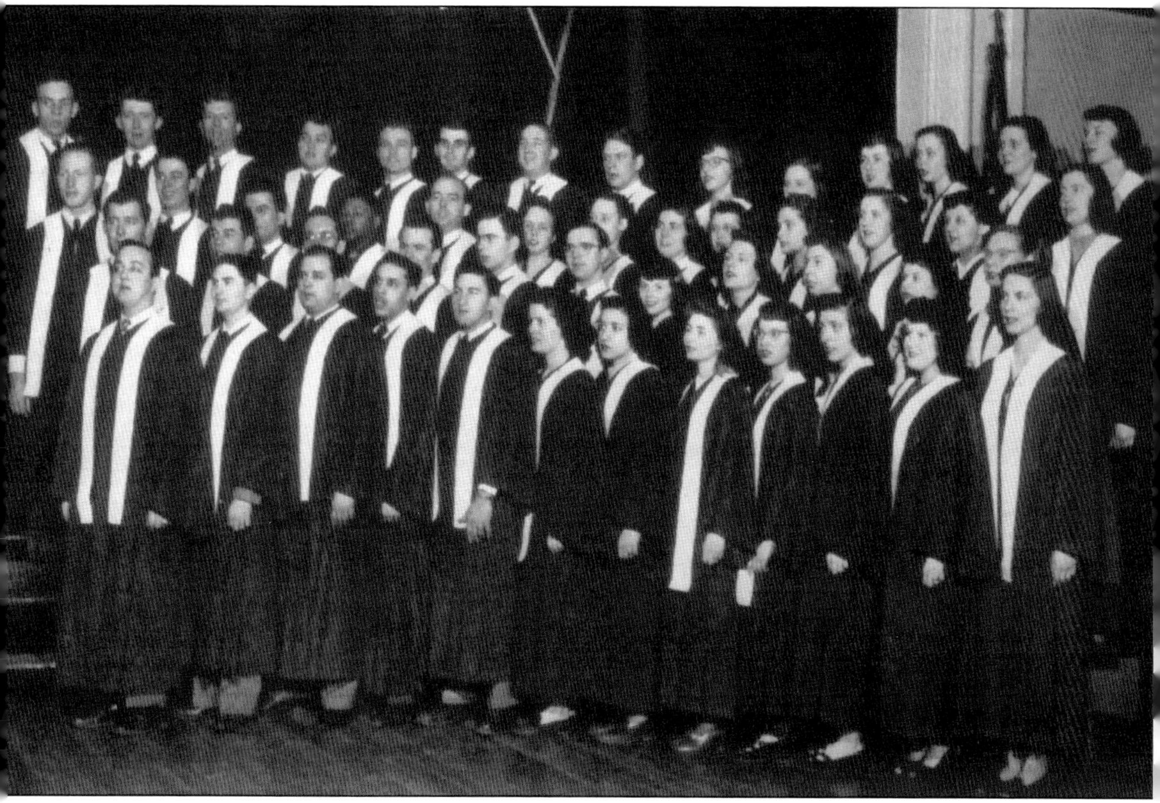

The highlight of this season was a program in Orchestra Hall in Chicago. In the first row, fourth from the right side, is James Helm. Sam Gibson is fourth in the first row, and George Hickman is fourth in the third row.

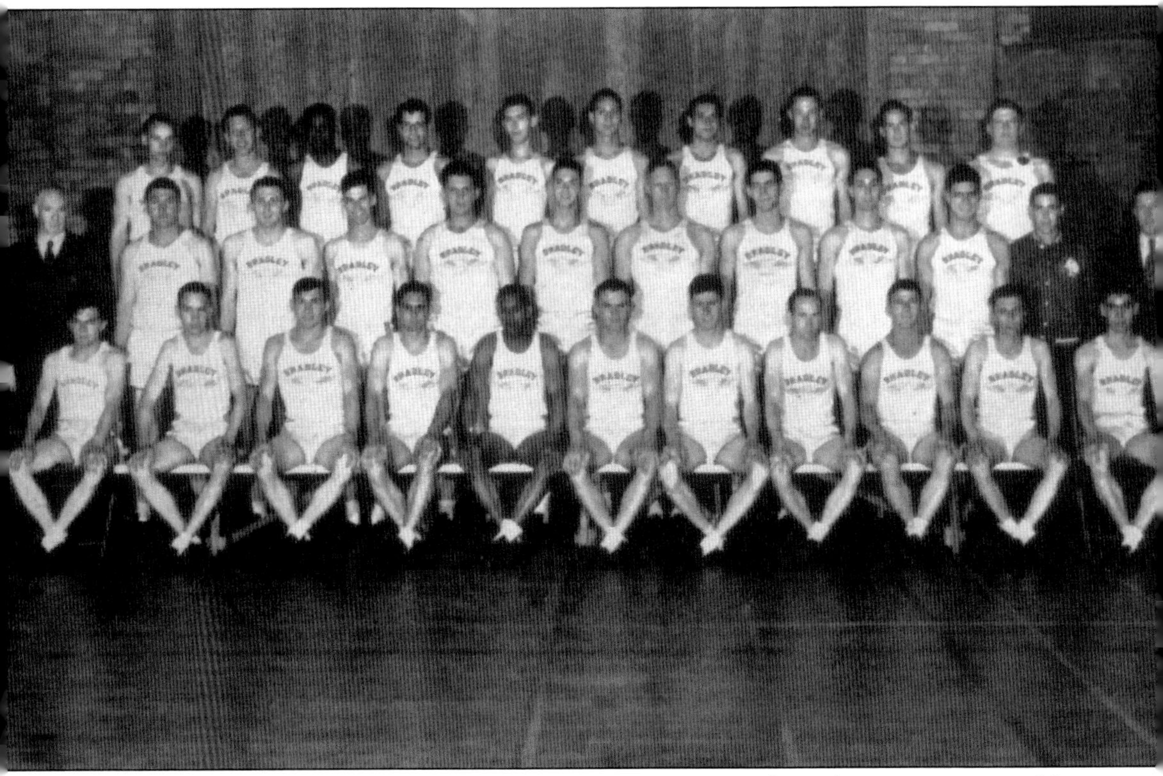

Up until the late 1940s and early 1950s, there were very few African-American athletes who played any sport for Bradley. Beginning with boxer Erskine Parker in 1938, many associated with the university began to question why this was so and encouraged the university to follow the lead of institutions such as Ohio State University by recruiting more African-American athletes. By 1948, there were two African-American members of the track and field team. Only last names are given, but the fifth person seated in the first row is Owen, and the third person in the third row is Connor.

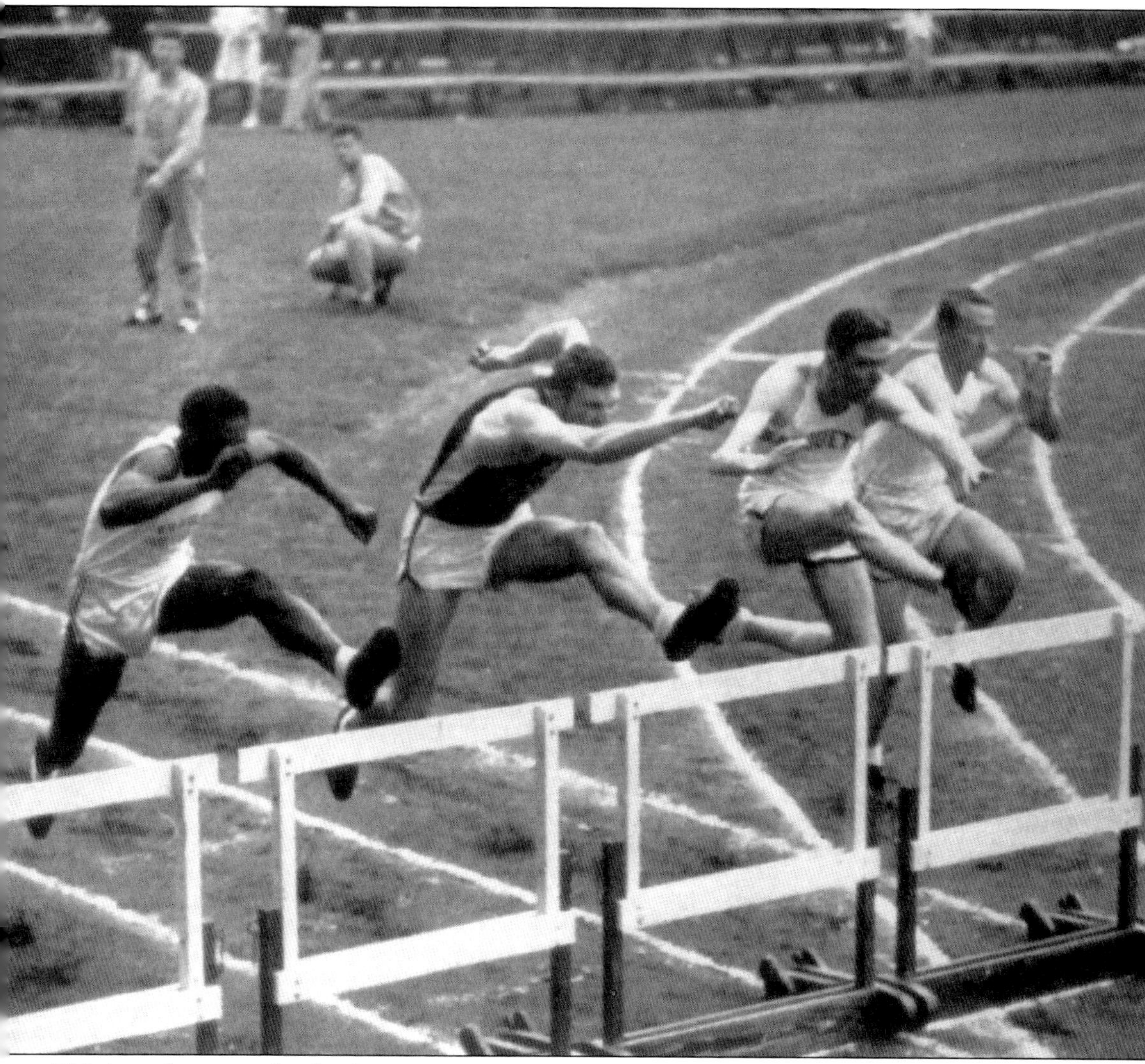

This is a photograph of either Owen or Connor competing in the hurdles in 1948.

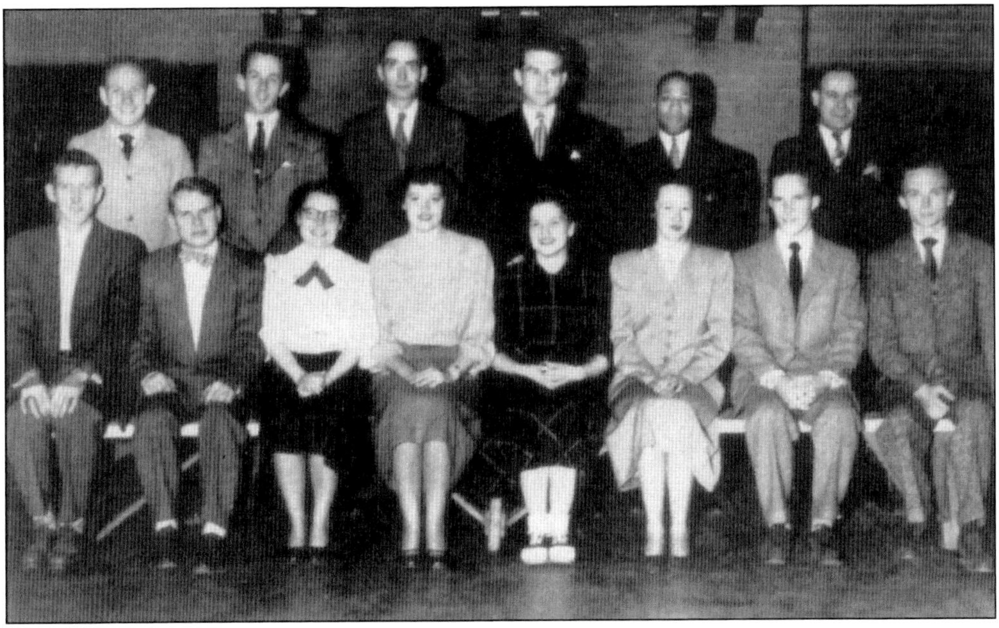

Although relatively small in number, African-American students were quite visible in a host of activities and organizations. As this photo shows, there were even members of the early debate team, which would establish itself as one of the best in the country by the 1990s. This team from 1949 includes Roy Norton and distinguished itself by competing that year with Notre Dame, Northwestern, the University of Illinois, the University of Chicago, and on April 7 of that year, an international debate with Cambridge University from England.

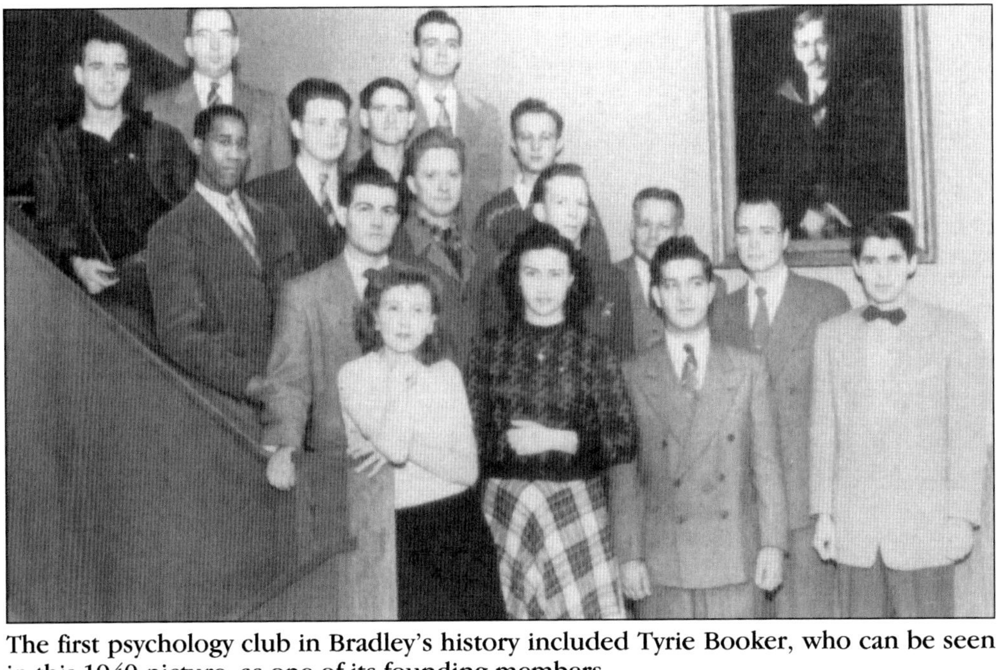

The first psychology club in Bradley's history included Tyrie Booker, who can be seen in this 1949 picture, as one of its founding members.

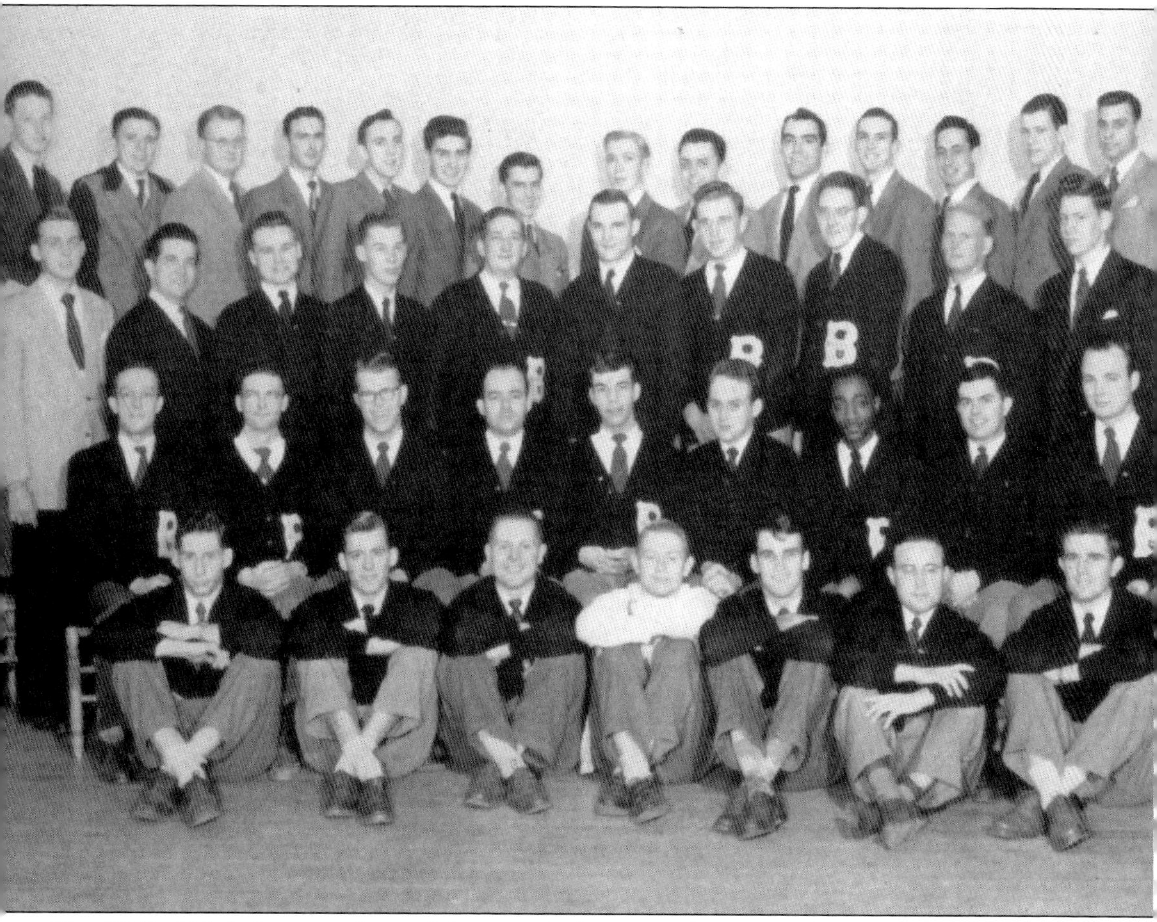

The 1949 Chieftains are pictured here including J. Helm, second row to the right in this photo.

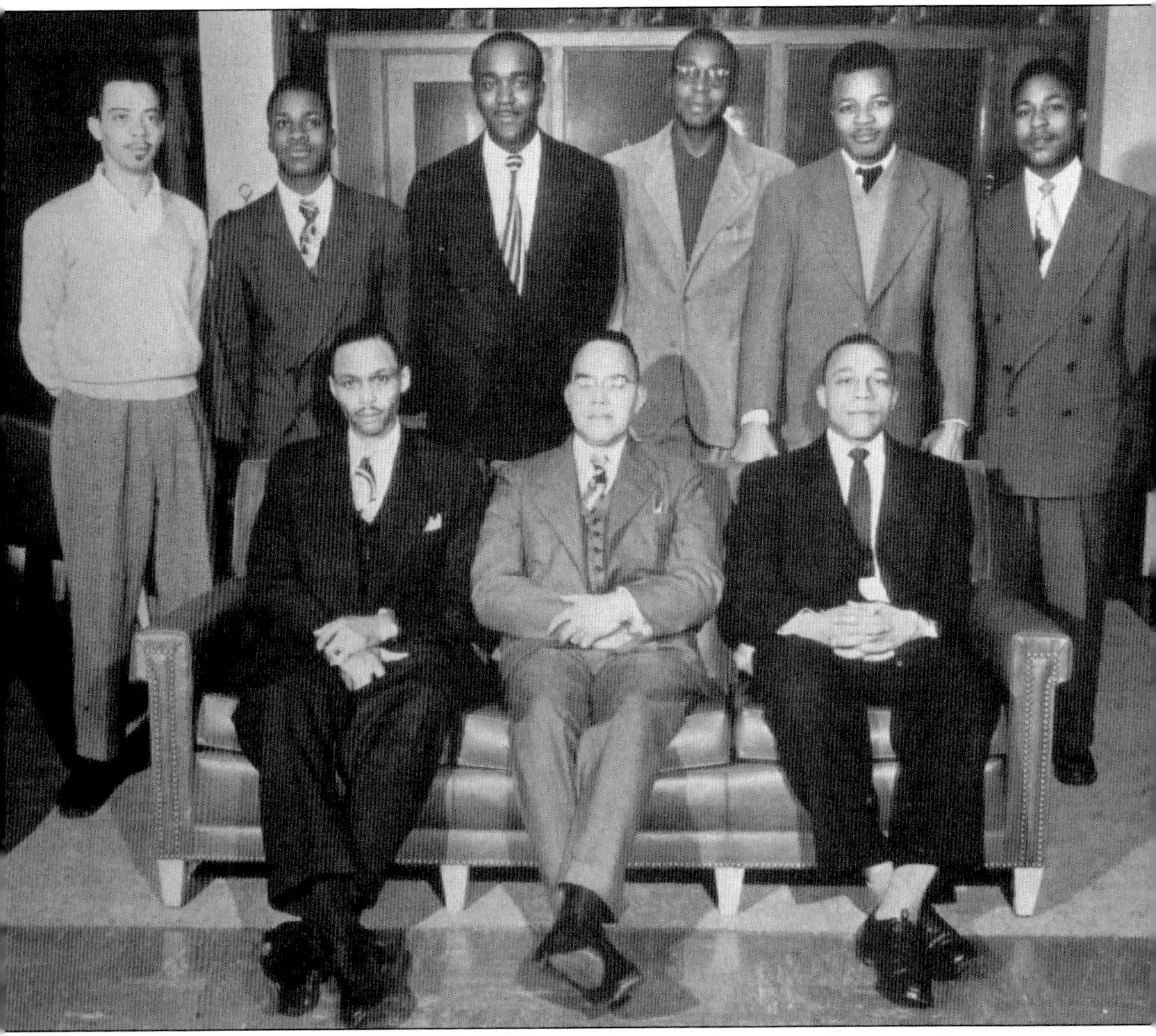

Several African-American male students are shown with Romeo Garrett, a former student of sociology and the first African-American faculty member hired in 1947. This picture was taken in 1949. From left to right are: (front row) John R. White, Romeo Garrett, Wilmer White; (second row) Jean Flowers, Thomas Johnson, Hayman Bell, Walter Richard, Willie Adams, and Henry Seward.

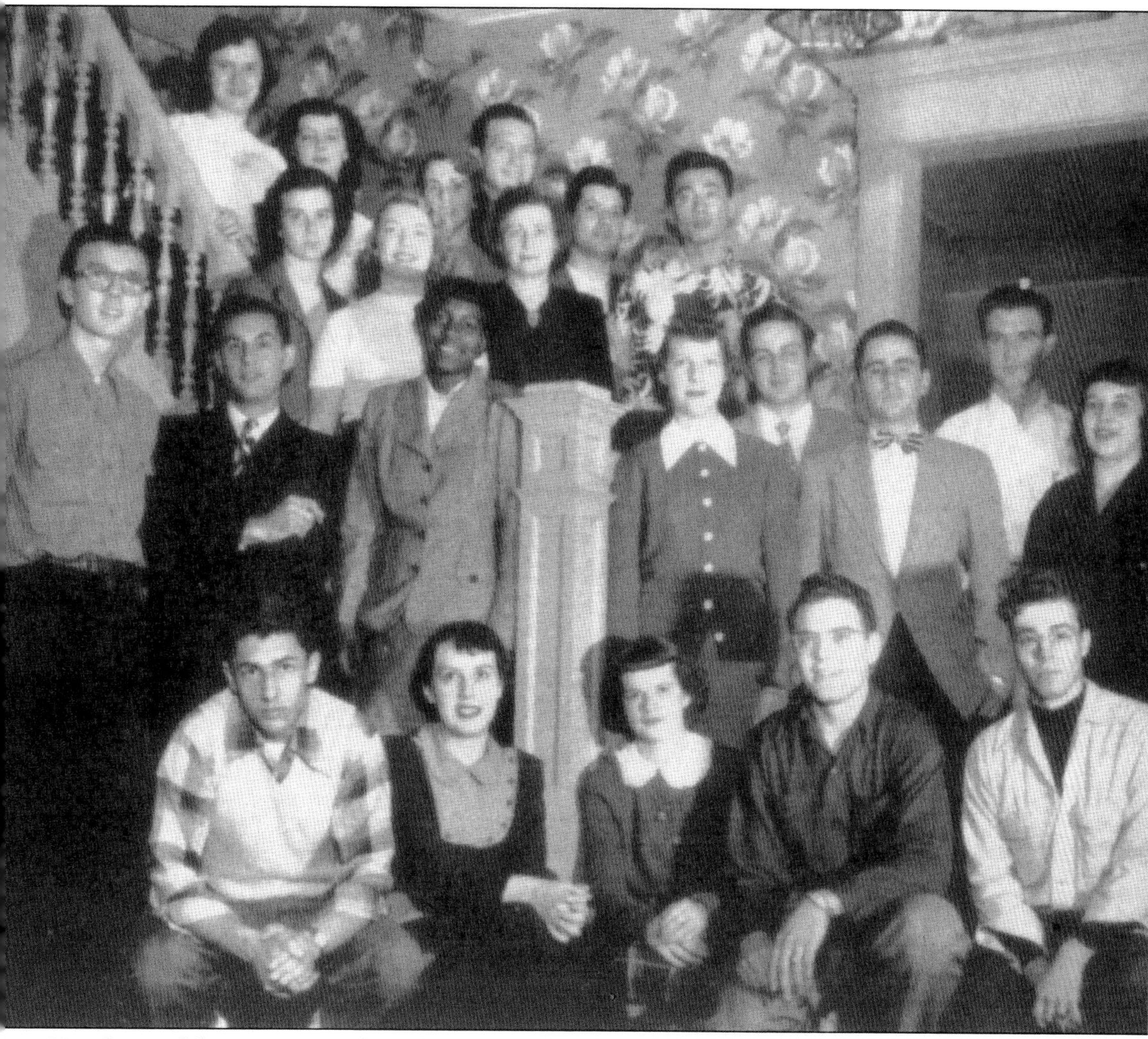

Members of the 1950 French Club. The club met once a week and held as its purpose to widen the interest in French culture, traditions, and language. Member Josephine Reese is depicted in this 1950 photo.

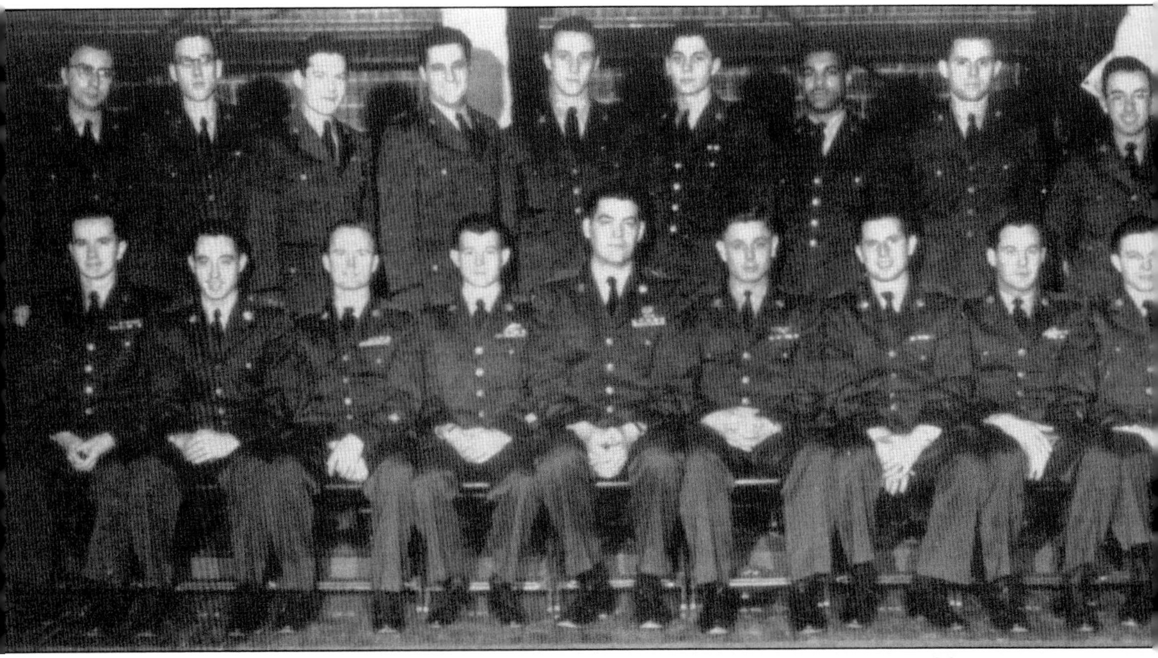

Members of the AFROTC Arnold Society are pictured here. The Arnold Society was organized in 1950, and was composed of members of the AFROTC program who were taking the advanced class of the program. African Americans have been members of the program since at least the early 1940s. In this photograph, R. Reid is visible in the back row.

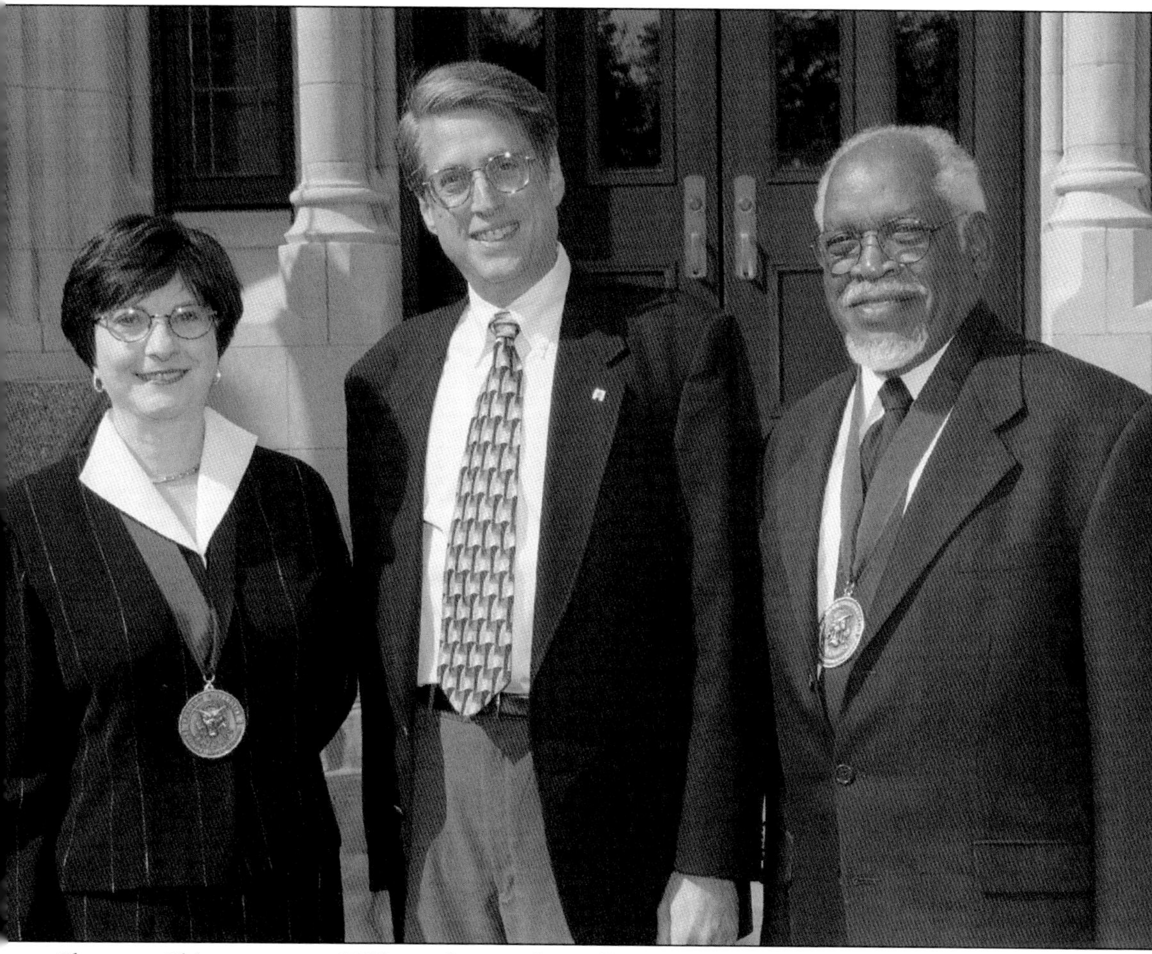

Clarence Shivers was a 1950 graduate of Bradley and one of the original Tuskegee Airmen. While a student at Bradley, he painted the mural at Peoria's Carver Center. He later became a well known artist and sculptor. He is pictured here in 1999 after being inducted into the Bradley University Centurion Society.

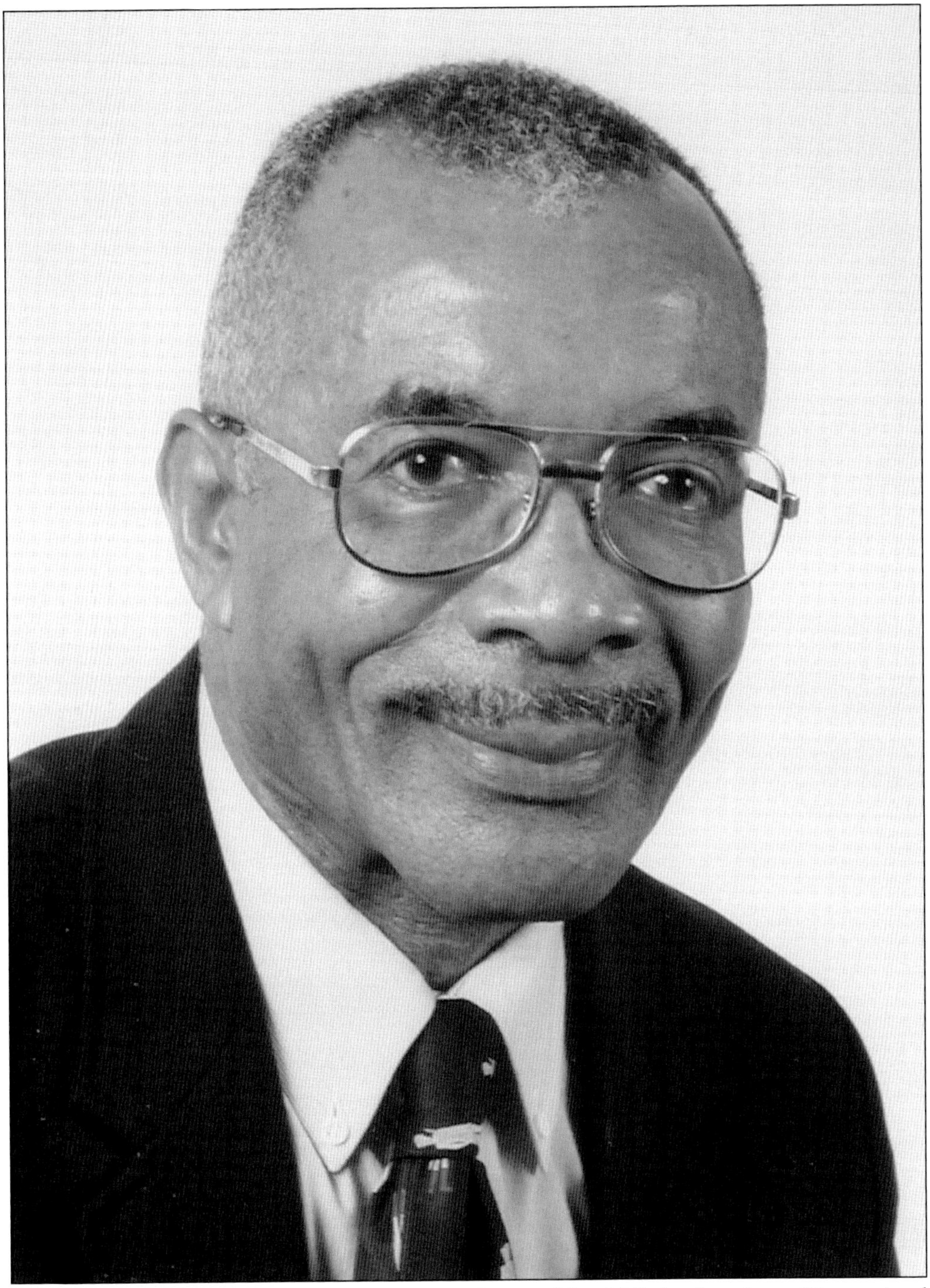

Dr. Benjamin Alexander was also a 1950 graduate with a M.S. in chemistry. He received his Ph.D in chemistry in 1957 from Georgetown University. He was president of Chicago State University and the University of the District of Columbia, a former member of Bradley's Board of Trustees, and a 1983 inductee into the Centurion Society.

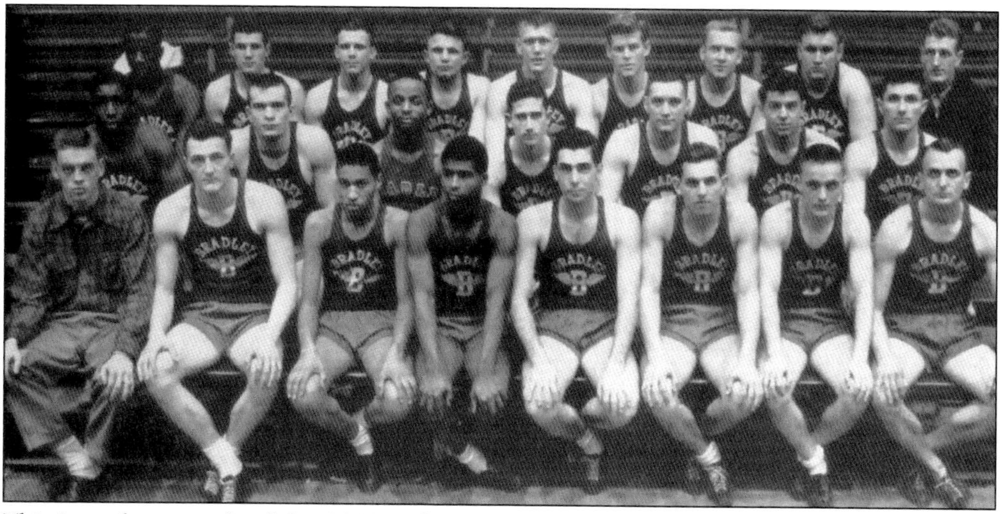

This is a photograph of the 1952 indoor track and field team. There were five African-American members of the team. It must be noted that although there were five members of the track and field team and five members of the 1952 football team, there were no African-American members of the Bradley basketball team except for Porter, who joined the team in 1951 as its manager.

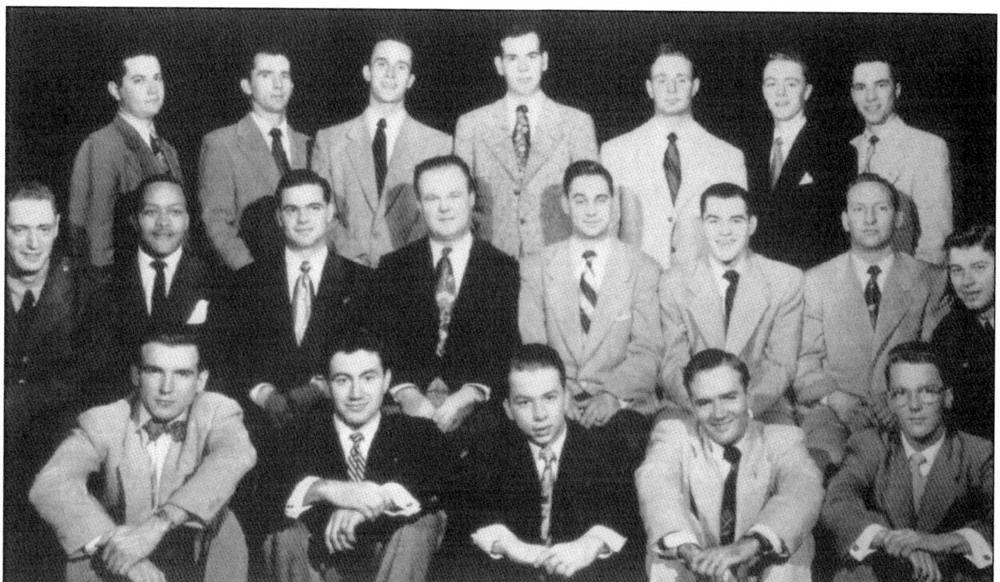

Members of the 1952 Interfraternity Council are pictured here. The second person in the second row is Grant Kinney. A member of Omega Psi Phi fraternity, he was the sole African-American member of the council.

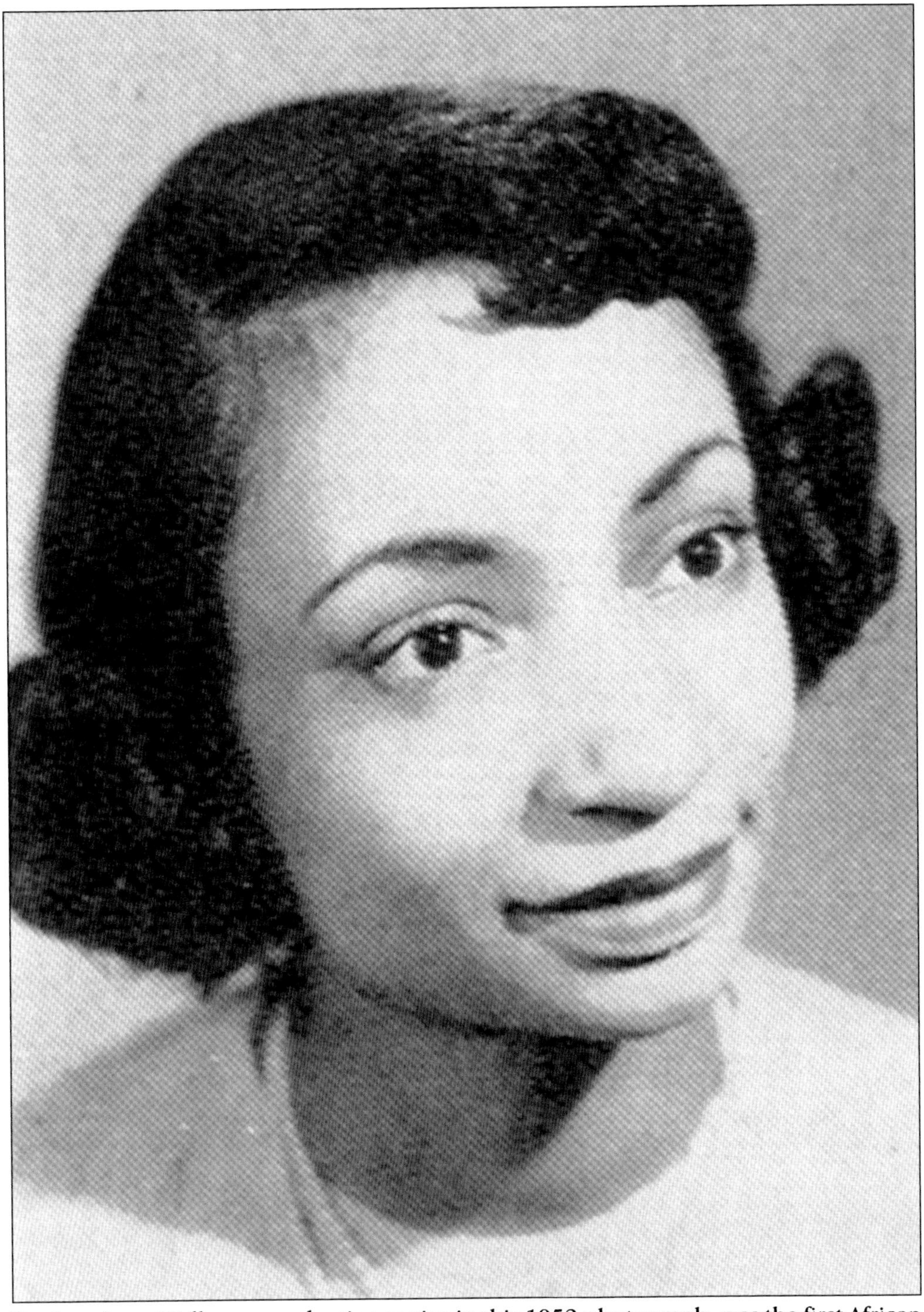

Dr. Joan Scott Wallace, a graduating senior in this 1952 photograph, was the first African American to live in one of Bradley's dormitories. In 1983, she was inducted into the Centurion Society.

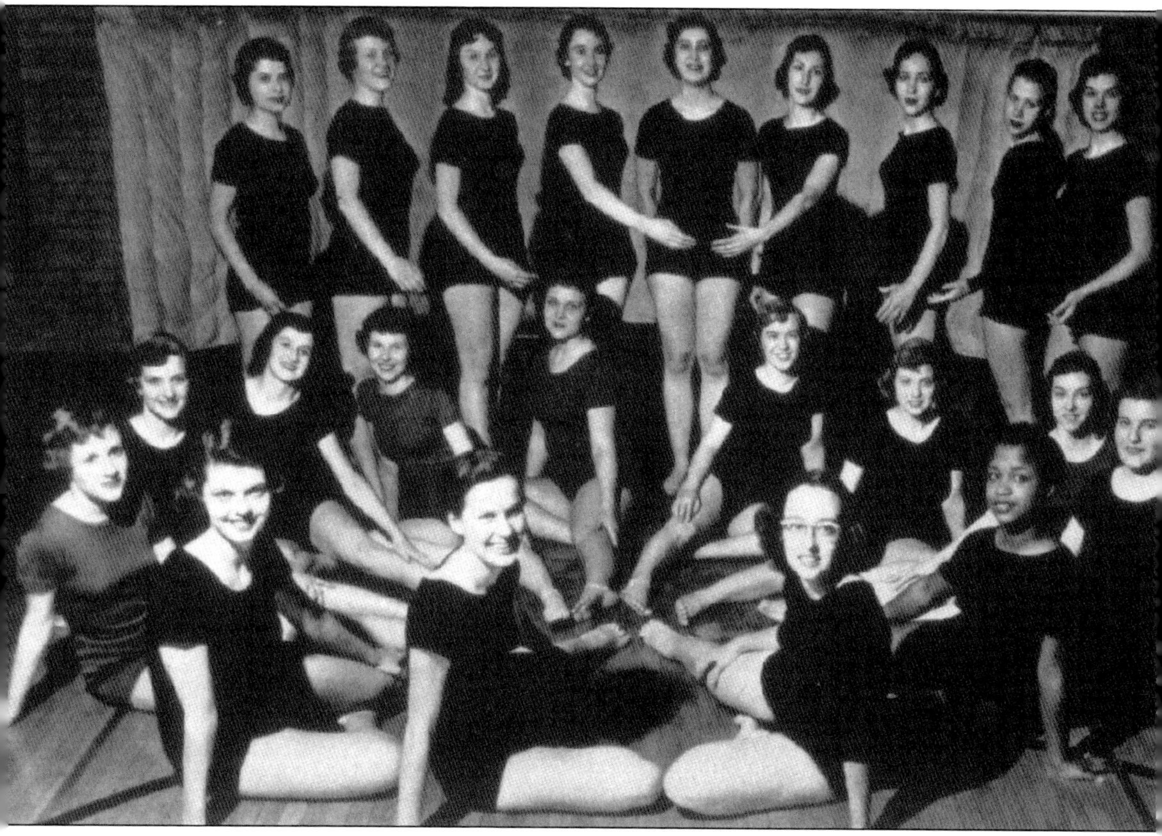

Jeanette Ray was the only African- American member of the newly established Orchesis, which was led by Mrs. Stegner. In this 1953 photograph, Ray can be seen seated on the far right side.

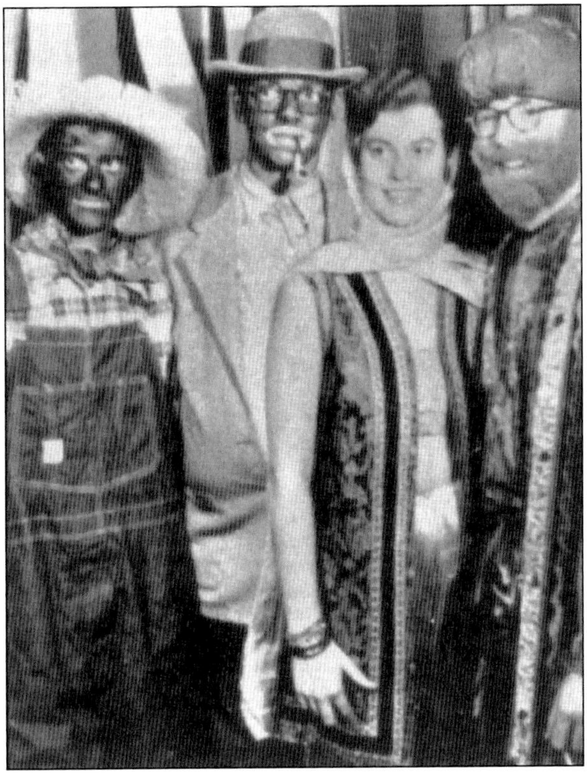

Pictured here are members of the Alpha Pi fraternity, which was established in 1898, making them the oldest on Bradley's campus. This image of two of its members in black face was taken from the 1953 *Anaga,* with the caption "Well aren't they cute. . . ." written under it. This example demonstrates that while African-American students attended Bradley and contributed to its various organizations and programs, they still endured racism, making their experience at Bradley mixed at best.

In spite of the increase in African-American students and athletes, racial insensitivity was still rampant on the campus, evident in this photograph from 1954. Fraternities continued to hold stunt shows where they painted themselves in black face during homecoming.

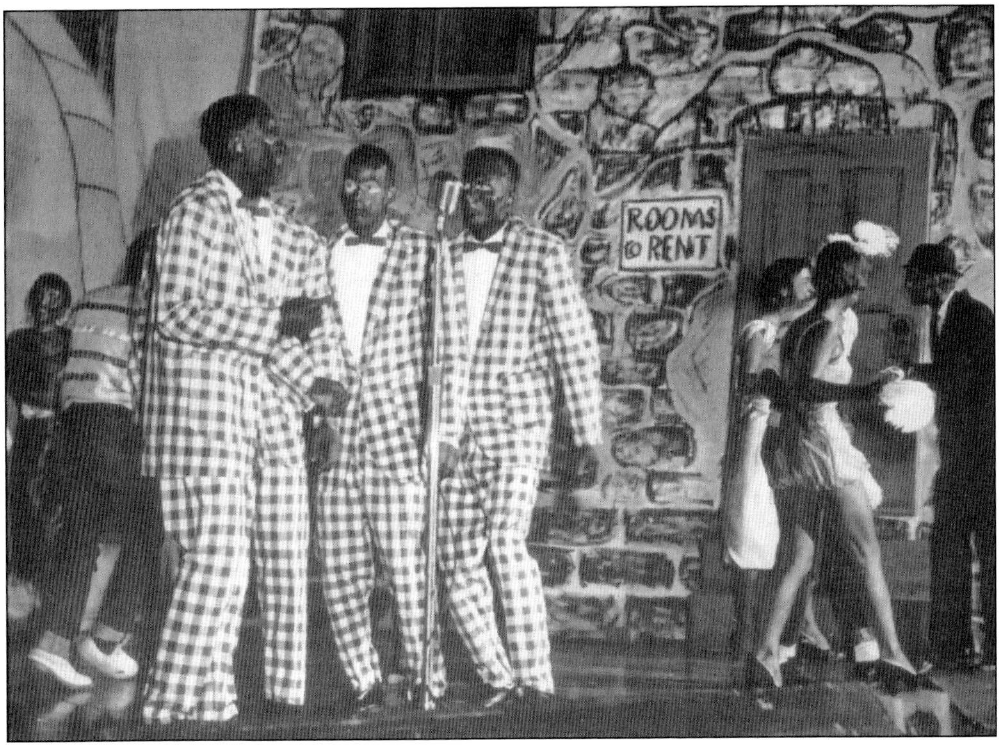

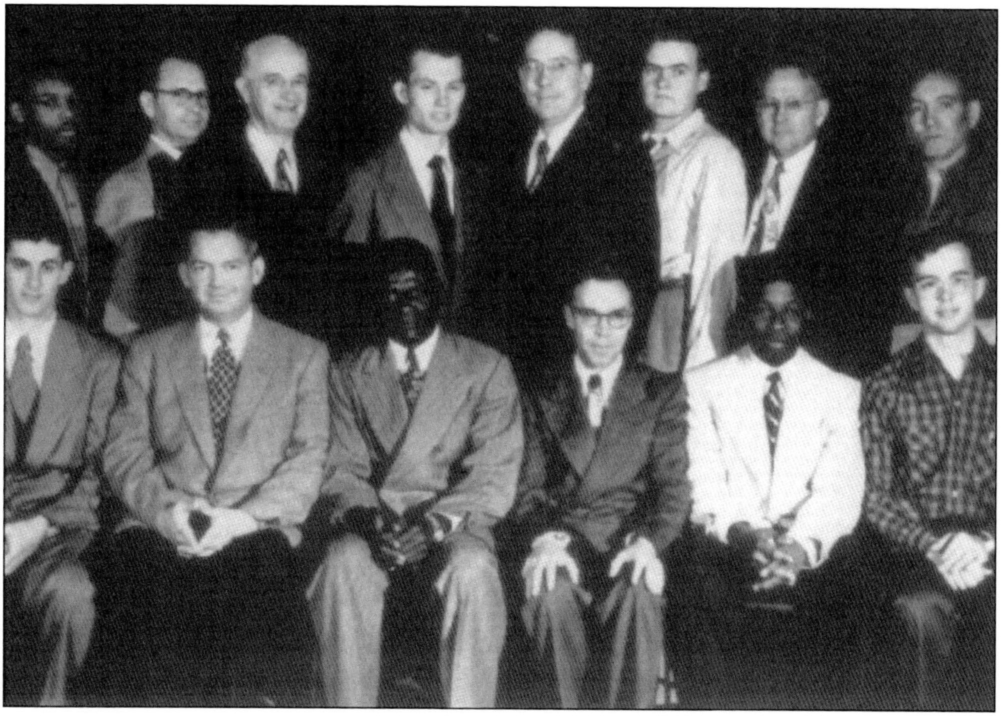

In this 1953 *Anaga* photograph, we see other students working together to improve the campus climate and to sponsor mixers for students to allow them to learn more about each other and listen to one another. In this image, members of the YMCA, including three People of Color, are shown. In the center of the first row are Augustus Kwabi and Henry Kaitell. The first person in the top row is Preston Bosley.

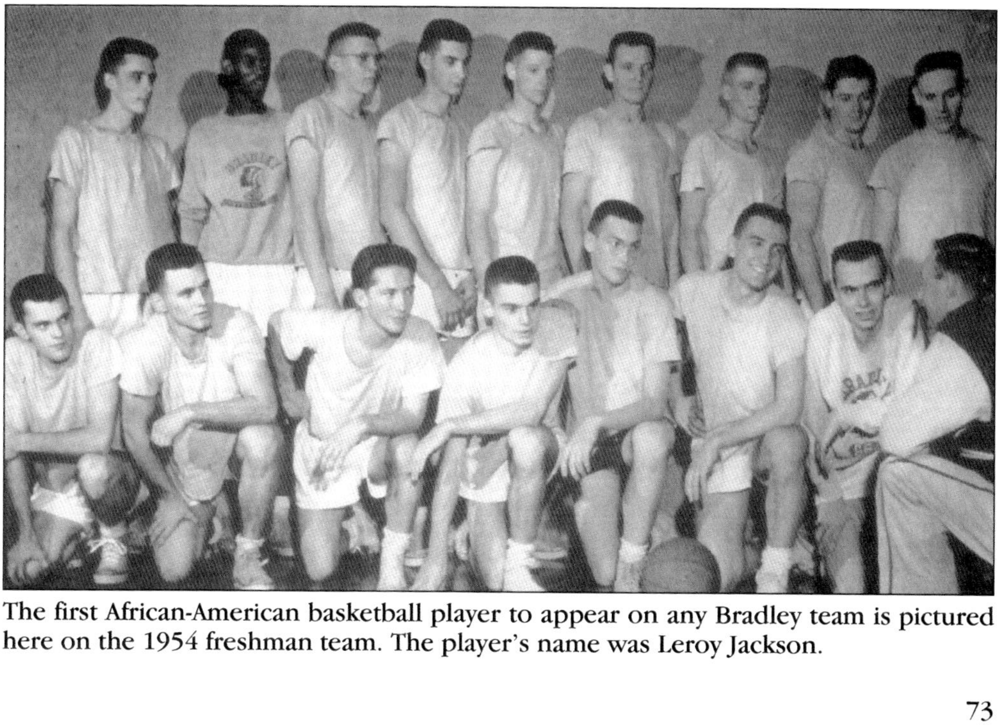

The first African-American basketball player to appear on any Bradley team is pictured here on the 1954 freshman team. The player's name was Leroy Jackson.

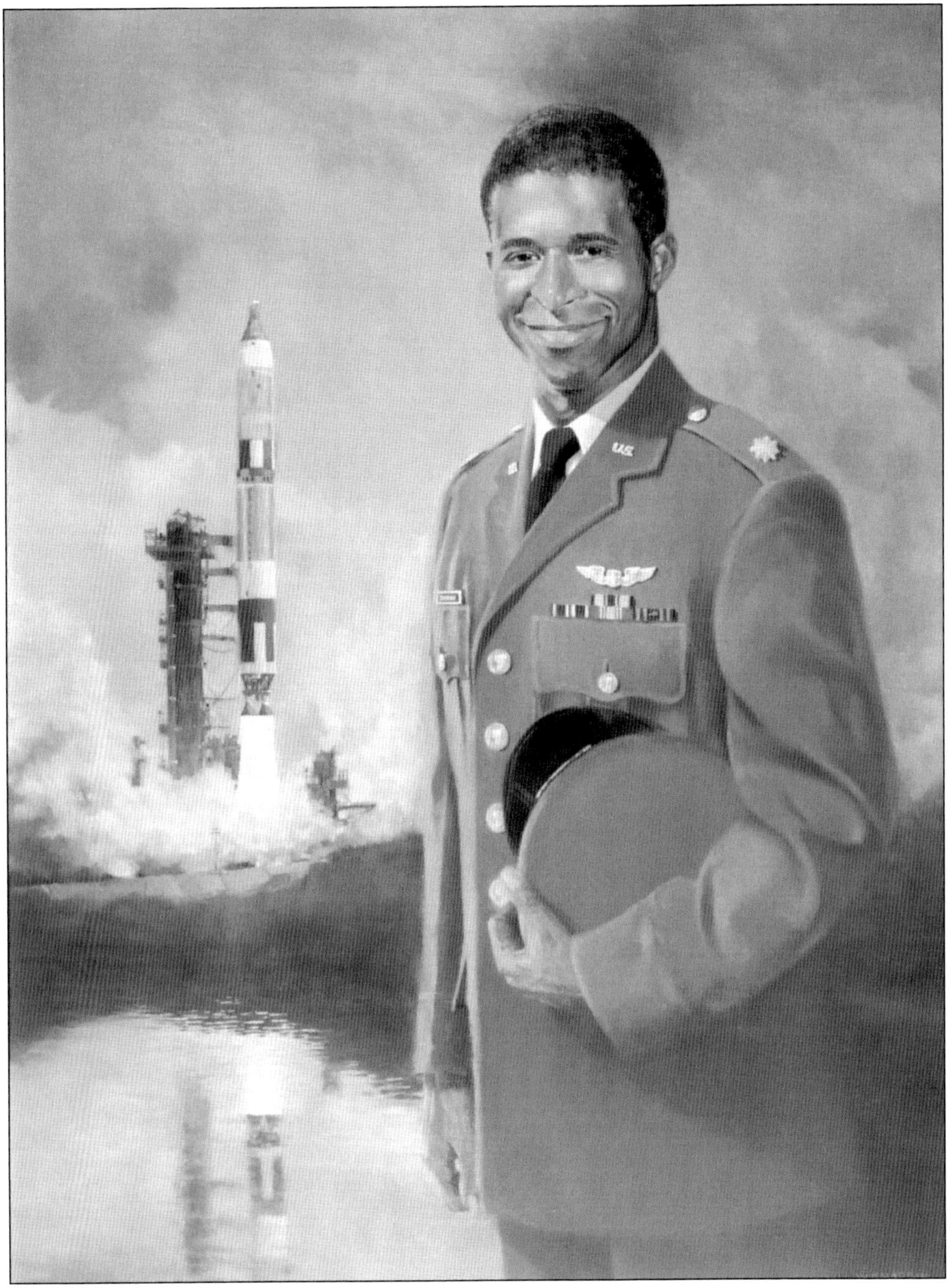

Major Robert L. Lawrence graduated in the class of 1956. He went on to receive his Ph.D. in Chemistry from Ohio State University in 1967. Major Lawrence was the first African-American astronaut. In 1990, a lectureship was begun at Bradley in his honor. His widow also established a scholarship in his name. Major Lawrence was inducted into the Centurion Society posthumously in 1982.

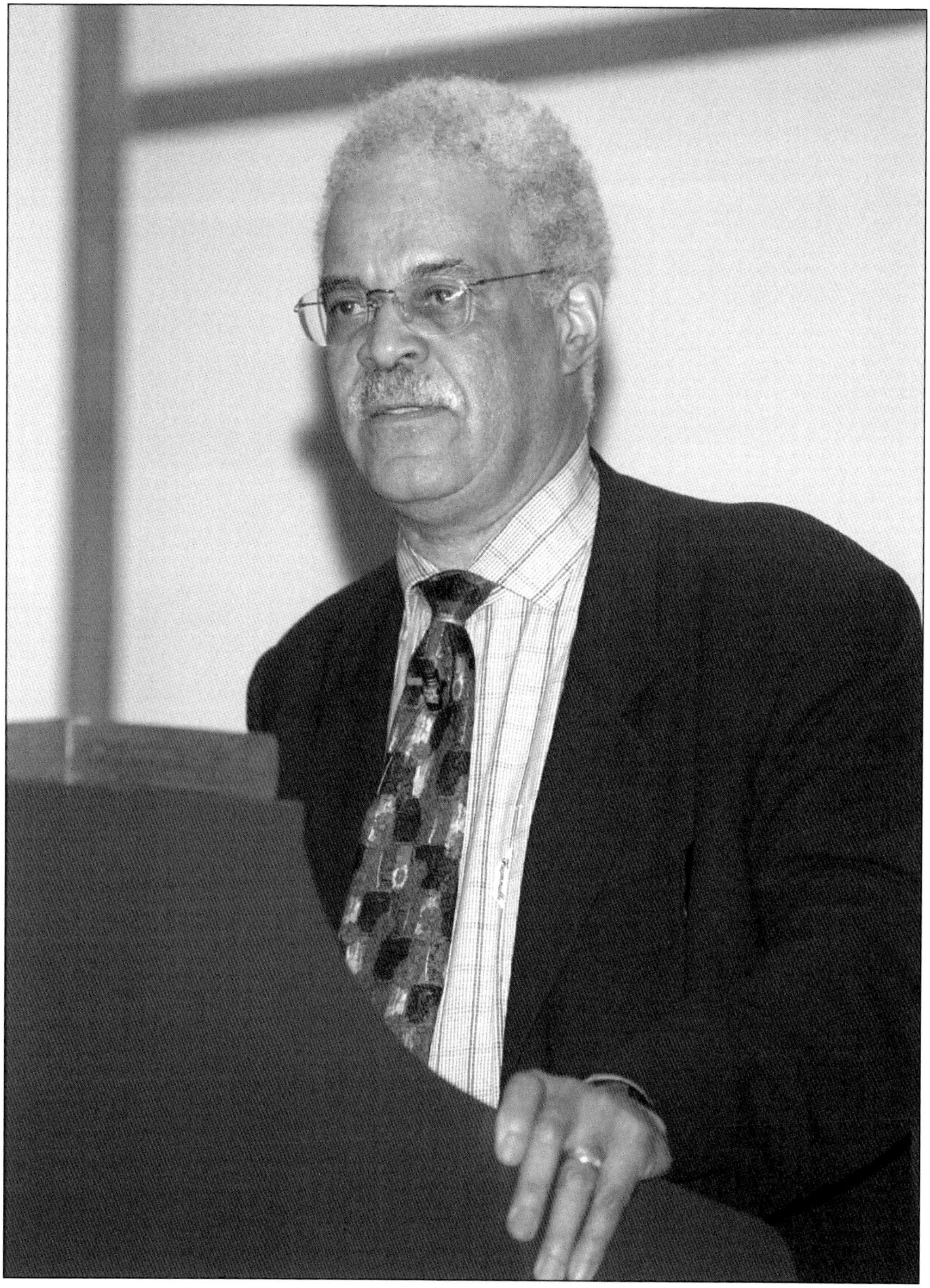

Douglass Alligood graduated in 1956. He is depicted in this 1994 photograph giving a lecture to students during his visit to Bradley when he was inducted into the Centurion Society.

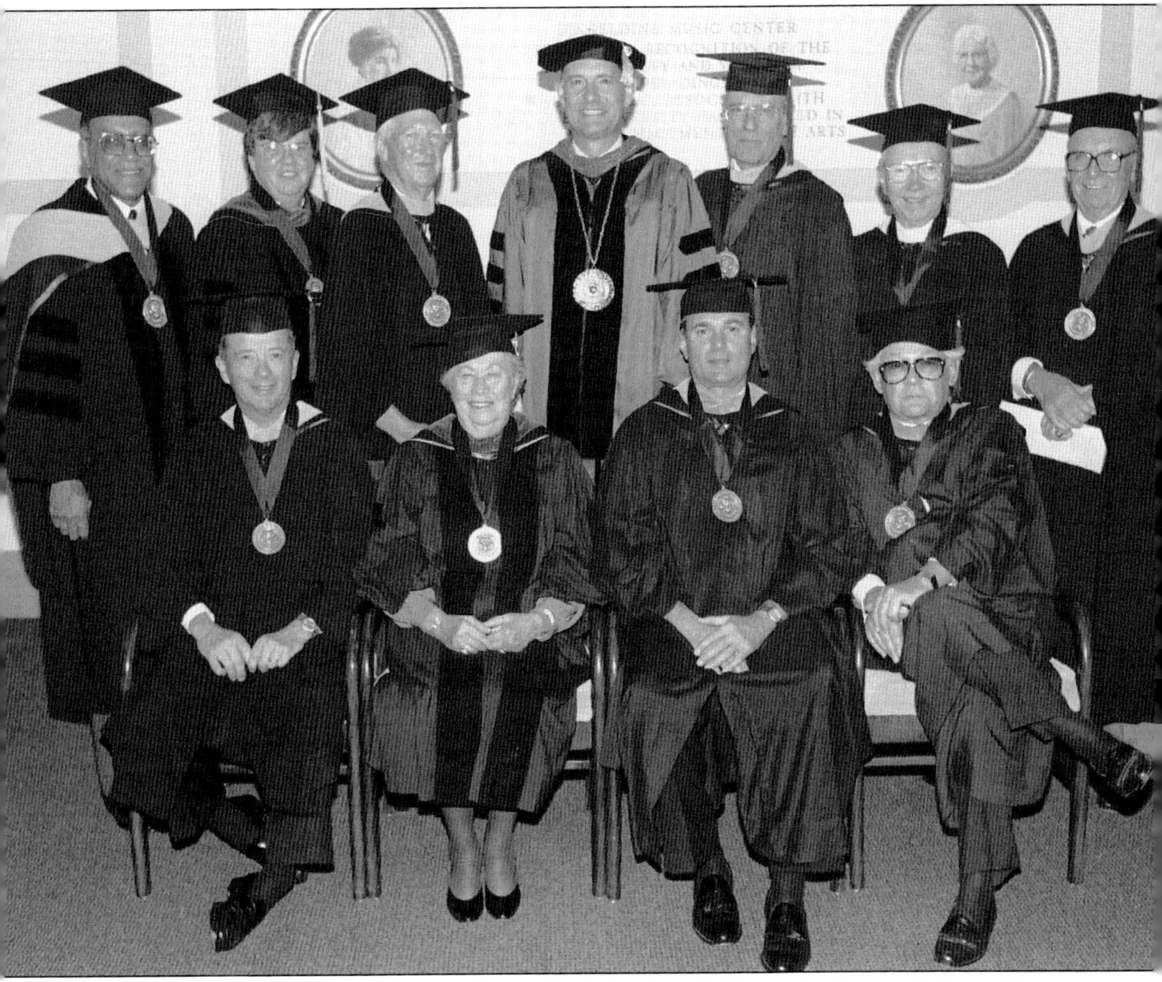

Linneaus Dorman, former president of Livingstone College, is pictured above. Dorman is a 1956 graduate of Bradley. He is seen here in 1993, along with several other individuals, being inducted into the Centurion Society.

Three

A Historic Moment
Blacks, Basketball, and Bradley's Rise to National Prominence 1955–1972

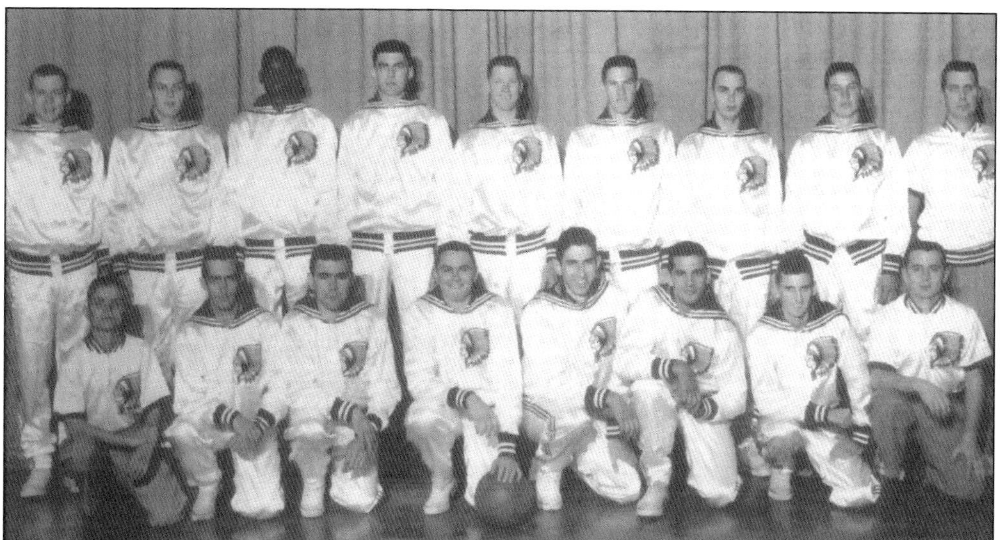

Members of the 1955 Bradley basketball team are pictured here. The only African-American member is Tony Davis.

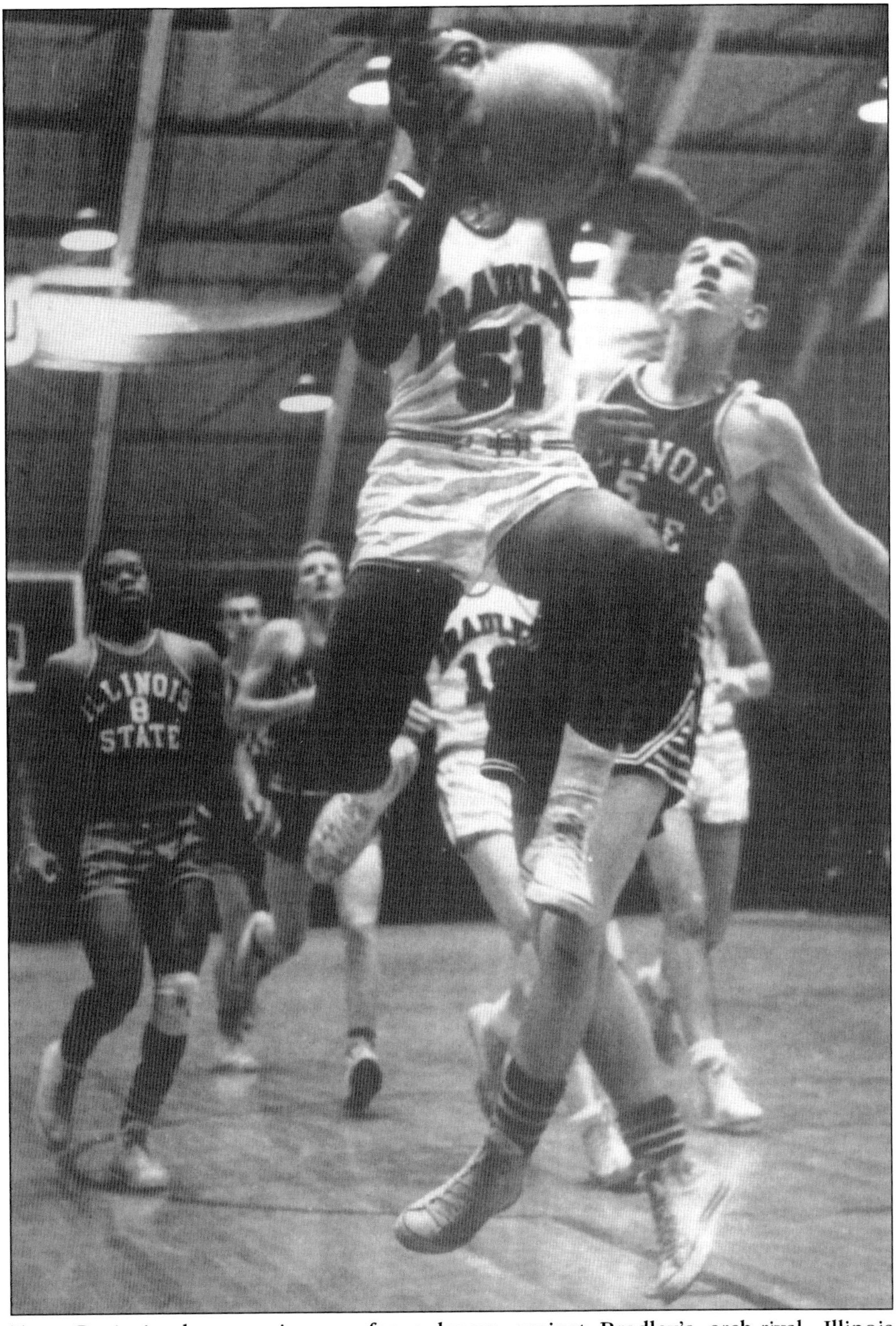

Tony Davis is shown going up for a lay-up against Bradley's arch-rival, Illinois State University.

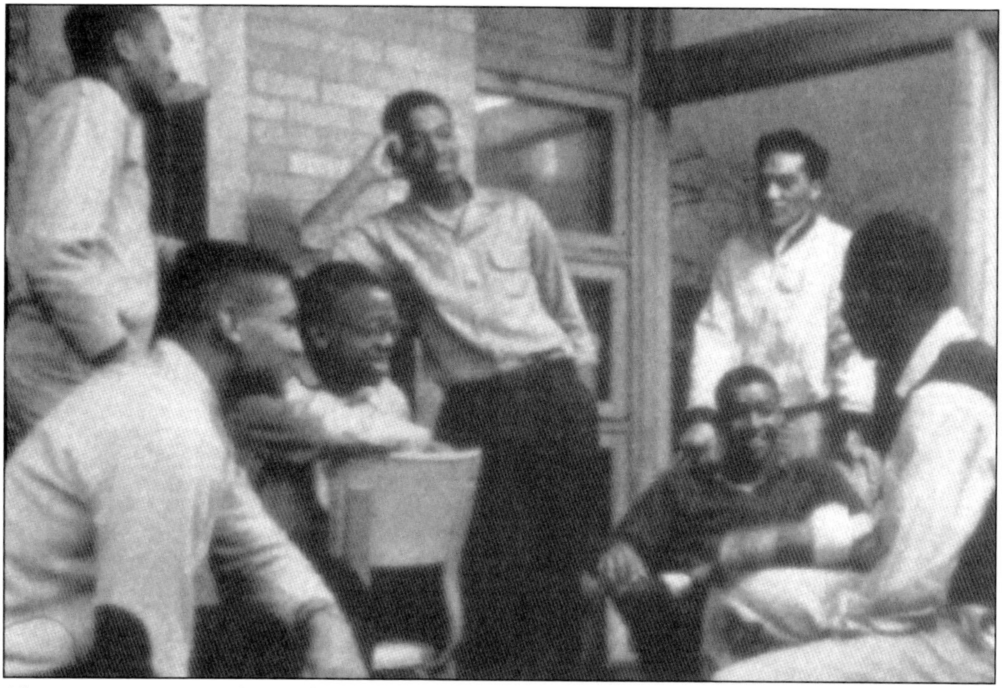

African-American male students are shown unwinding in a dormitory room.

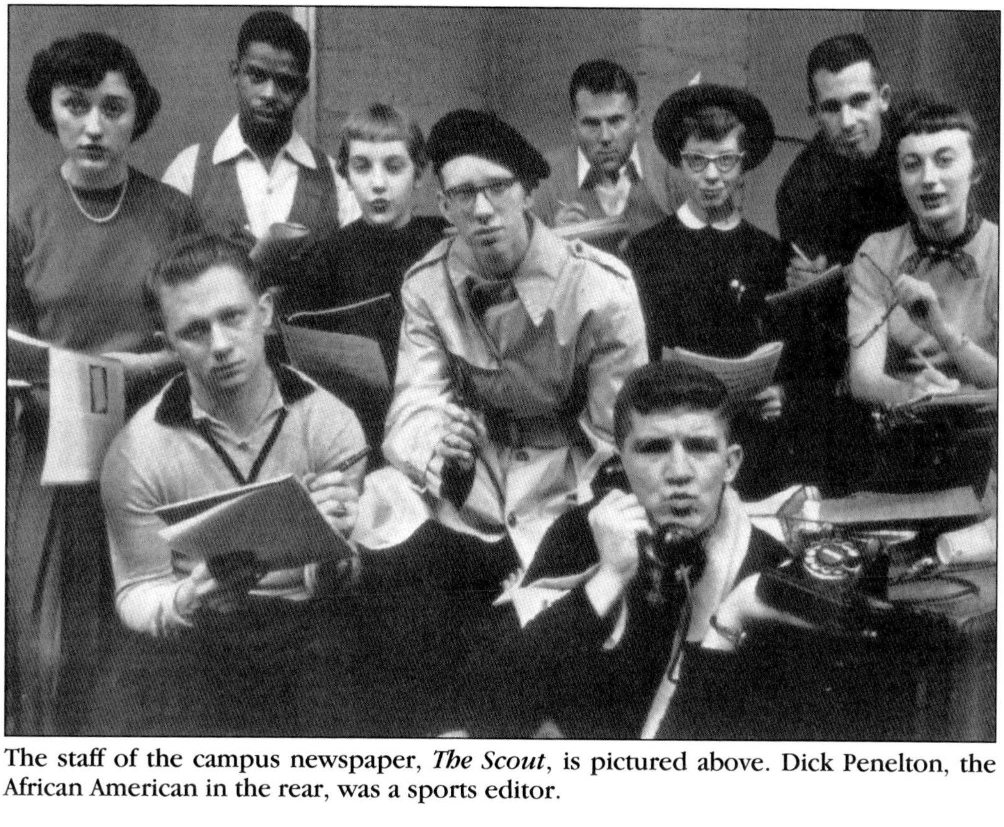

The staff of the campus newspaper, *The Scout*, is pictured above. Dick Penelton, the African American in the rear, was a sports editor.

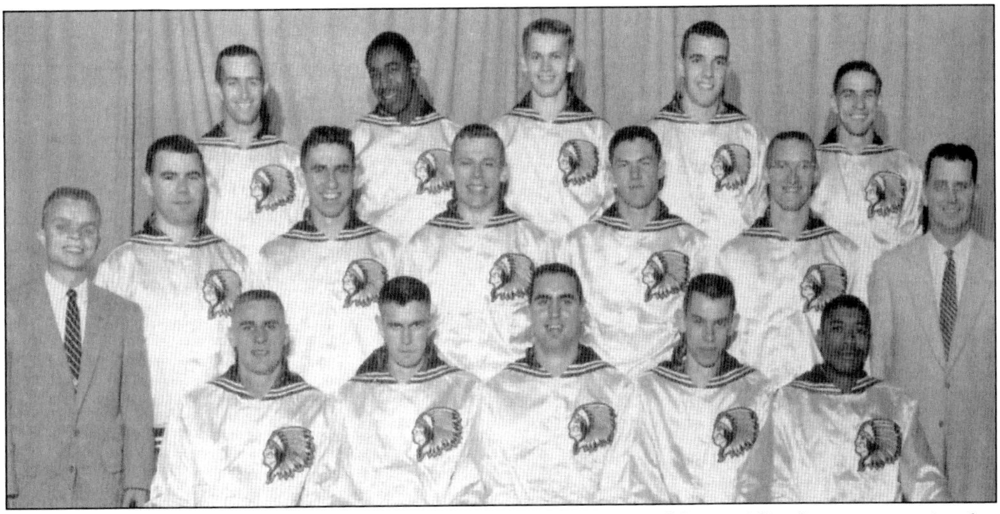

Members of the 1956 Bradley basketball team are pictured here. The last person in the first row is Shellie McMillon. The second person in the top row is Curley Johnson, who would later play with the Harlem Globetrotters.

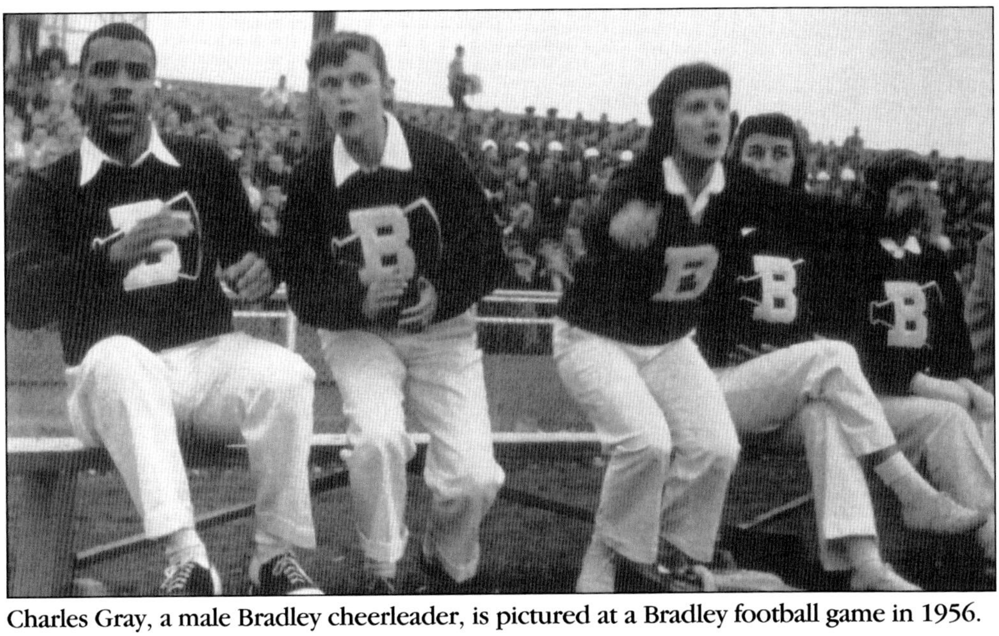

Charles Gray, a male Bradley cheerleader, is pictured at a Bradley football game in 1956.

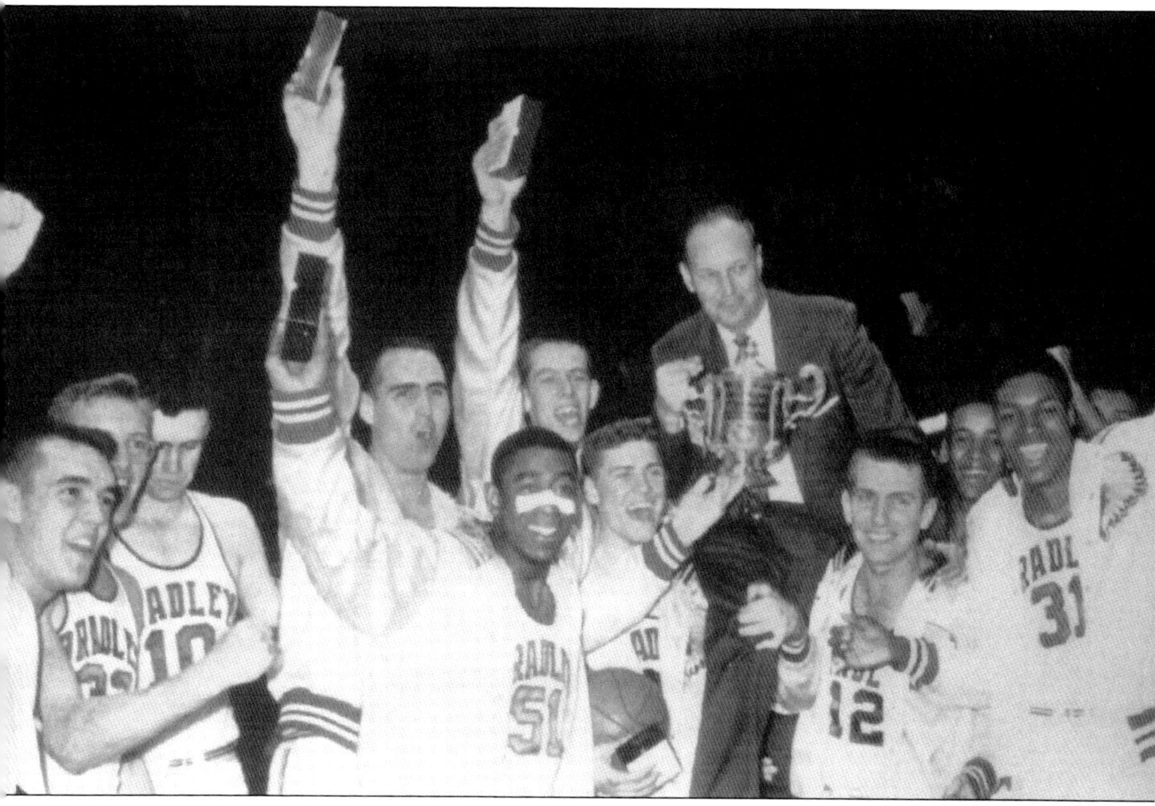

Members of the 1957 N.I.T. championship team are shown here returning from Madison Square Garden, New Jersey, where they defeated the Temple Owls 94–66. The game was broadcast live on CBS. Shellie McMillon sank a field goal and a free throw with 29 seconds left in the game to seal the victory and Bradley's first national championship.

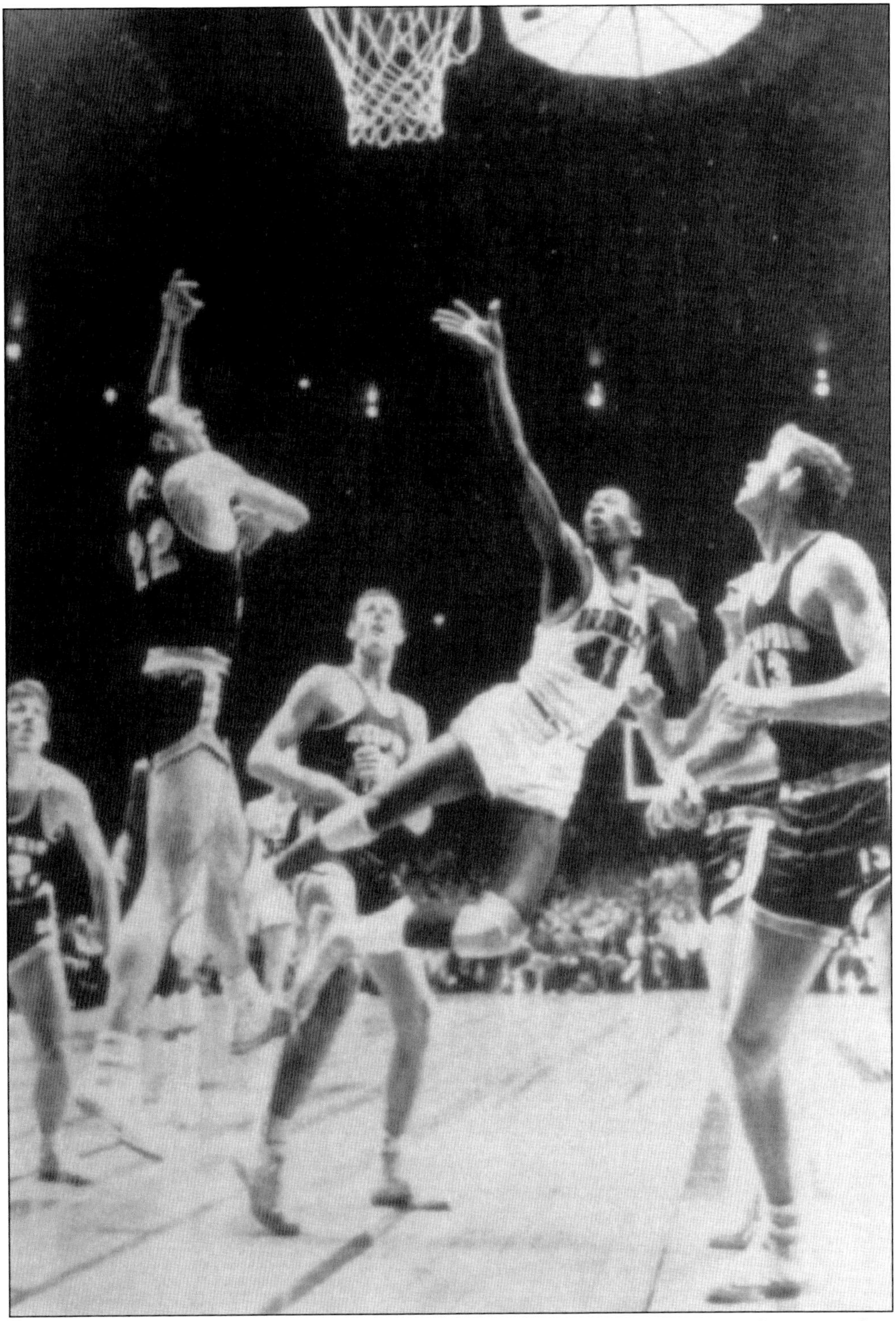

Pictured above is Shellie McMillon's winning shot in the 1957 N.I.T. championship game against Temple.

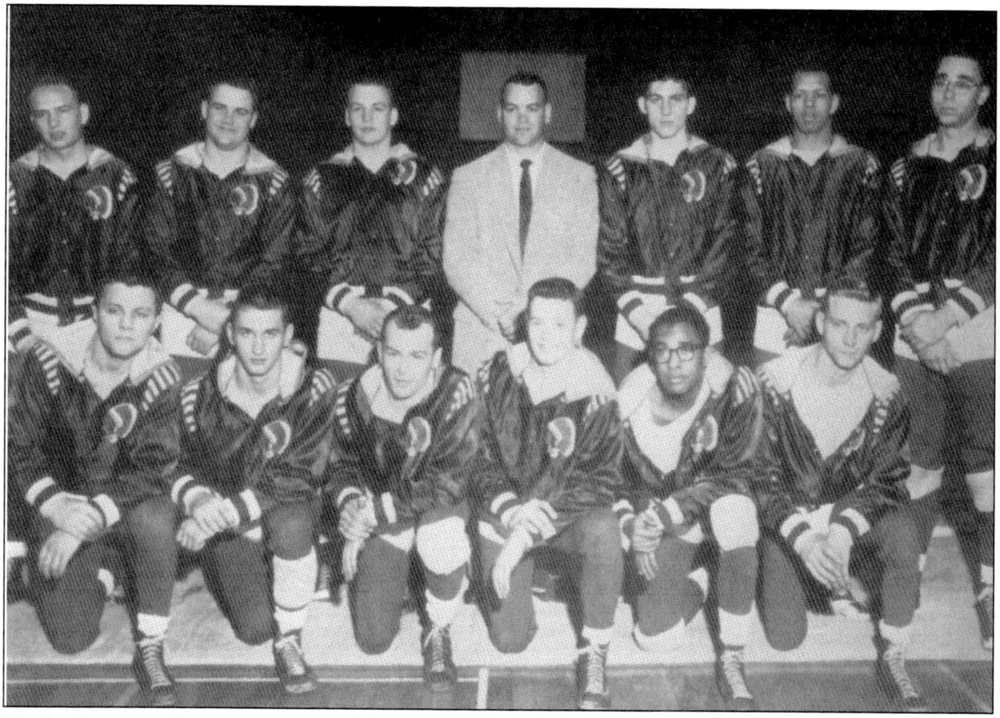

Myrle Cooper, first row, second from right, was a member of the 1958 Bradley wrestling team coached by Bill Zimmer.

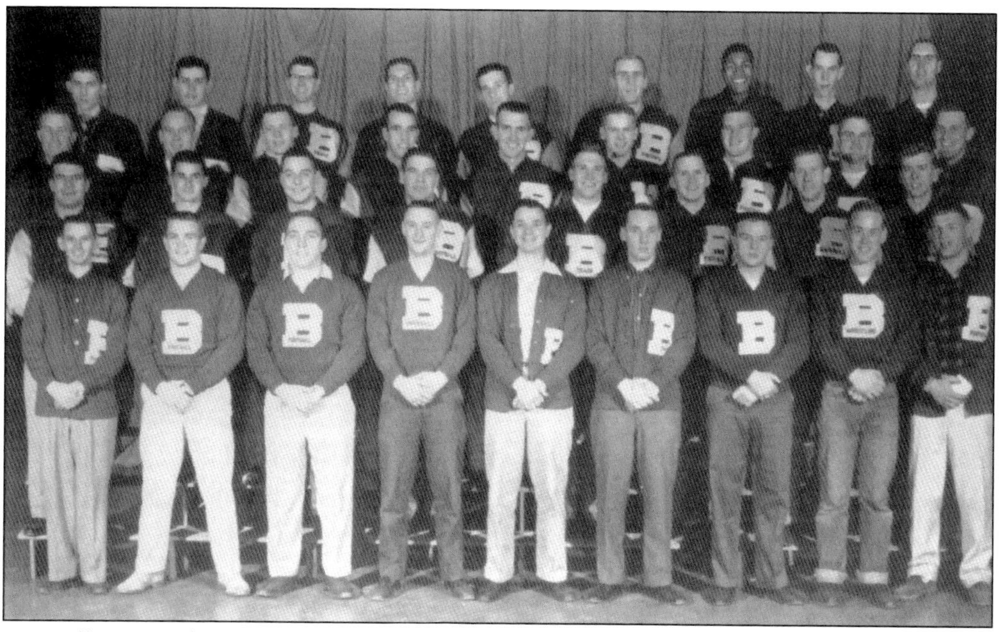

Joe Billy McDade, who was a star athlete and letterman, is depicted in this 1958 photograph. The lettermen sold programs at football games, sold concessions, sponsored the beanie sales, and sold homecoming tags as well as those for awards dinners and spring dances.

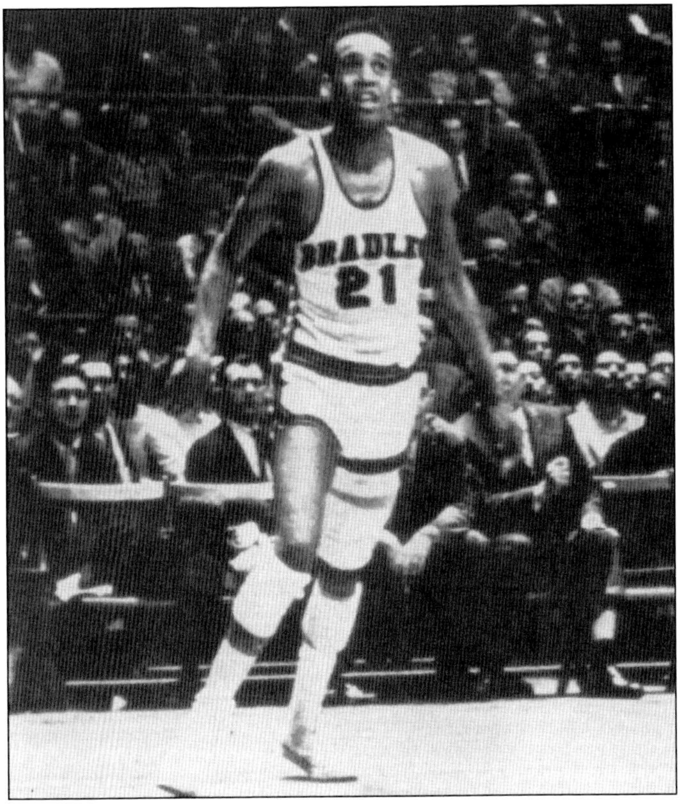

Bobby Joe Mason was voted most valuable player during the Braves' 1959 season. This photograph was taken during the 1959 N.I.T. championship game against St. John's. Bobby Joe Mason later played for the Harlem Globetrotters, and in 1972, he returned to Bradley to play before a packed fieldhouse.

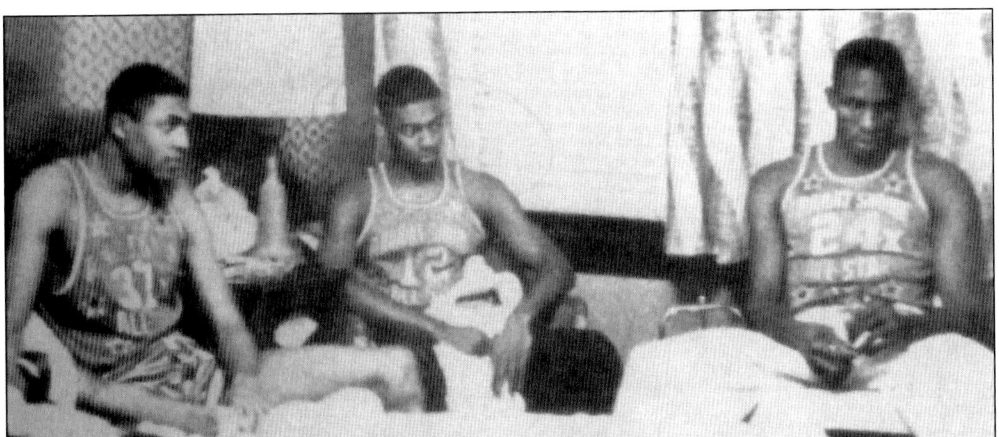

All-American Joe Billy McDade, who played with Bobby Joe Mason, was invited to play in the East-West basketball game. He is shown here relaxing before the game with Oscar Robinson of Cincinnati and Johnny Green of Michigan State.

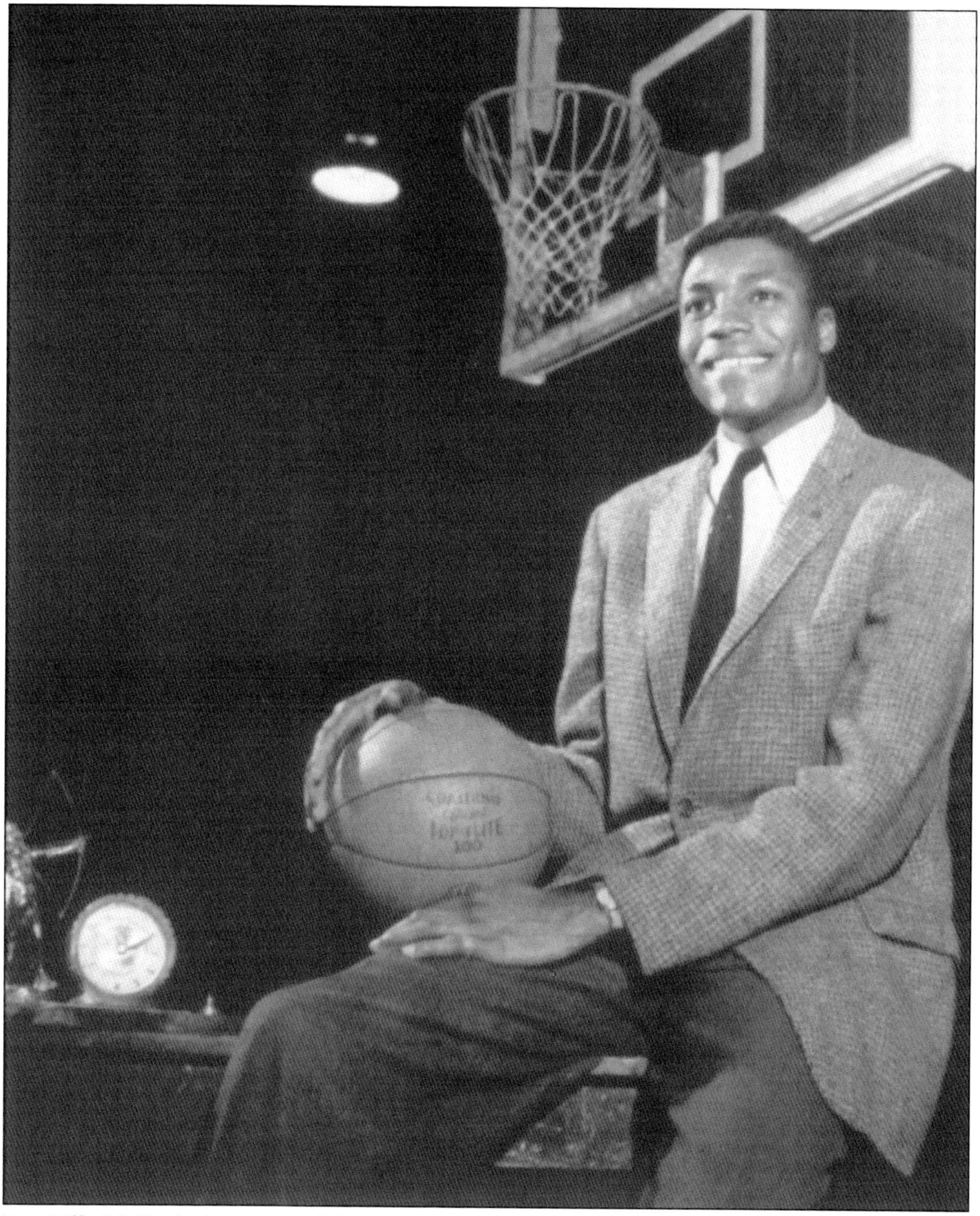

Joe Billy McDade is pictured here in 1959, his senior year. During this year, McDade, who was a stellar athlete and student, won the Waconda Award. He also played tennis and was homecoming king in 1959.

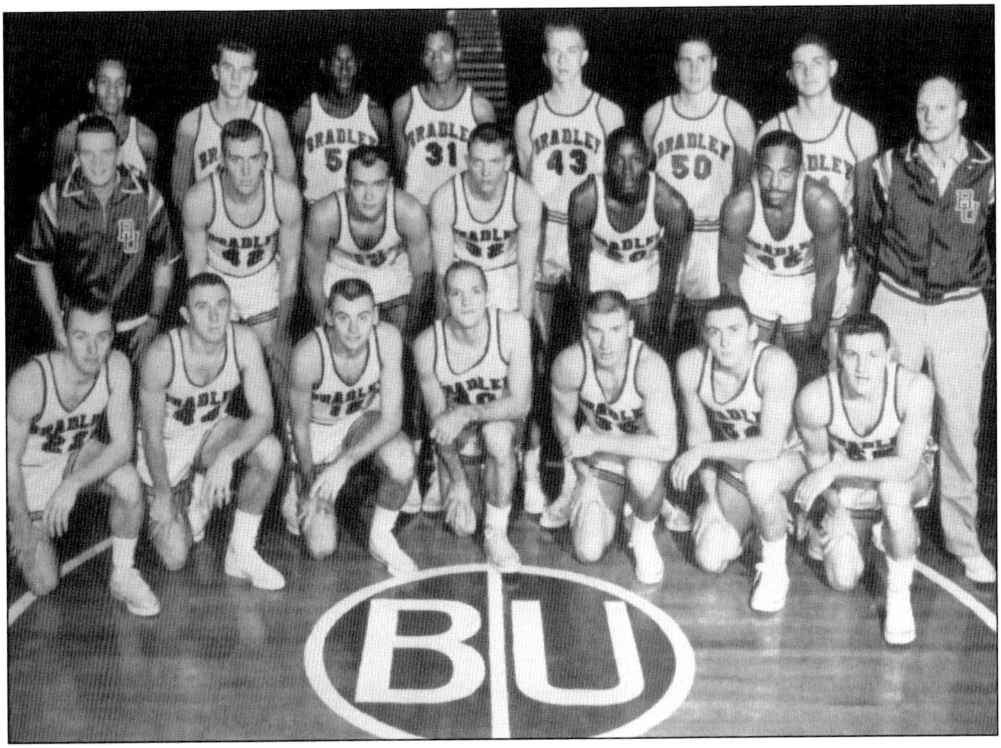

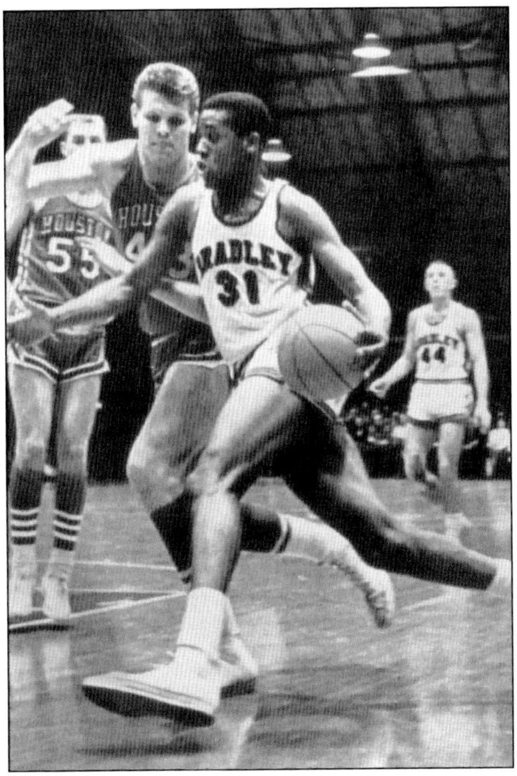

The 1959-60 Bradley basketball team, ranked second in the nation through much of the season, finished the season ranked fourth in the nation behind California, Cincinnati, and Ohio State. Led by All-Americans Chester Walker, Bobby Joe Mason, and Al Saunders, the Braves finished the season 24–2. In this photo, Bobby Joe Mason is the first person in the last row, the third person is Mack Herndon, the fourth person is Chester Walker, and on the second row, far right, are Al Saunders, Chuck Gramby, and Coach Chuck Orsborn.

All-American Chet "The Jet" Walker is shown here during the 1959-60 season getting around Houston's Bill Hathaway. Chet Walker helped Bradley win its second N.I.T. Championship in 1960. Chet Walker went on to have a very successful professional basketball career. He later wrote in his autobiography about the struggles against racism he experienced while at Bradley.

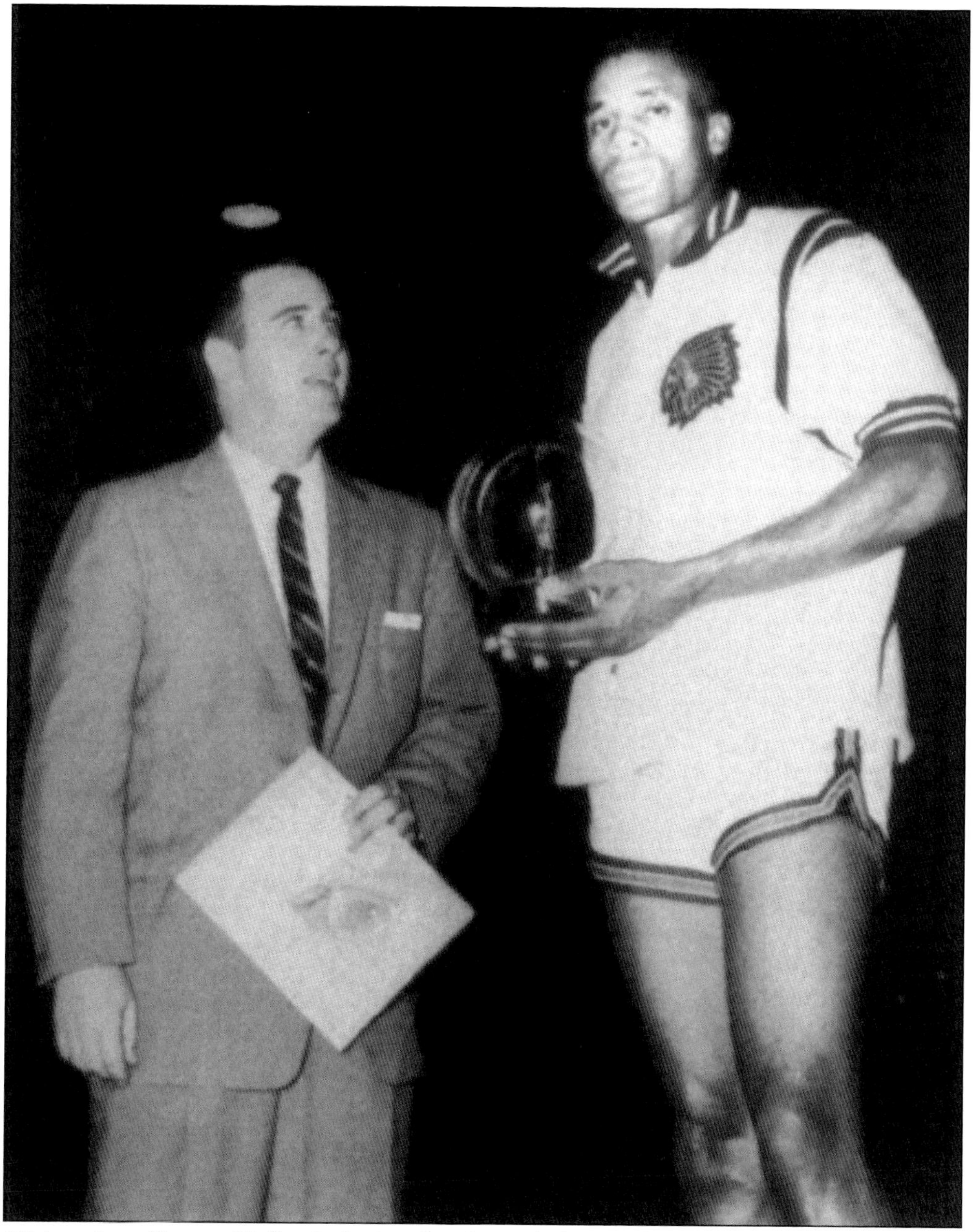

All-American Chester Walker is depicted at the end of the 1960-61 season receiving the Dell Publishing Award as their choice for the best player in the nation. Although Bradley did not have as good a season as the year before, Walker had a record-breaking season.

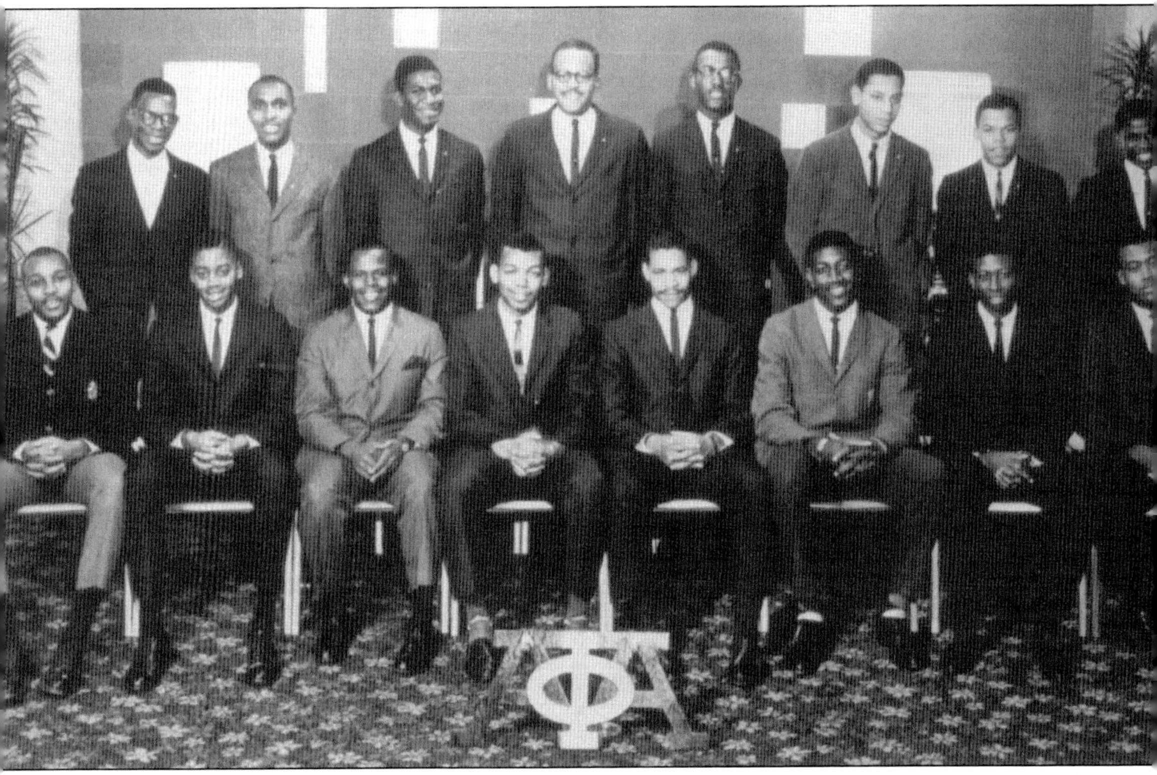

Pictured above are the founding members of the Bradley chapter of Alpha Phi Alpha fraternity, which was established on the campus in the fall of 1962. They are, from left to right: (front row) Judson Mitchell, Roger Ford, Tom Banks, Henry Waples, Larry Cowling, LeVern Tart, Joe Mongomery, Len Harris; (second row) James Ellis, Tyron Smith, Clayton McNindra, Lee Edwards, Dave Stroud, Earl Wells, Roger Hutchins, and Ted Coles.

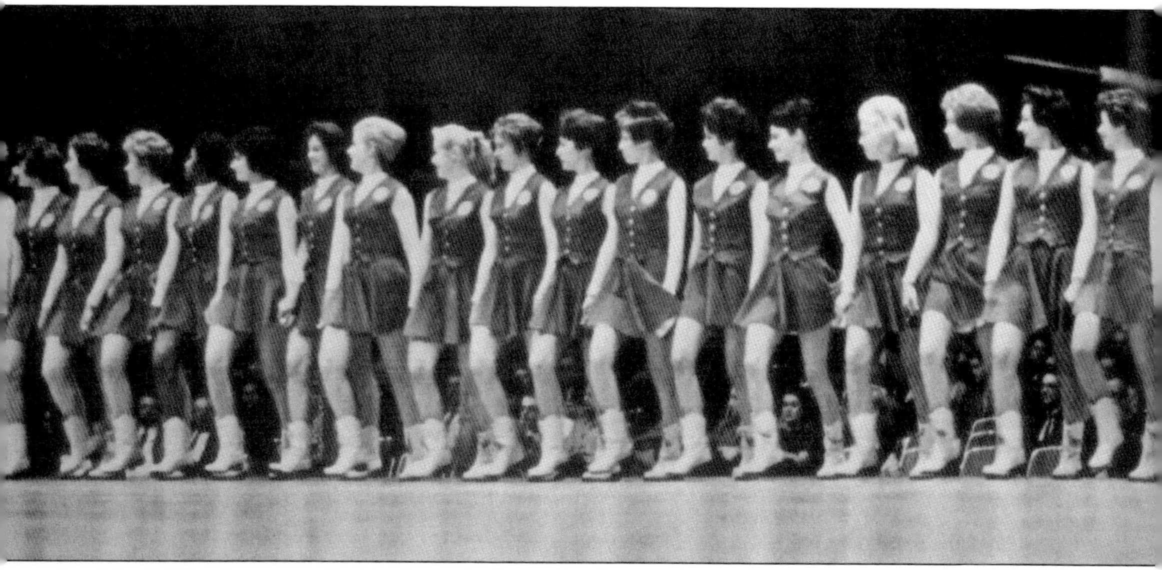

In this 1963 photograph, Ruth Binkele is the lone African-American cheerleader at a Bradley basketball game.

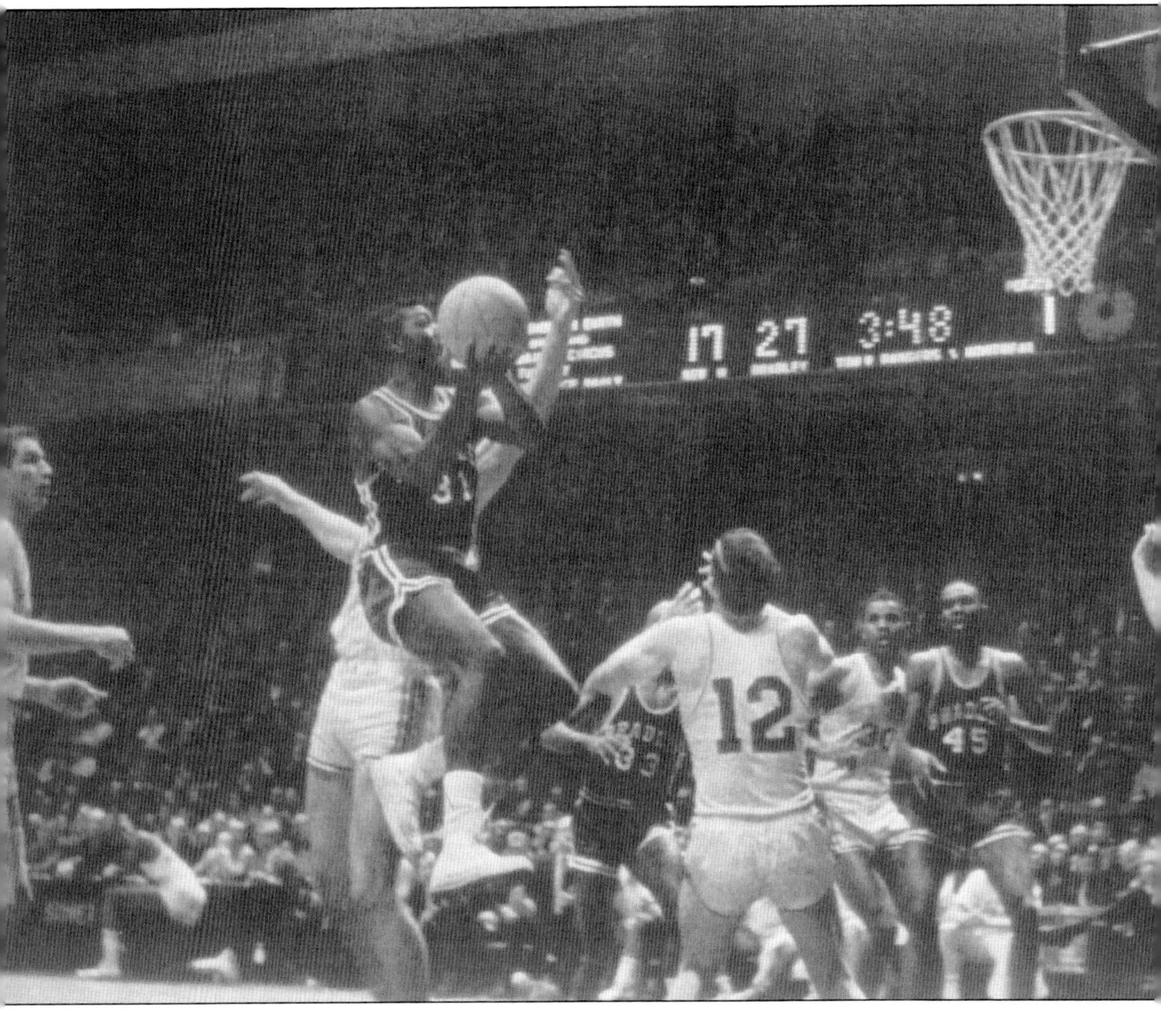

Levern Tart is shown shooting a basket in the 1964 N.I.T. championship game against the University of New Mexico. Tart was voted the Most Valuable Player for his role in helping Bradley secure its third N.I.T. Championship.

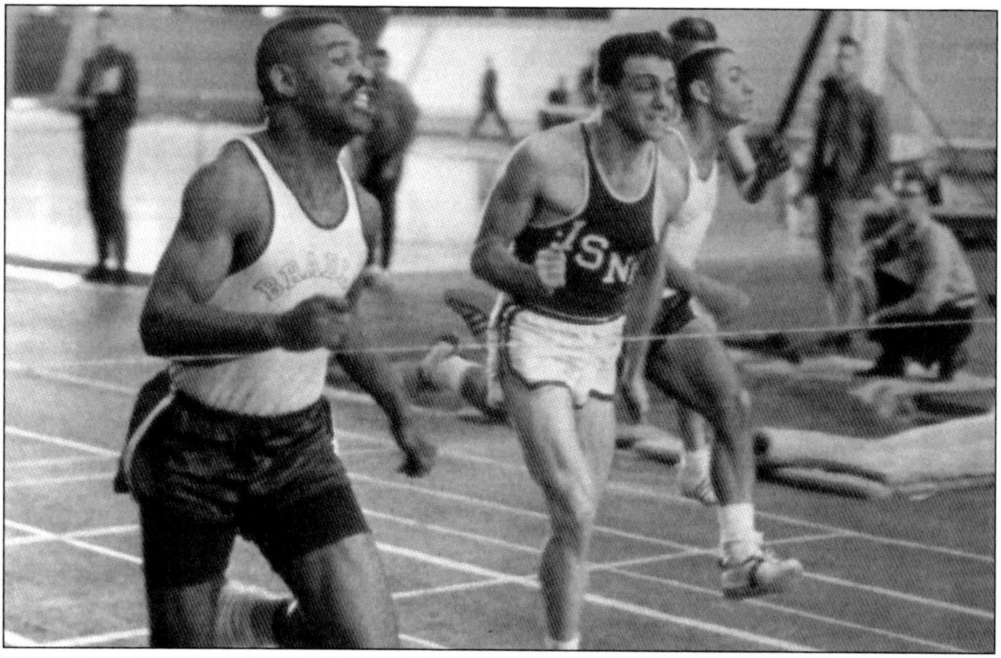

Larry Cowling, a member of the Bradley track and field team, is shown advancing against his competition in this 1964 meet.

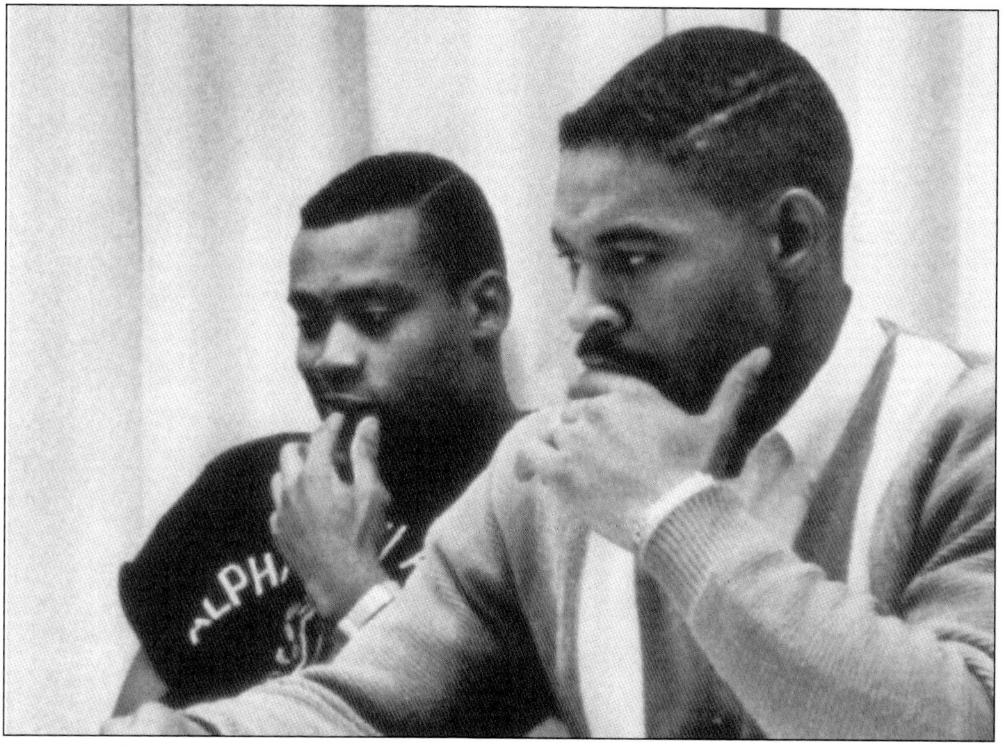

Larry Cowling was also a member of Alpha Phi Alpha fraternity, and he is shown here hard at work in the classroom with one of his fraternity brothers.

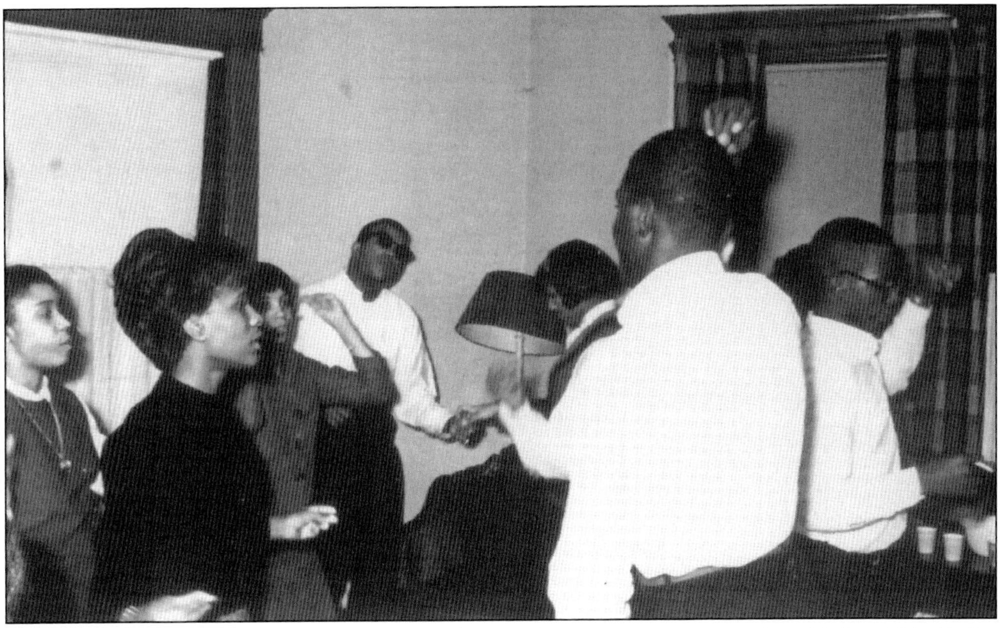

African-American students are pictured relaxing at a party at the Alpha Phi Alpha fraternity house in 1965.

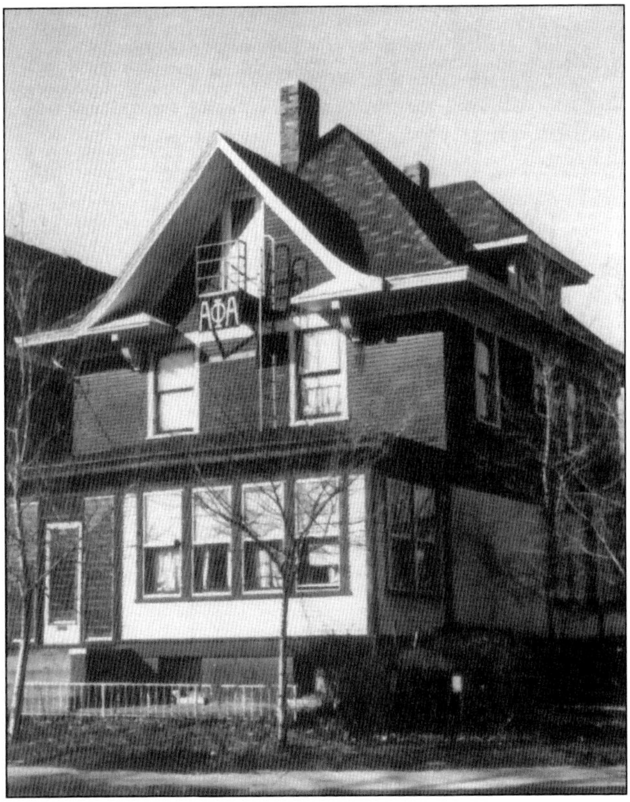

The Alpha Phi Alpha fraternity house is pictured here. The Alphas were the only Black Greek organization to have a house. This picture was taken in 1965.

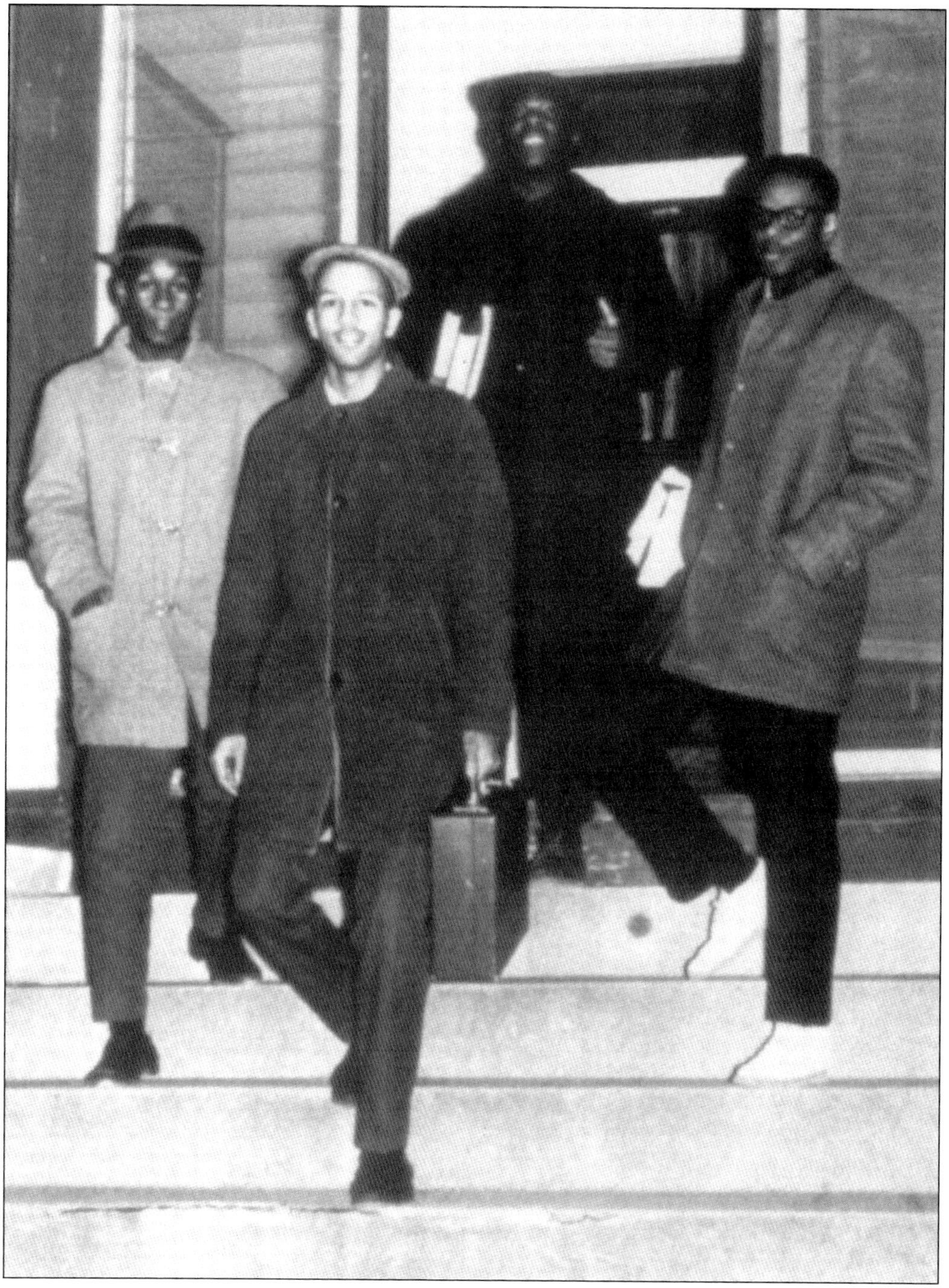

African-American students are pictured on their way to class in 1966.

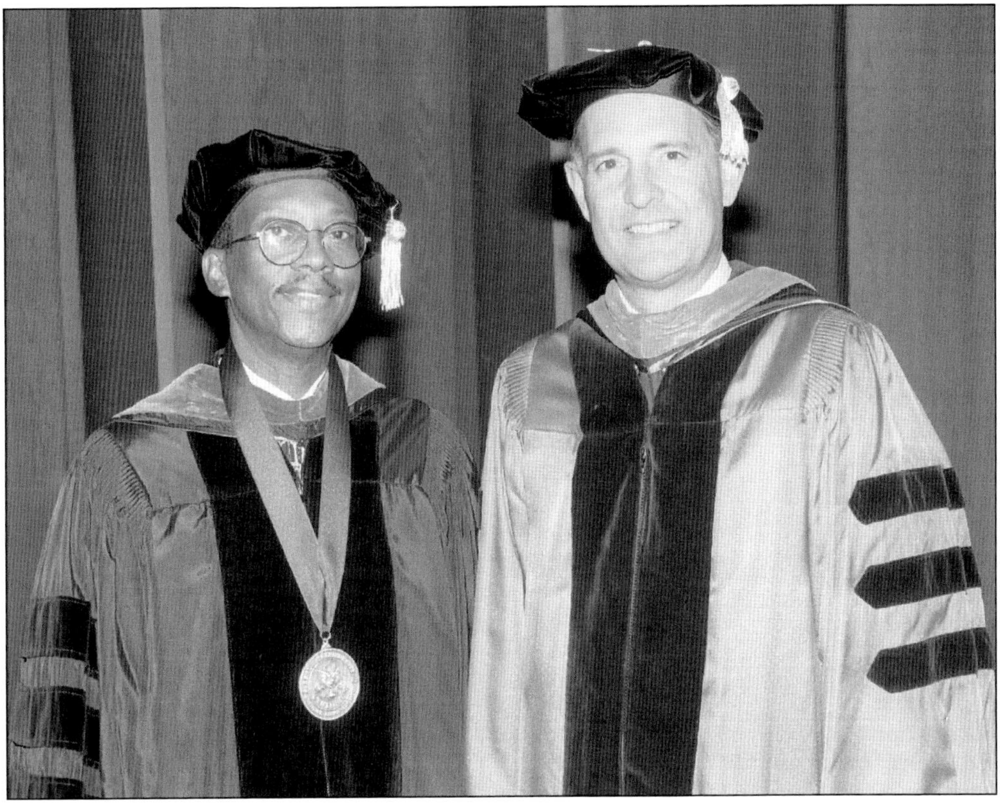

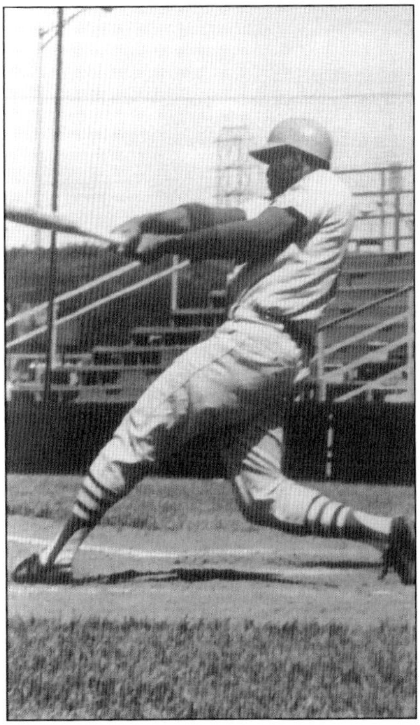

Burnett Joiner Jr., class of 1968, is standing next to former president John Brazil after being inducted into the Centurion Society in this 1995 photo.

Al Smith shows how he earned his .320 batting average. As a member of the 1969 Bradley baseball team, Smith helped to lead the team to a Missouri Valley Baseball Championship.

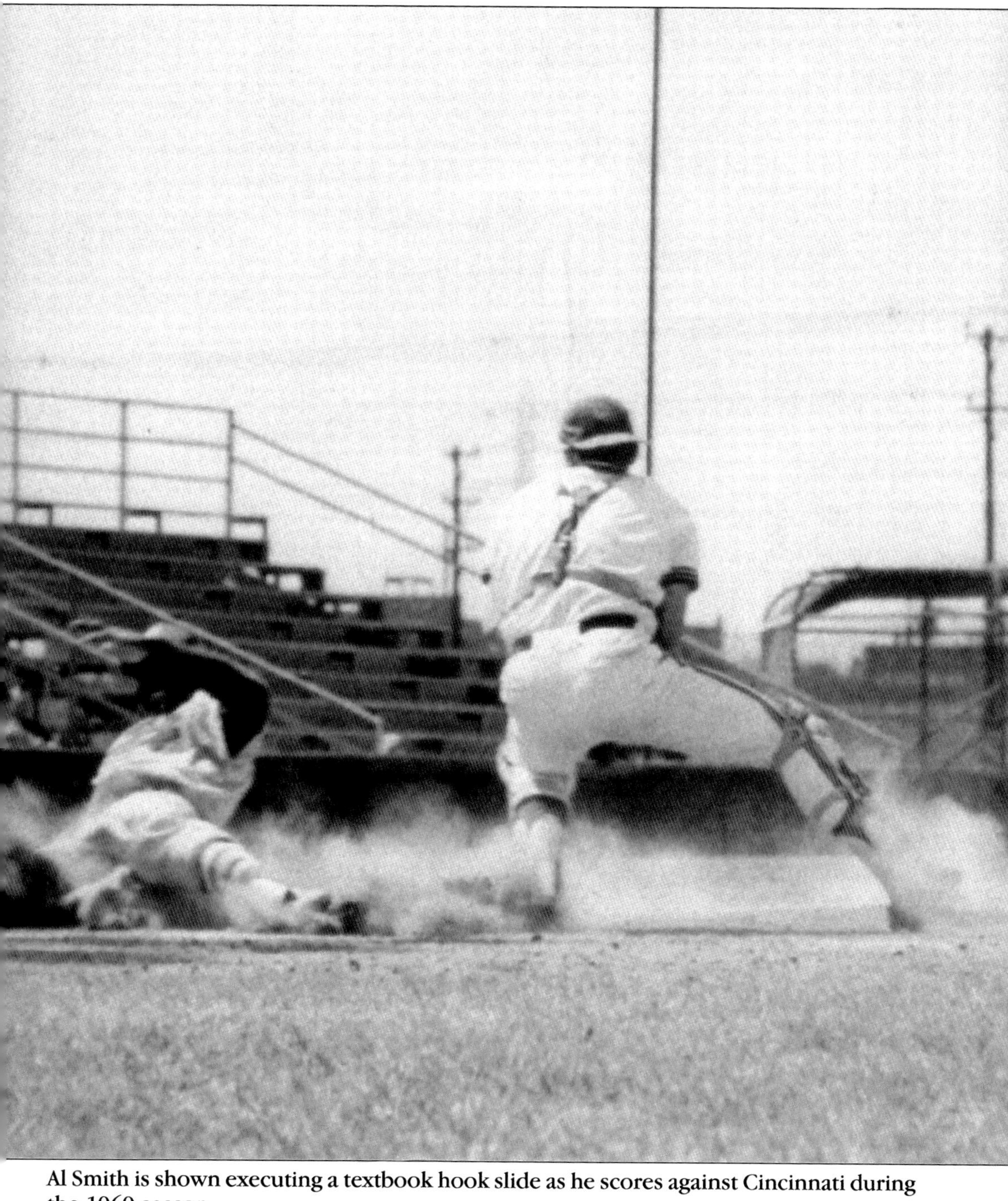

Al Smith is shown executing a textbook hook slide as he scores against Cincinnati during the 1969 season.

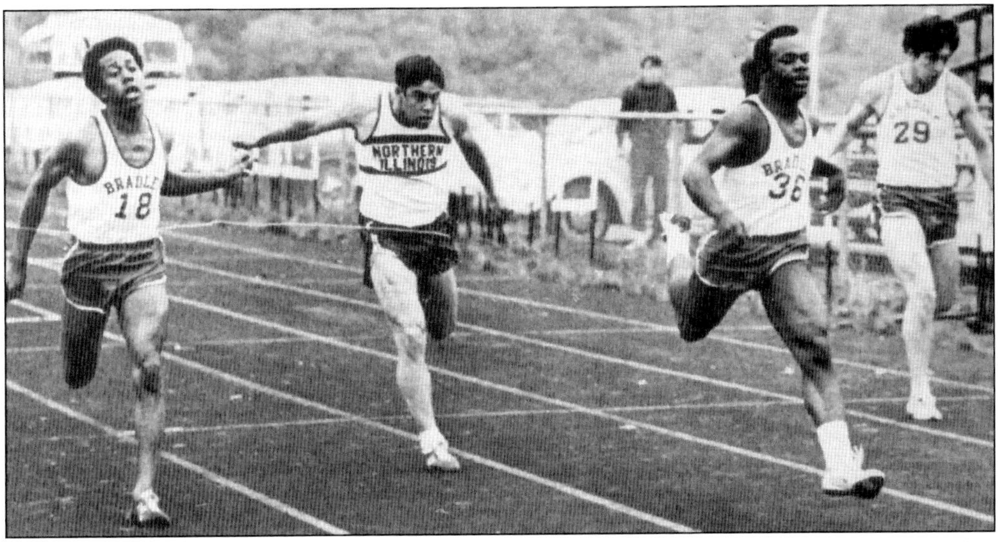

Other African-American athletes continued to do their best for Bradley as well. In this 1969 photograph, Bill Willingham, number 36, comes in first just ahead of his teammate Joe Williams, number 18.

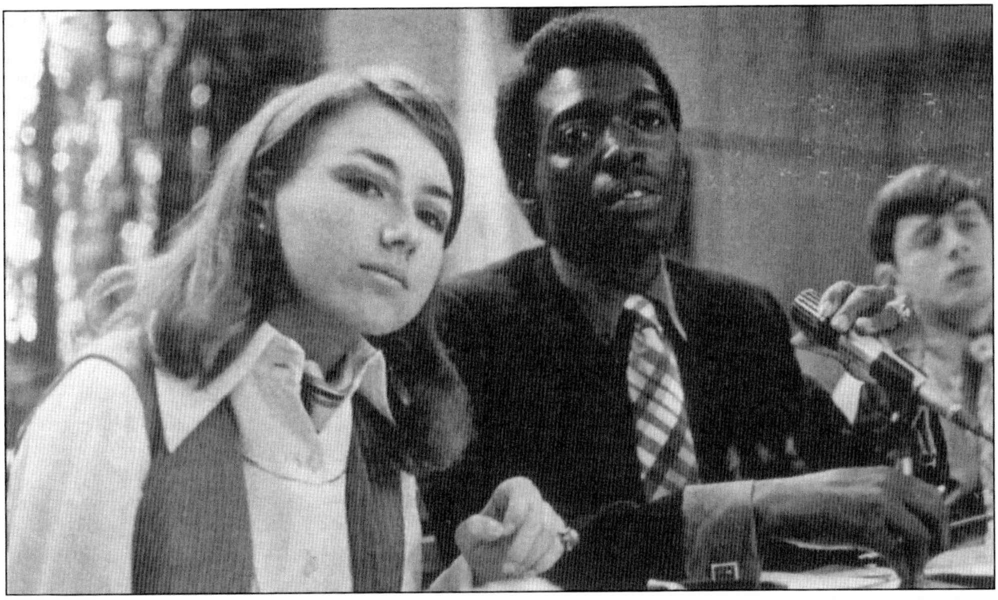
Although there was tension on Bradley's campus as on all campuses during the late 1960s, some African-American students worked to change the university from within. Willie States, the sophomore class president, is shown in this photo, taken in October 1969, with Linda Rassel, sophomore class vice-president, listening to members of the sophomore class at a meeting.

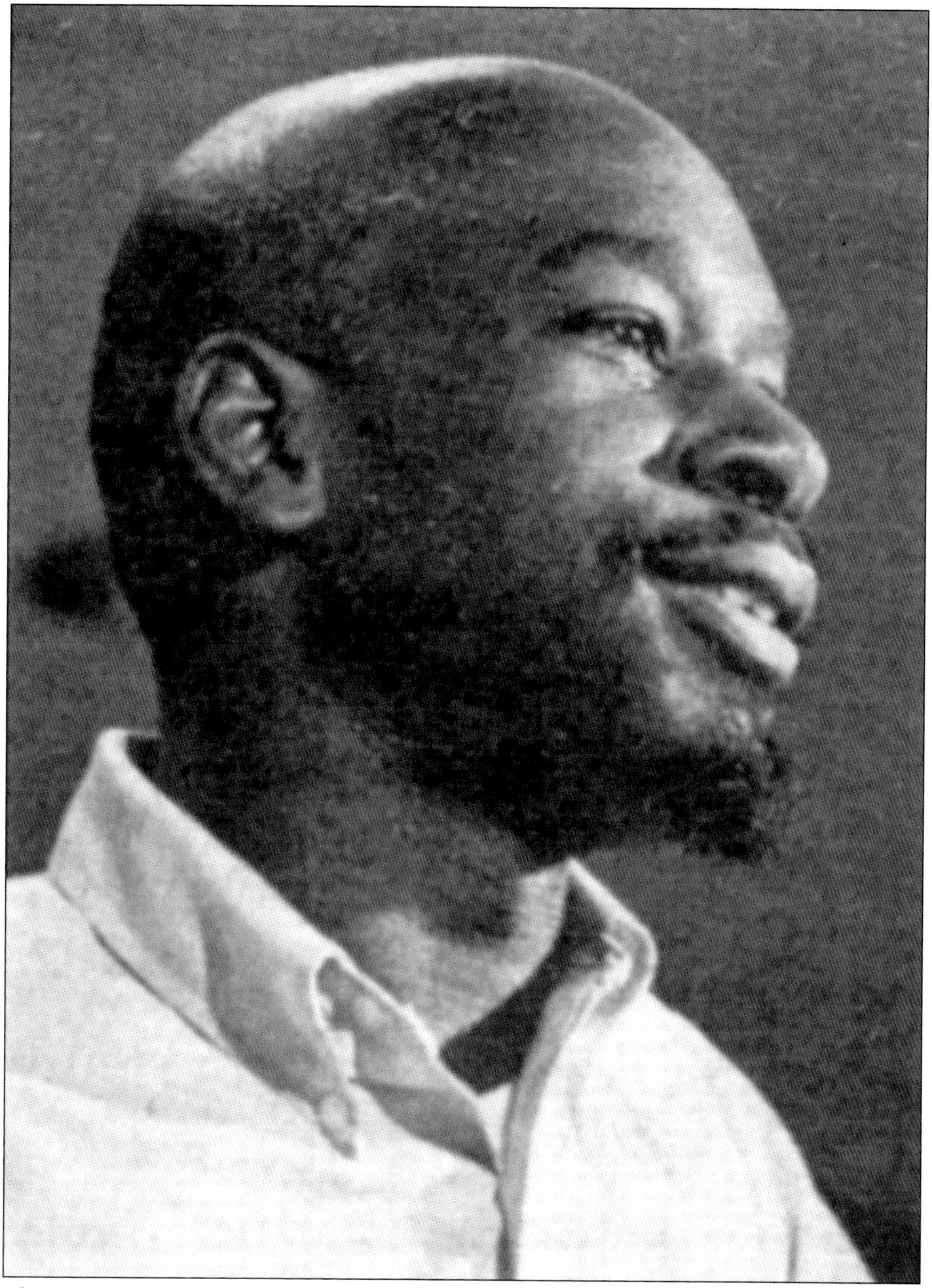

African-American students also used the Black Student Alliance, led by Charles Burke, to force change at the university. The BSA helped organize the student protest in 1969, and gave the administration a list of nine demands, including the establishment of Black Week. Burke is shown here in this November 1969 photo chastising the administration for not doing all it could to improve the racial climate on campus.

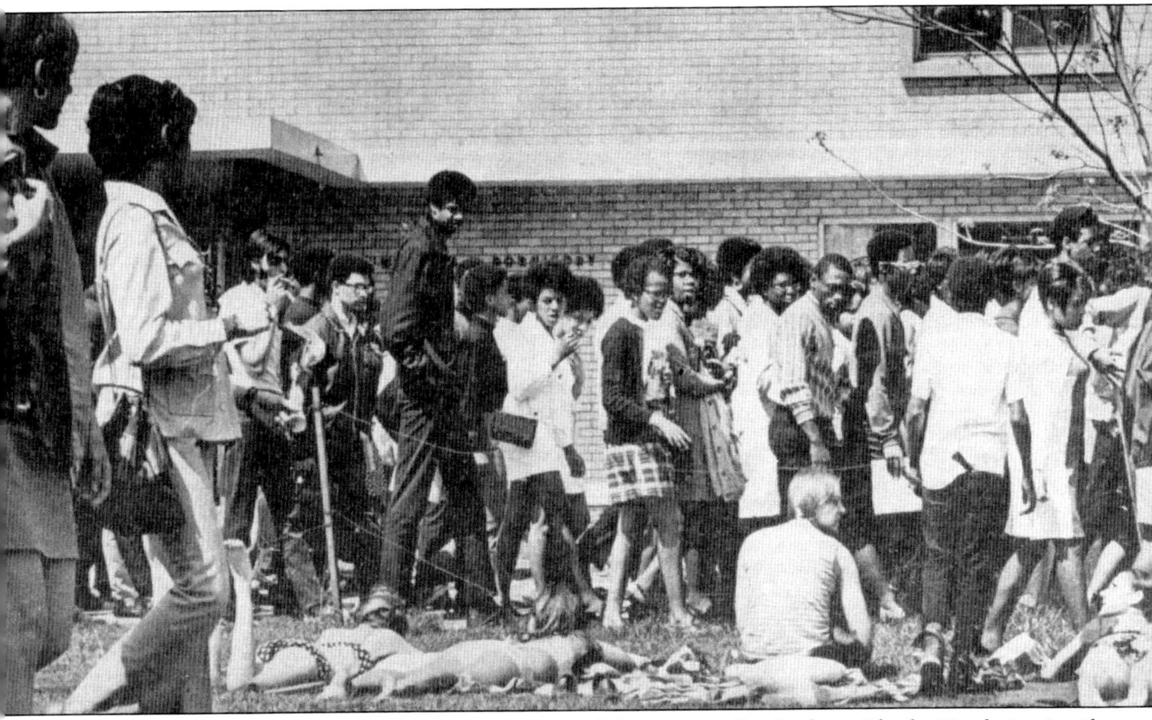

African-American students marching to celebrate Bradley's first Black Week in April 1969 are pictured above. The week would later be called Garrett Week, named in honor of Dr. Romeo B. Garrett, Bradley's first African-American faculty member. During the week, African-American history, culture, and current issues were showcased. Although there was some participation by White students and faculty, the attitude of most can be gathered from the students who took the opportunity to sunbathe on this warm April day.

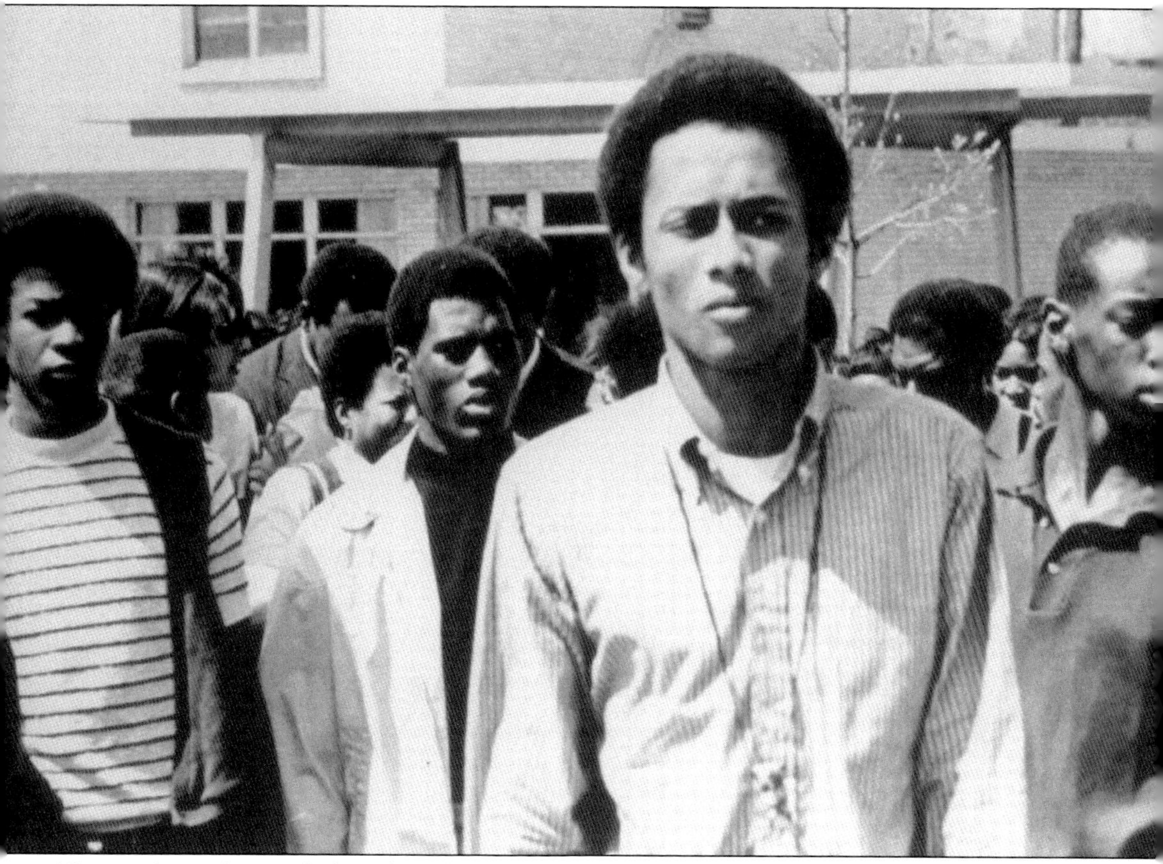

The apathy and outright hostility of some faculty, administrators, and students continued to disillusion African-American students on the campus. Many graduated during this period feeling unwanted and unappreciated. Many students began to become more radical and to embrace the Black Nationalist movement and the ideas of groups such as the Black Panthers.

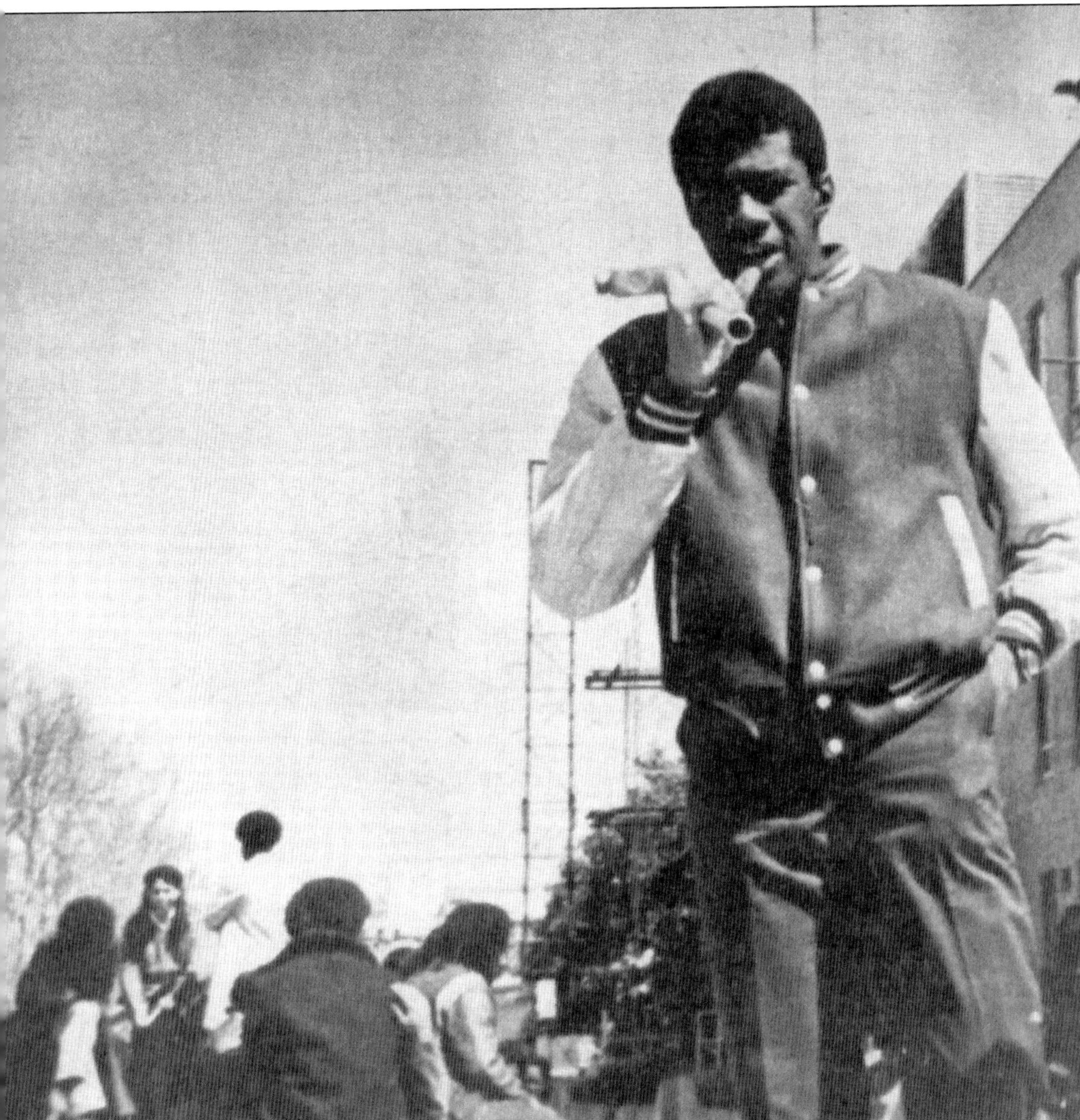

By May of 1969, many African-American students on campus became fed up with the racism they confronted at Bradley on a daily basis. As a result of this anger and frustration with the administration's inability or unwillingness to listen to their concerns, students began an angry protest over new construction projects that involved no Black workers. Students also orchestrated takeovers of Swords Hall, the administration building on campus, and the student union, where a considerable amount of damage was done.

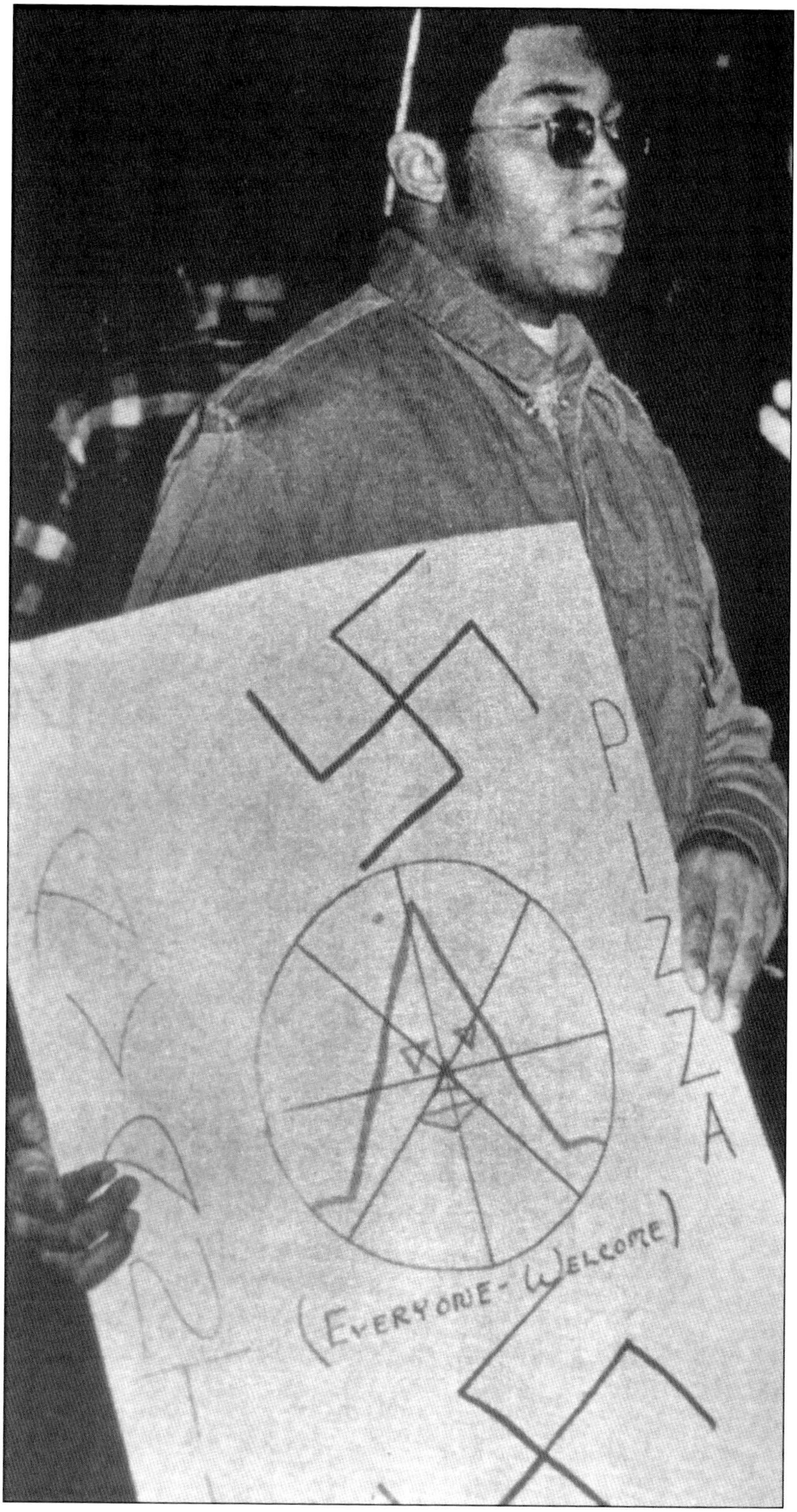

Racial incidents on the campus and in the nearby community that had gone unchallenged in earlier years became catalysts for major protests. In this photo taken outside Avanti's Pizza in October of 1970, about 40 African-American students protested alleged discrimination by the restaurant.

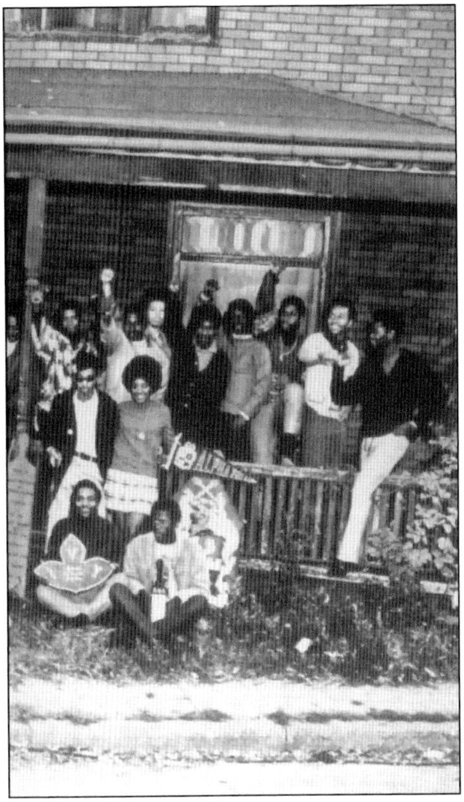

Perhaps due to a lack of concern by White students, faculty, and administrators, by the late 1970s many of Bradley's Black students, particularly the sororities and fraternities, adopted the positions of many radical Black students around the country. Following the stalling of the civil rights movement, many students began to turn to the more confrontational messages of individuals like Stokely Carmichael and the Black Panthers. In this 1970 image of members of Alpha Phi Alpha, it is clear from their afros and their Black power salute, the fraternity had departed from its earlier, more conservative posture for this more radical approach.

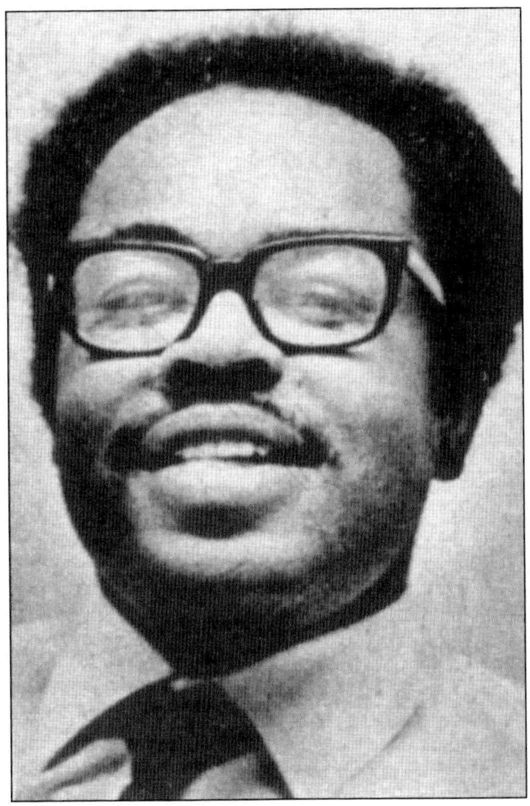

As a result of these types of protests on and off campus, a number of student demands were eventually met, beginning with Black Week—later known as Garrett Week. Students also influenced the opening of the Garrett Center, the establishment of the Multicultural Student Services Office, and the creation of the Black Studies Program. In this photo, the first director of the Black Studies Program (now the African-American Studies Program), Oscar Williams, is interviewed by *The Scout* about the purpose of the program and many of the obstacles to getting the program started.

Four

Contributors to Change
Black Students, Alumni, Faculty, and Staff 1972–1989

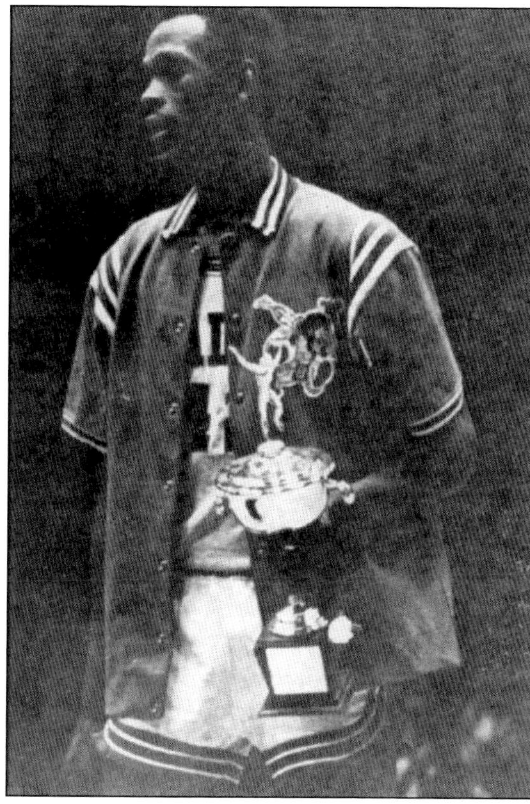

In the midst of charges of discrimination and racism and an increasingly militant Black student body, many African-American students, and particularly athletes, tried to stay focused and do their best. The troubles undoubtedly took a toll on everyone. This is a photo of Sam Simmons after receiving the Illinois Collegiate Classic award in March of 1972.

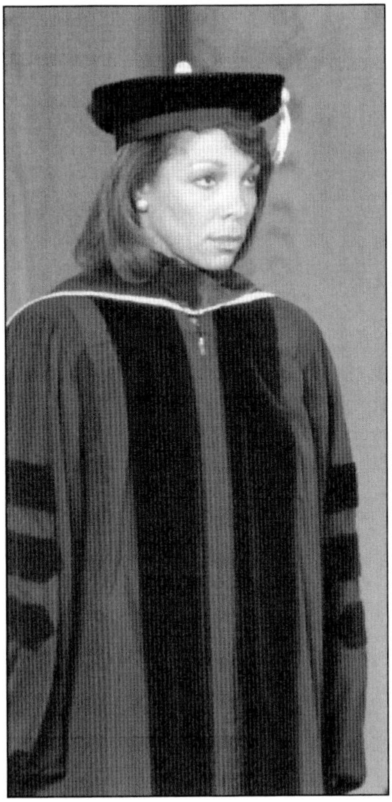

Carol Coram, a 1972 graduate of Bradley is preparing to be inducted into the Centurion Society.

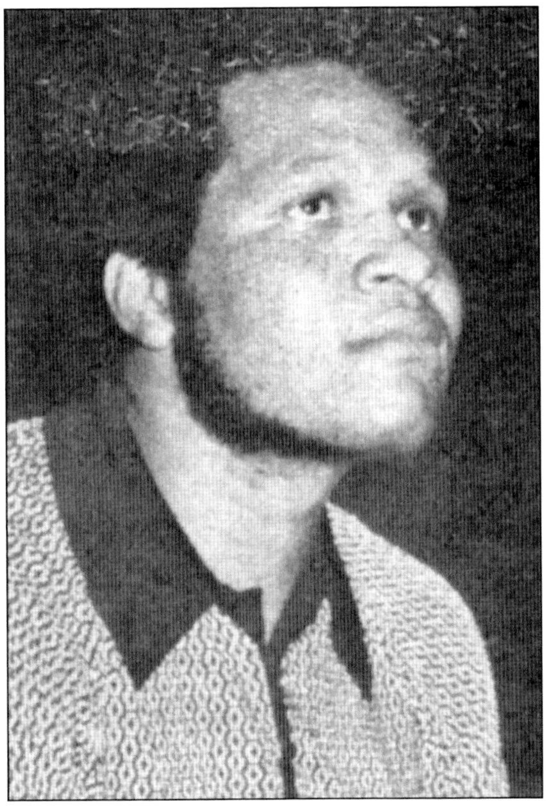

In spite of much criticism by current students and faculty, Bradley did make an effort to employ many of their former star athletes when possible. This is a photo of Joe Allen, an outstanding member of the basketball team who was hired by Bradley as an assistant coach. Allen, who was voted most valuable player in the Missouri Valley Conference in 1967 and 1968, was drafted by the NBA and later coached in Italy. He scouted new players for Bradley, primarily in Chicago.

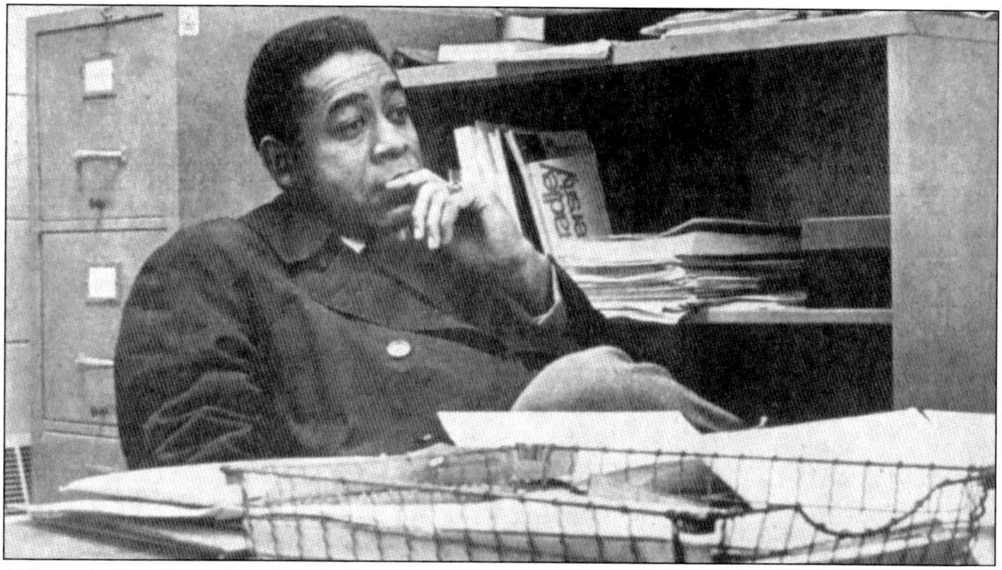

Although Bradley also hired Curley Johnson, who had played basketball, as director of campus security, Vice President Richard M. Trumpe, who resigned shortly after the incident, later dismissed him without proper notice. Johnson's firing renewed cries of racism by Black students, faculty, and community leaders. Johnson found his termination particularly hard due to the fact that he was not given a chance to defend himself. The outcry over Johnson's firing led to the creation of a special search committee that hired another African American, David Baer, to the post in March of 1973. Baer was a former U.S. Naval Master of Arms and Southern Illinois University graduate in Justice Administration.

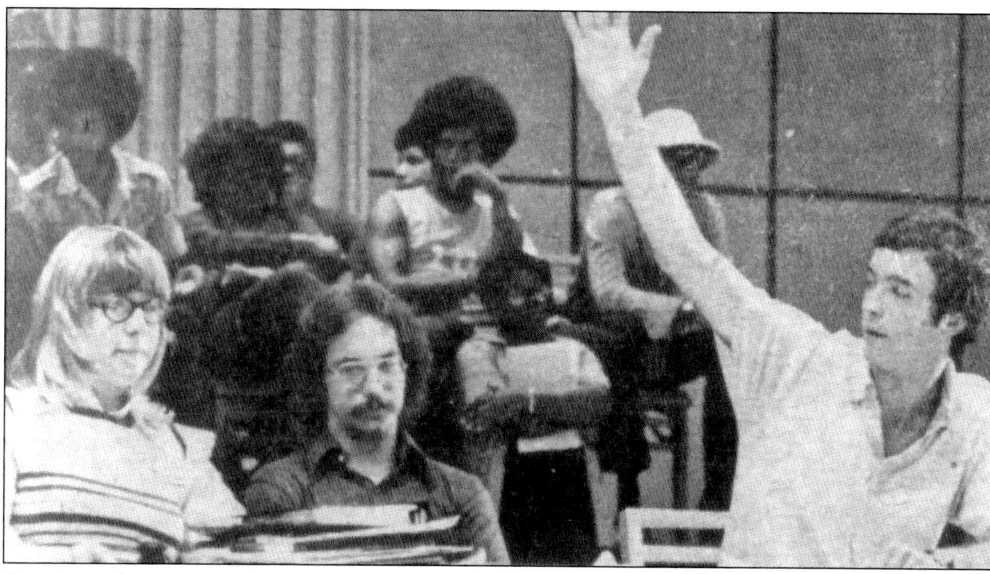

Tensions between African-American students and Whites continued throughout the 1970s. In September of 1973, Black student senator Aldon Morris, now Professor of Sociology at Northwestern University, led a walk out of one hundred Black students at the student senate meeting to protest changes to the student constitution, which he believed reduced the voting power of African-American students.

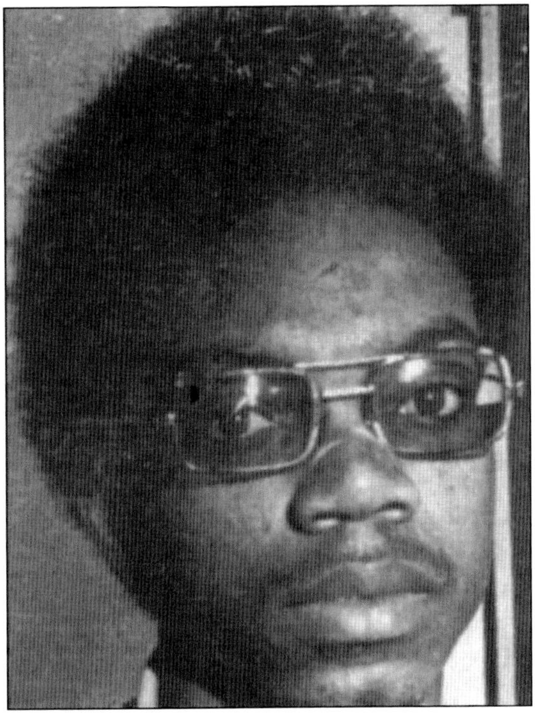

This is a photo of David Driver, the 1973 sophomore class president.

The mother of senior psychology major Cherie Bagley, Joyce Bagley was named Mother of the Year during the annual Mom's Day luncheon in the spring of 1974. She is shown here receiving the honor by then Assistant Professor of Teacher Education Dr. Barbara Penelton (later University Ombudsman) in front of an overflow crowd of 550.

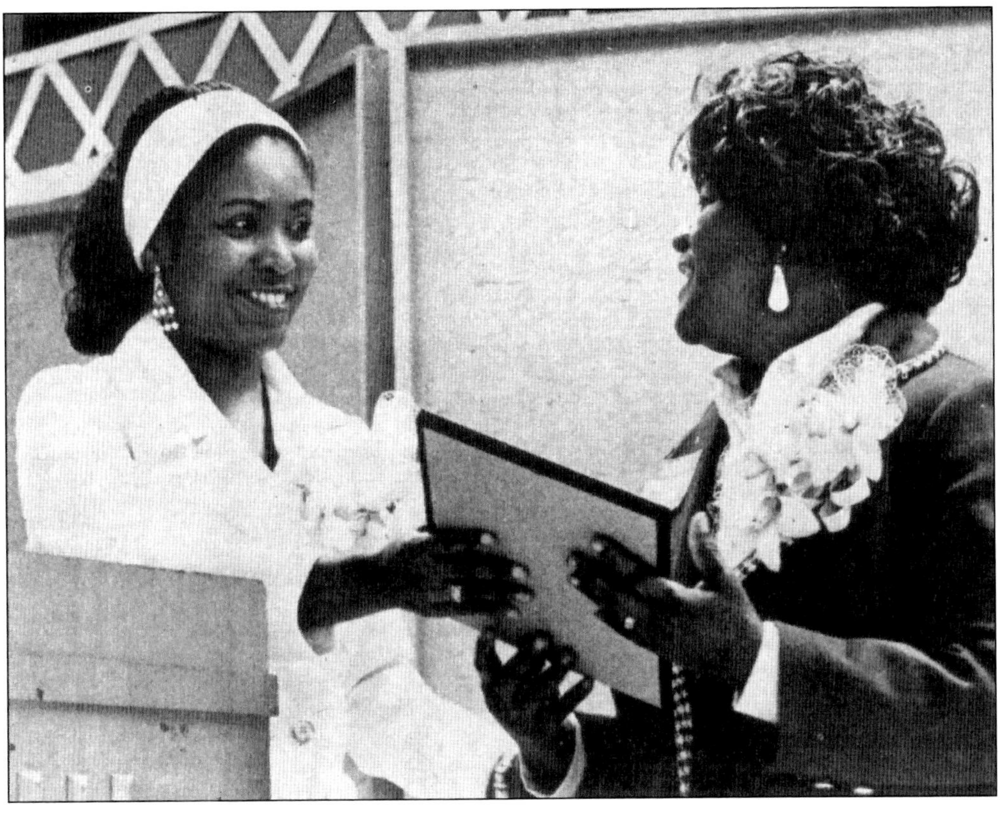

Jory Luster, a 1975 graduate, is now president and CEO of Luster Products, Inc. in Chicago, Illinois.

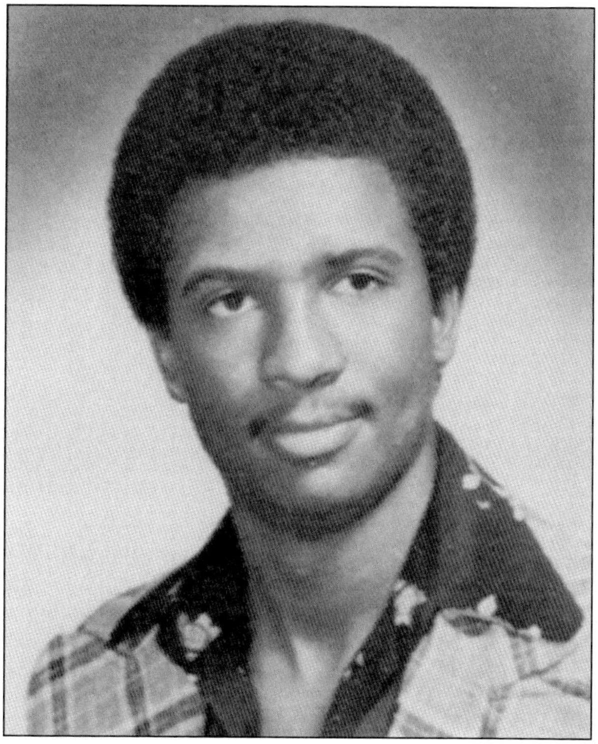

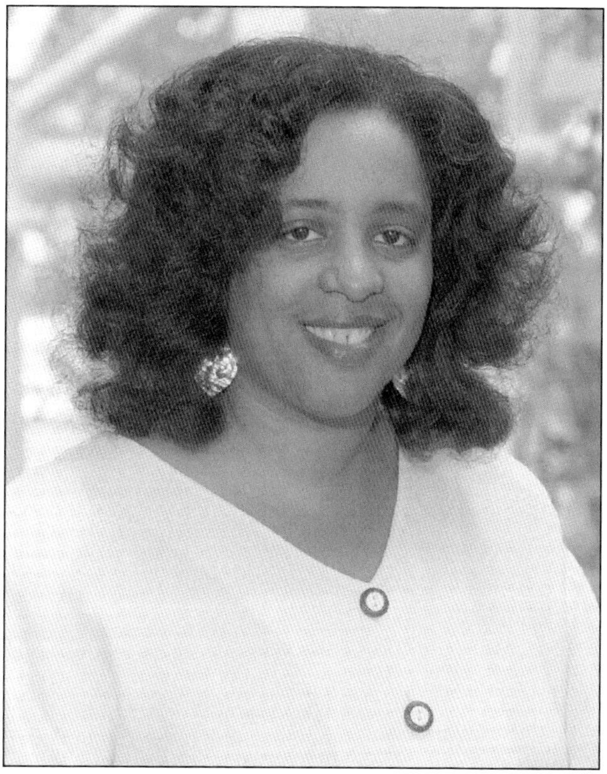

Cheryl Corley was a member of Bradley's championship forensics team. The team's dramatic performances entertained crowds and helped Bradley to begin a string of national titles and rankings that the university still enjoys today. Corley is now a correspondent for National Public Radio in Chicago.

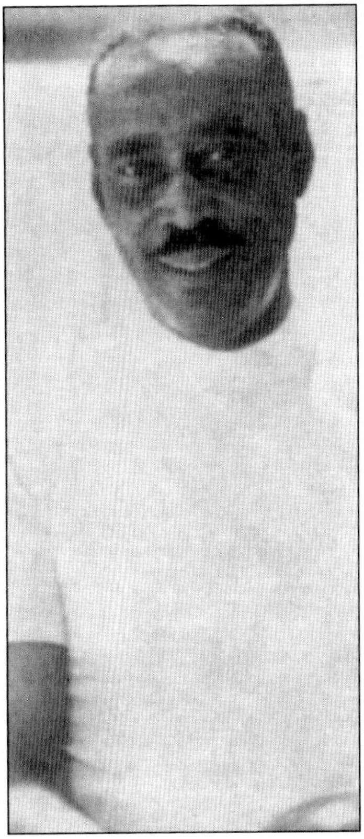

Joseph Delemore Russell, who was known on campus as "J.D." and was featured in this September 1977 issue of *The Scout,* was a well liked physical education instructor. Russell had been invited to the 1936 Olympic trials for the 800 and 1500 meter runs but could not accept because of a pulled leg muscle. He was the first Black coach in an integrated high school in Illinois. He received the Illinois High School Basketball Coach of the Year award, Outstanding Achievement award for coaching, and is in the Illinois Basketball Coaches Hall of Fame. Orville Nothdurft and Chuck Orsborn recruited him to Bradley.

In 1977, several years after the first Black Week, Bradley University refurbished and established the Romeo B. Garrett Cultural Center. The center being named in honor of Bradley's first African-American professor was the second university honor bestowed upon him. In 1964, while still teaching at Bradley, the university established the Garrett Scholarship, which was awarded to African Americans within a 100-mile radius of the campus. The first recipients of the scholarships—five of which were to be offered every academic year—were Carol Daugherty, Marilyn Hinton, Frederick Horne, Dean Rogan, and Rosalind Zanders.

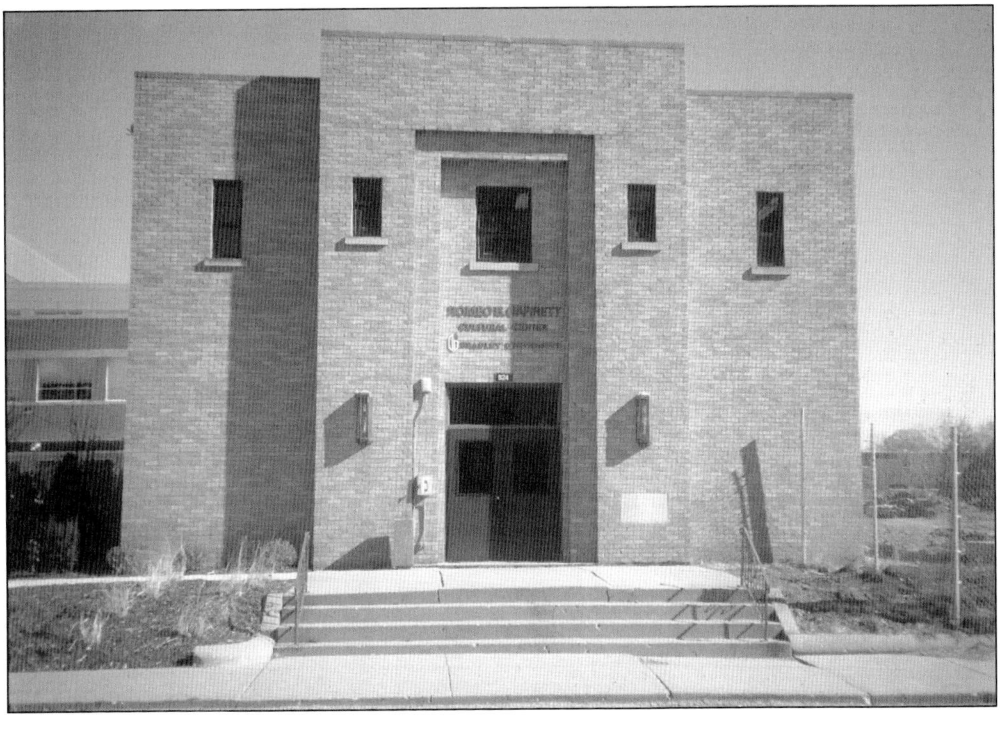

Dr. Garrett is pictured here attending the opening of the center. Even in retirement, he attended many cultural events on campus. The impact of Dr. Garrett is still felt by the countless students he touched, inspired, and mentored during his tenure at Bradley University.

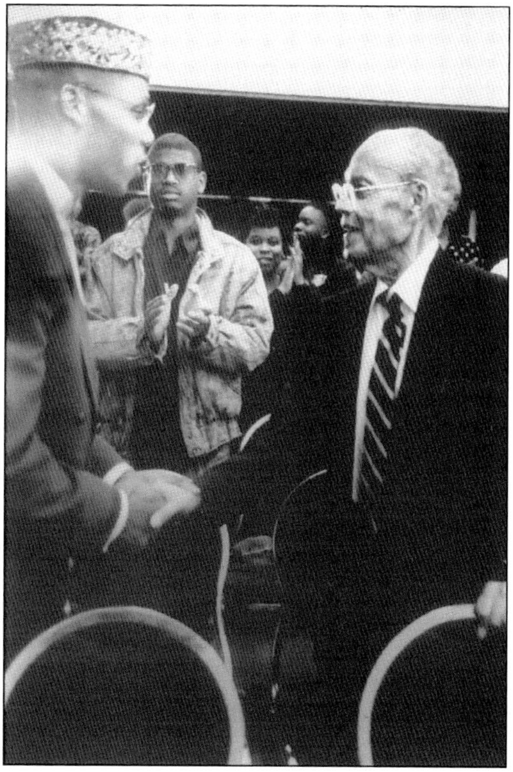

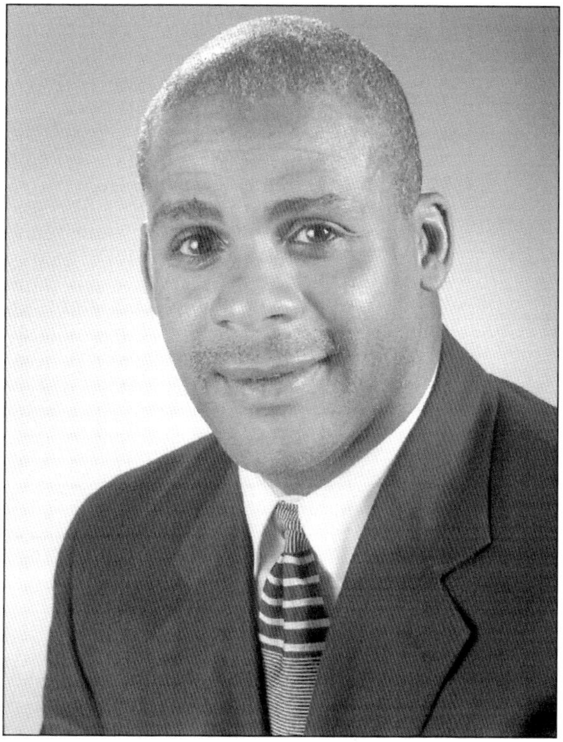

Wayne McClain, a 1977 graduate, coaches the Peoria Manual Rams high school basketball team. At Manual, his teams won four Illinois High School Association state championships.

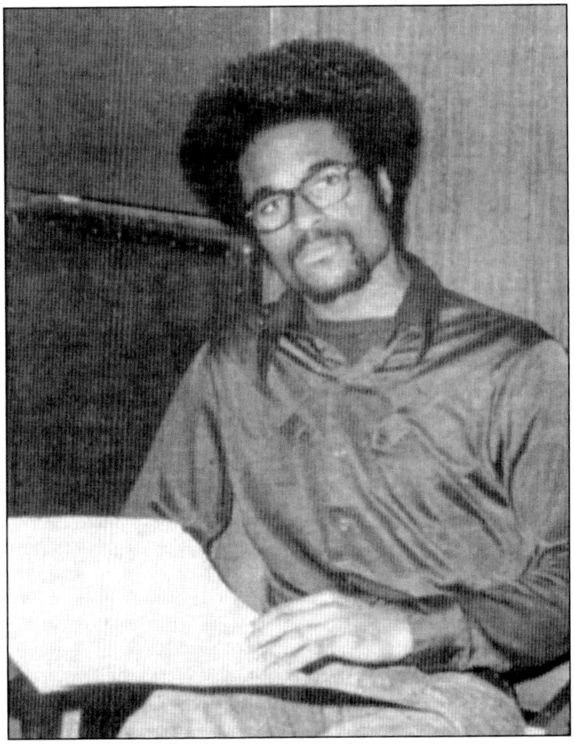

Ron Barker was a Bradley student and founder of the Jazz combo "bej." This group, made up of all Bradley students, was among nine judged outstanding at the annual Midwest College Jazz Festival in the spring of 1978, held at Elmhurst College. Members of the group often wrote and composed their own materials and were well received by Bradley students and throughout the community. Members of "bej" included: Don Gardner, drummer, who received an outstanding at the Annual Midwest College Jazz Festival; David Keys, bassist, who won two outstanding awards; Tom Bishop, who earned one outstanding award for his composition *Exploration,* written on the way to the semi-finals of the talent contest; and Ron Barker, who also wrote material for the group.

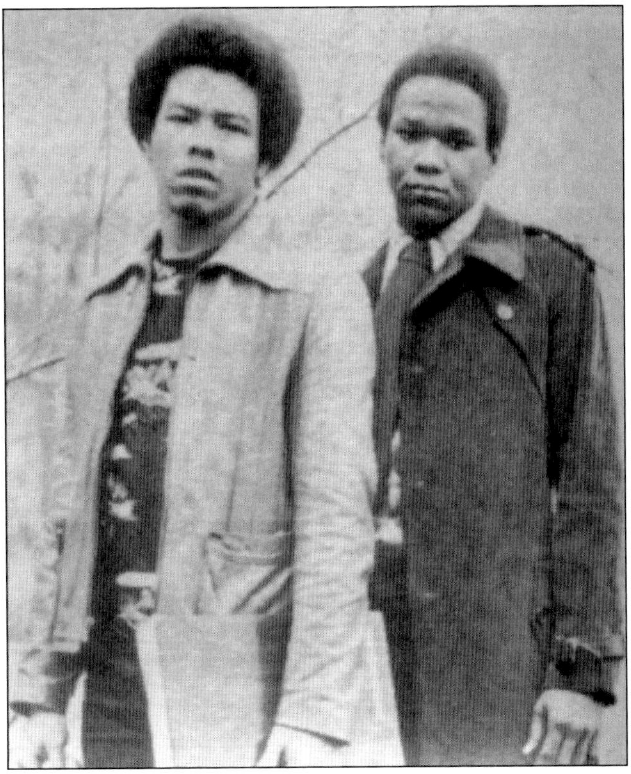

Pictured from left to right are: Donald Havis, a candidate for vice president of the student body; and Wendell Hayes, candidate for president of the student body. Hayes eventually lost the presidency after a runoff in the spring of 1978.

William Hollman Jr., M.D. was a graduate from Bradley in 1978. He became Medical Director at St. Mary's Endoscopy Center, Racine, Wisconsin in 1994.

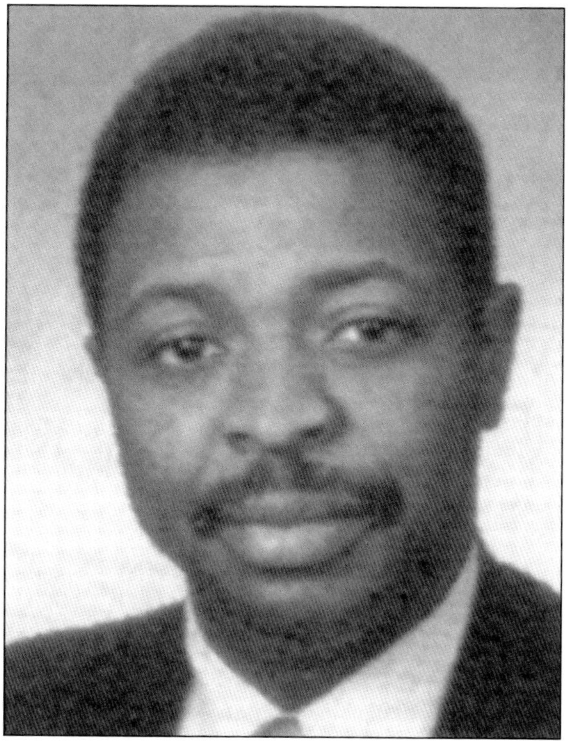

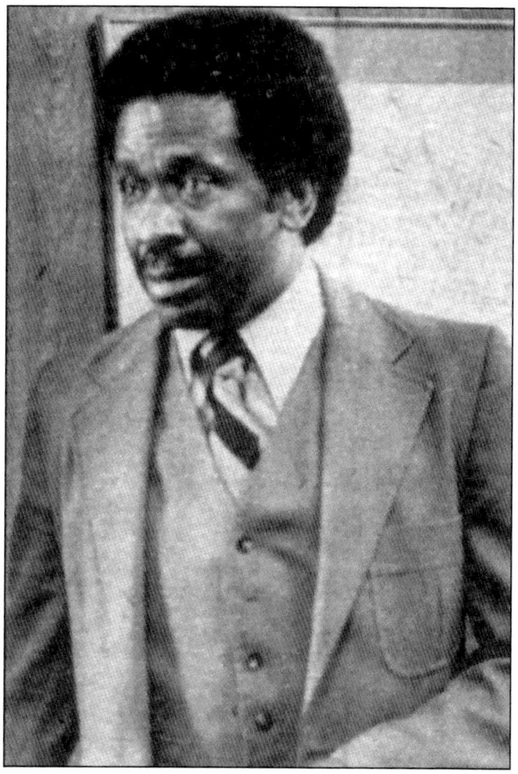

John Gwynn, president of the Illinois and Peoria chapter of the NAACP, became well known among African-American Bradley students for his civil rights work at Bradley and in the Peoria community. Gwynn is also known in folklore among African-American students for being denied a haircut in 1965 at Big B Barbershop on Main Street, across from the Bradley campus, because he was Black. Gwynn, in response to this, led a several day protest in which songs were sung and the business picketed by Bradley students—Black and White. In this photograph taken in 1978, Gwynn is pushing Bradley administrators to comply with federal standards for affirmative action. Gwynn, perhaps more than any other individual, was responsible for many of the gains made by African-American students and faculty during the 1960s and '70s.

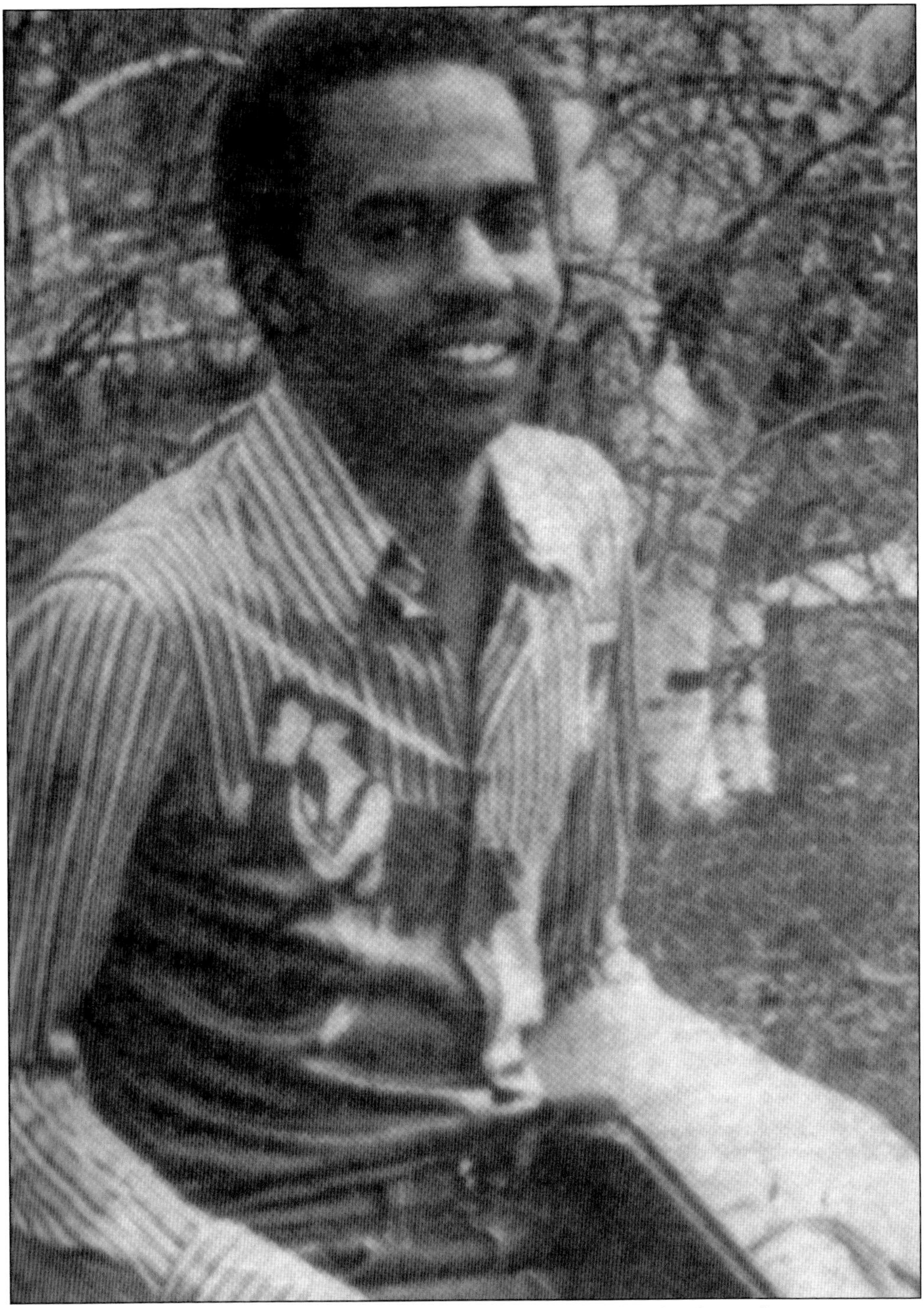

Tony McBride, a junior economics major, was chosen to be the first African-American chairman of the Student Activities Budget Review Committee (SABRC) in April of 1978. SABRC was the committee responsible for allocating student activities funds and at the time had a budget of over $57,000.

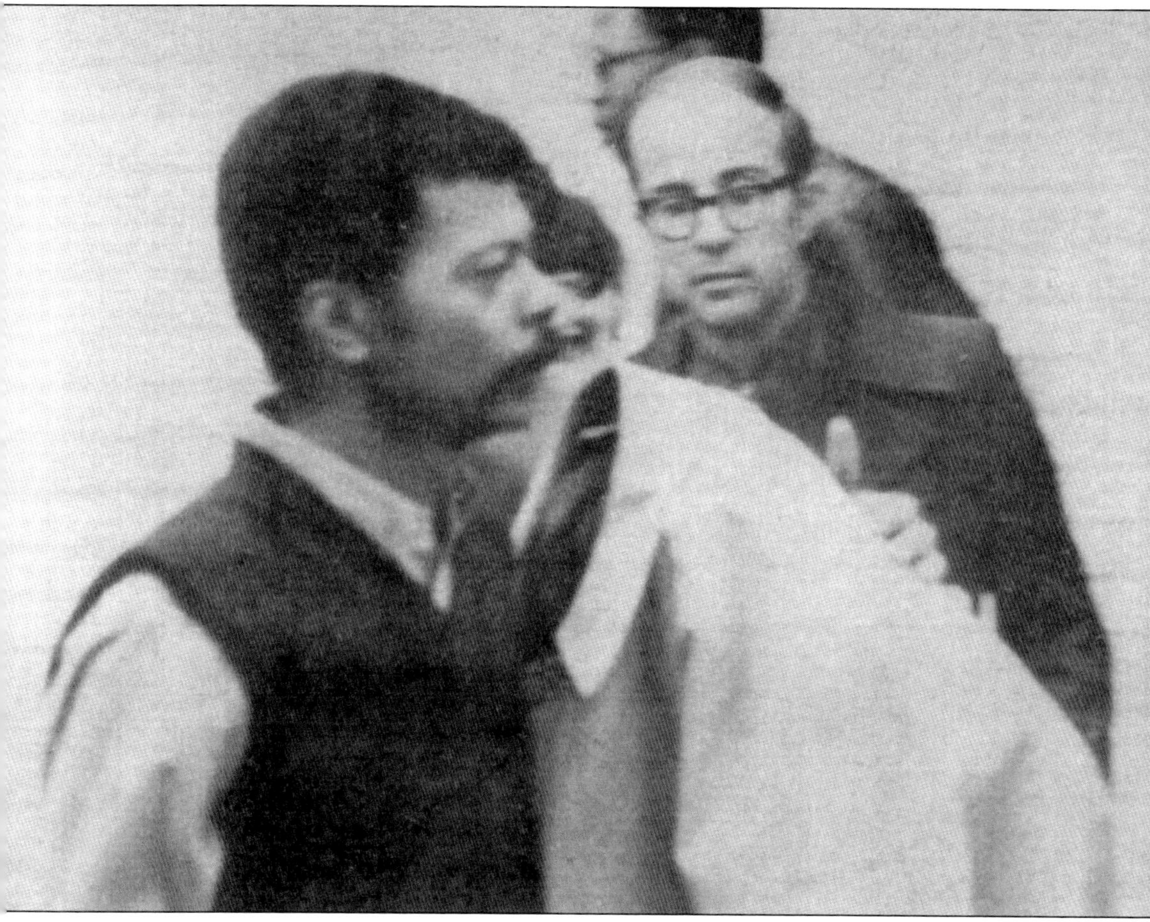

In November of 1978, Bradley security director David Baer became a hero when he disarmed a female Bradley student, senior Sharon Spurlin, who was armed with a loaded .38 caliber revolver and holding fellow student Jim LaFreniere hostage on the first floor of Wyckoff Hall for almost 90 minutes. Baer, who had known Spurlin since her freshman year, calmed the unnerved student who became increasingly uneasy as a crowd of over five hundred students, faculty, and police gathered outside the building. When she relaxed her guard, Baer took the weapon and surrendered her to police.

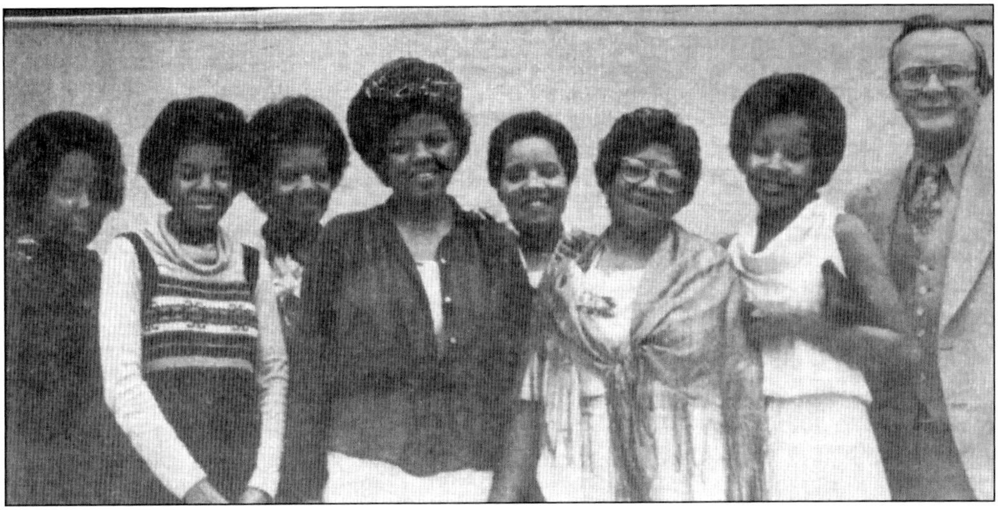

Mrs. Eugene Banks of Markham, Illinois, third from right, was the 1978 winner of the Mom of the Year award at Bradley University. Banks, the mother of 11 children, 10 of whom at that point had completed or were completing college, is standing with her daughters and granddaughters and then-University President Martin G. Abegg. Three of her daughters studied at Bradley.

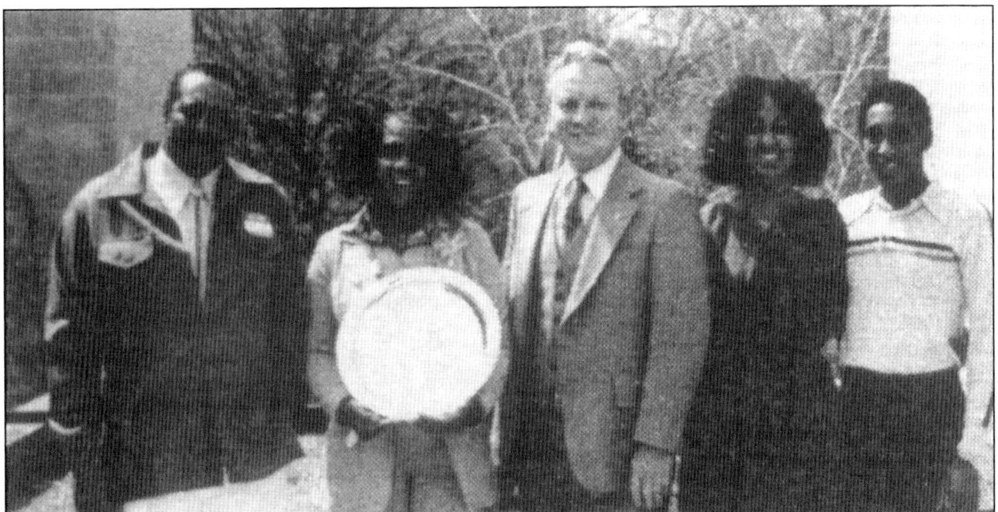

In the spring of 1979, Elizabeth Moore was selected as Bradley Mom of the Year. She is pictured here with her husband, President Abegg, her daughter, and her son.

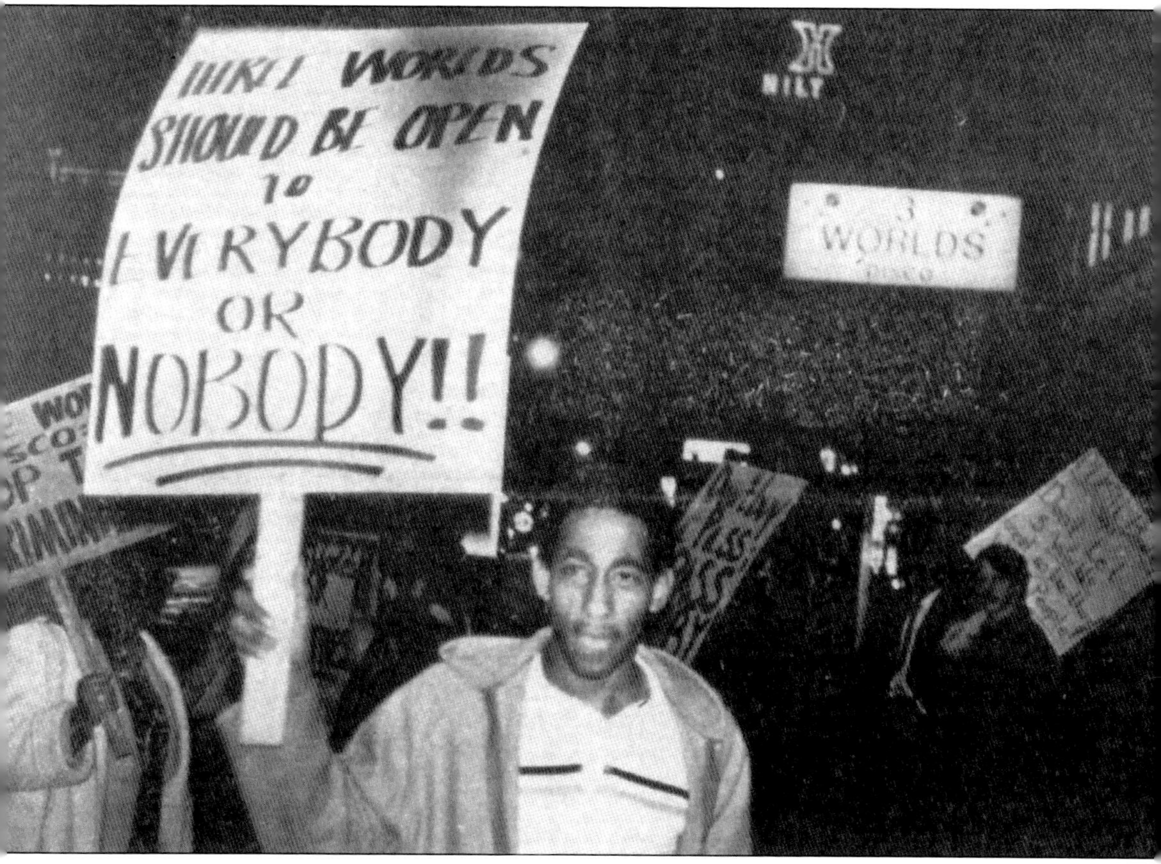

In spite of gains made, racism was still a problem for students on and off the campus. In this 1979 photograph, Allyn Moore joined over 75 students protesting discrimination by Three Worlds Disco. According to a lawsuit filed by three Bradley students, Lydia Cortes, Rodney Washington, and Tina Cancel, the popular hangout for Bradley students denied admission to the three because they were Black. The protest that followed was supported by John Gwynn, president of the state and local chapter of the NAACP; Gene Young, then director of Black Studies; and by the Bradley student body, represented by Judy Rybicki, All-School President.

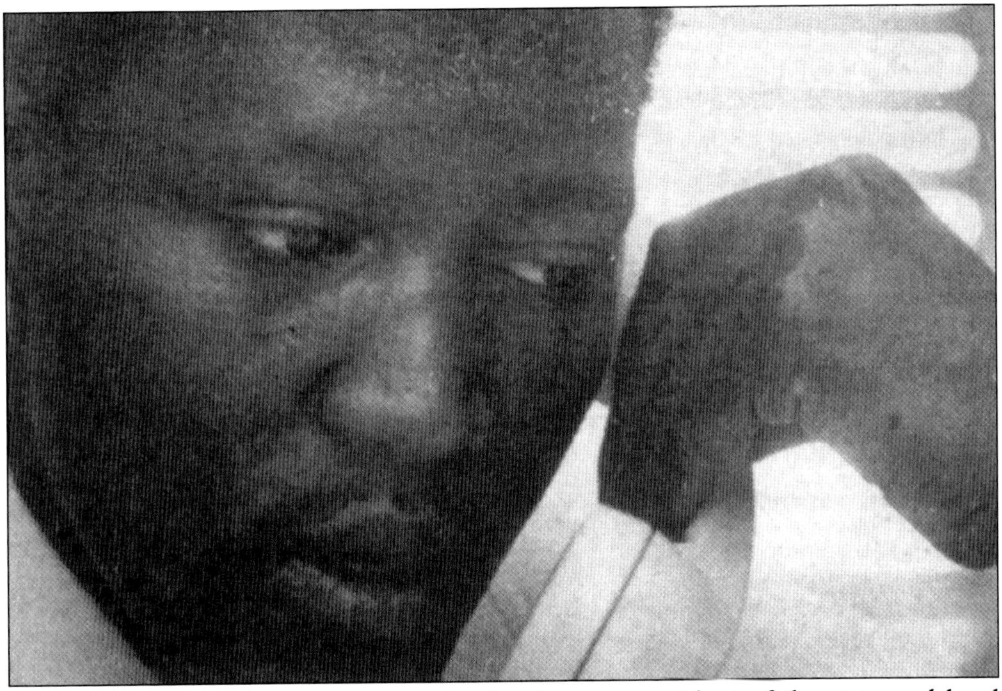

Following pressure from students and John Gwynn, president of the state and local chapter of the NAACP, Bradley hired Clarence Brown as the Director of Affirmative Action in the fall of 1978. Brown, who had been a counselor since 1970, is shown in this 1979 photograph hard at work bringing Bradley in line with federal guidelines for affirmative action.

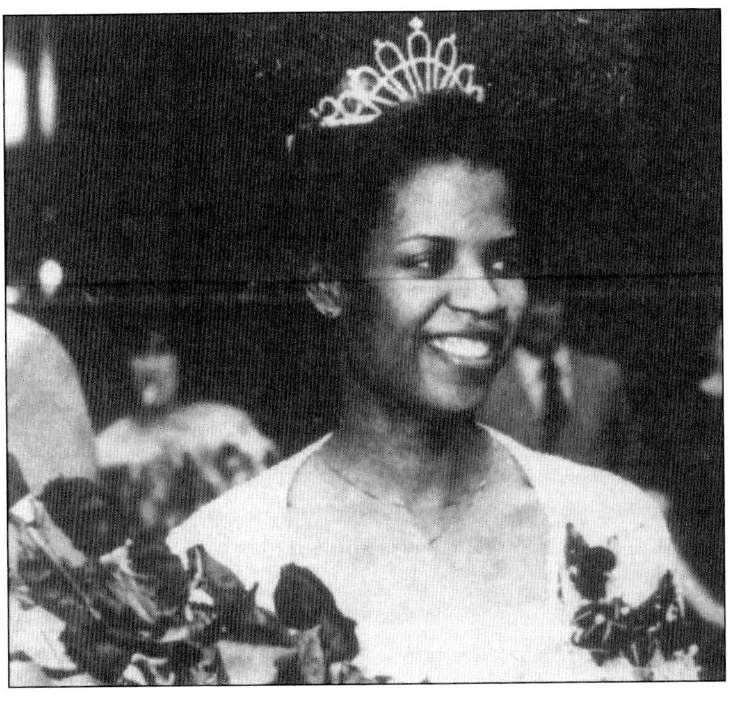

Demetrice Worley, a sophomore, is depicted as the 1980 Homecoming Queen. Worley, who participated in track during 1978-79 school year and was a Merri-N-ette, represented Phi Beta Sigma fraternity. Worley went on to receive a Ph.D. in English, and by 2000 was Associate Professor of English at Bradley and the author of a popular anthology used by students of African-American literature around the country.

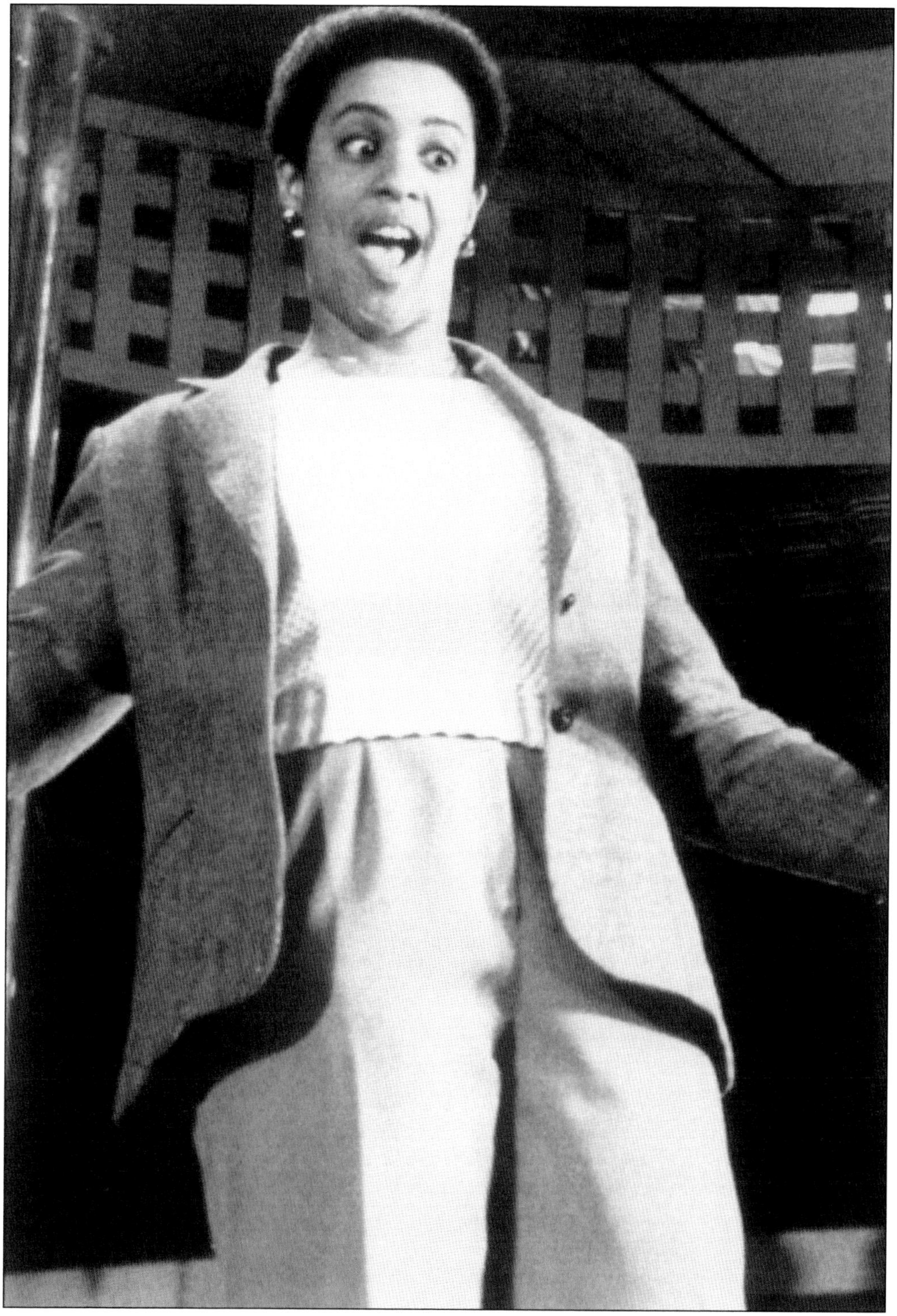

Cheryl Corley, of Bradley's championship speech team, is entertaining a crowd at Sully's Pub in this 1984 photo.

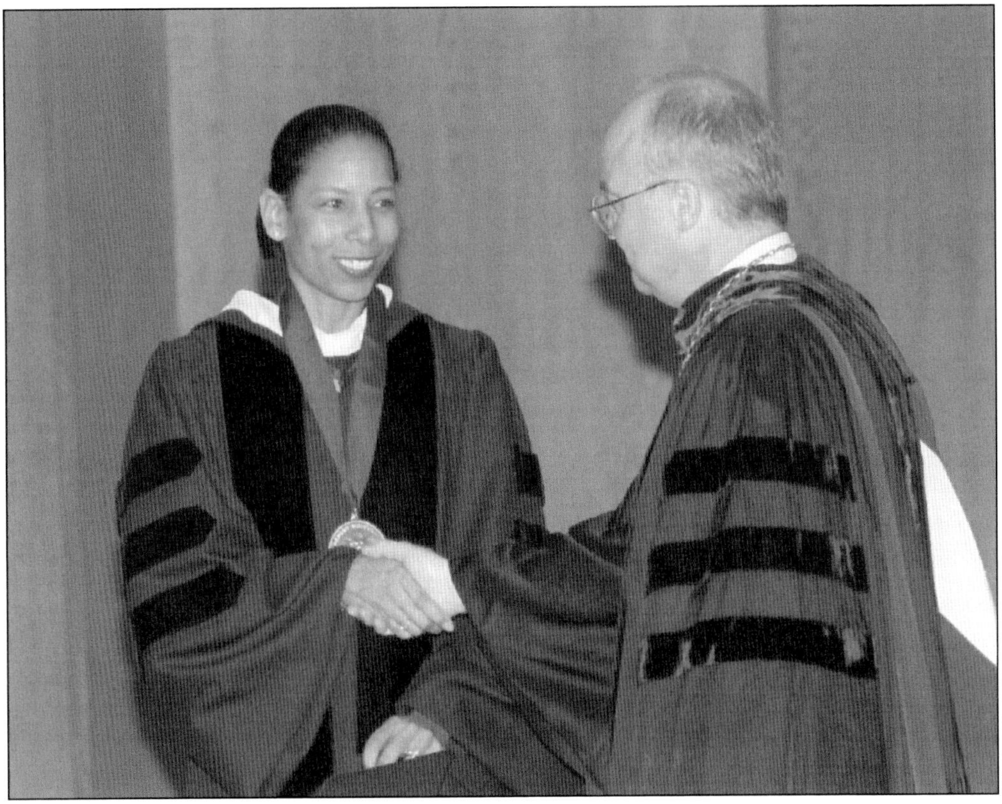

Charlene Dewey, a 1985 graduate of Bradley, is shown being inducted into the Centurion Society by current president David Broski in this 1985 photo. Dewey is now Assistant Professor of Medicine at Baylor College of Medicine.

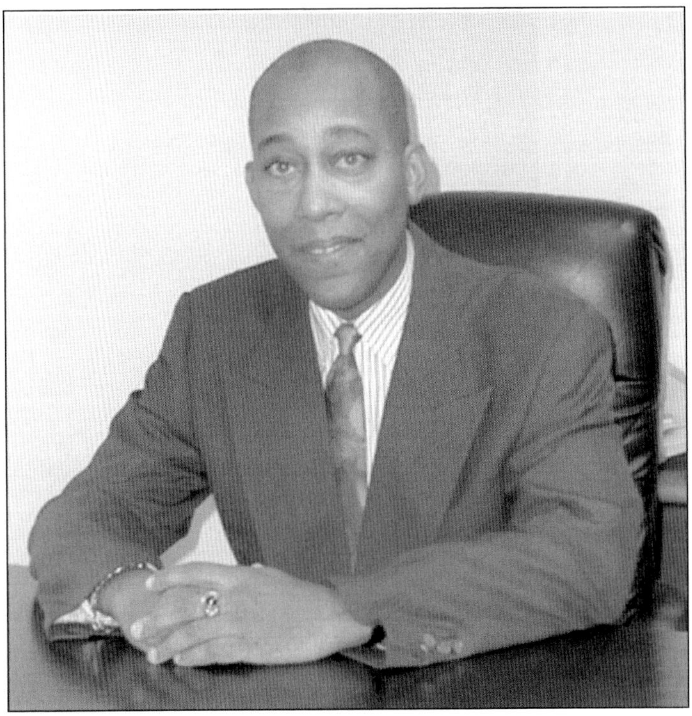

Lester Blair was a 1986 graduate of Bradley. Blair is Chief Investment Officer for Blair Capital Management in Chicago.

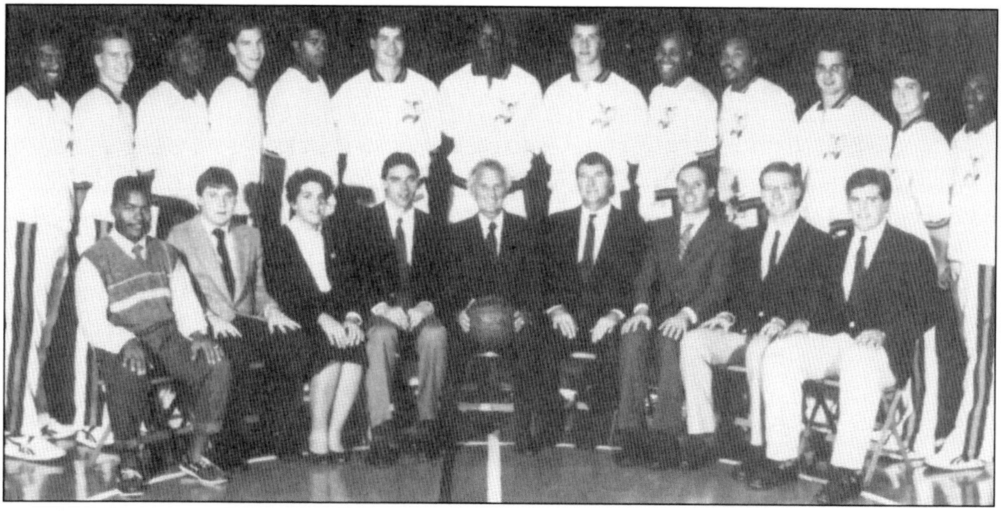

Members of the 1987-88 Bradley basketball team, which won the Missouri Valley Conference Title and is remembered for its star player Hersey Hawkins, are pictured here. The African-American players, beginning in the second row, and standing left to right are: Hersey Hawkins, first; Steve Bayless, third; Donald Powell, fifth; Luke Jackson, seventh; Paul Wilson, ninth; Greg Jones, tenth; and the last person in the back row standing, Deon Butler.

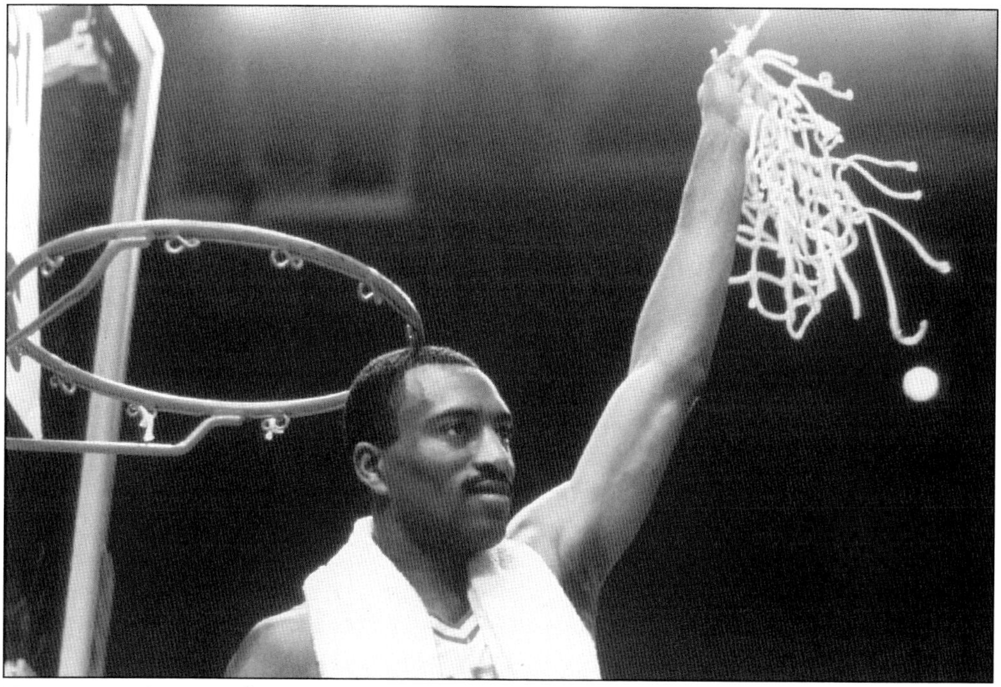

Hersey Hawkins is shown in this 1988 photo after cutting down the net following Bradley's victory of the Missouri Valley Conference Title. Hawkins would go on to have a distinguished basketball career playing for the Chicago Bulls, among other teams. He would also be inducted into the Centurion Society for alumni who have brought national and international distinction to Bradley University.

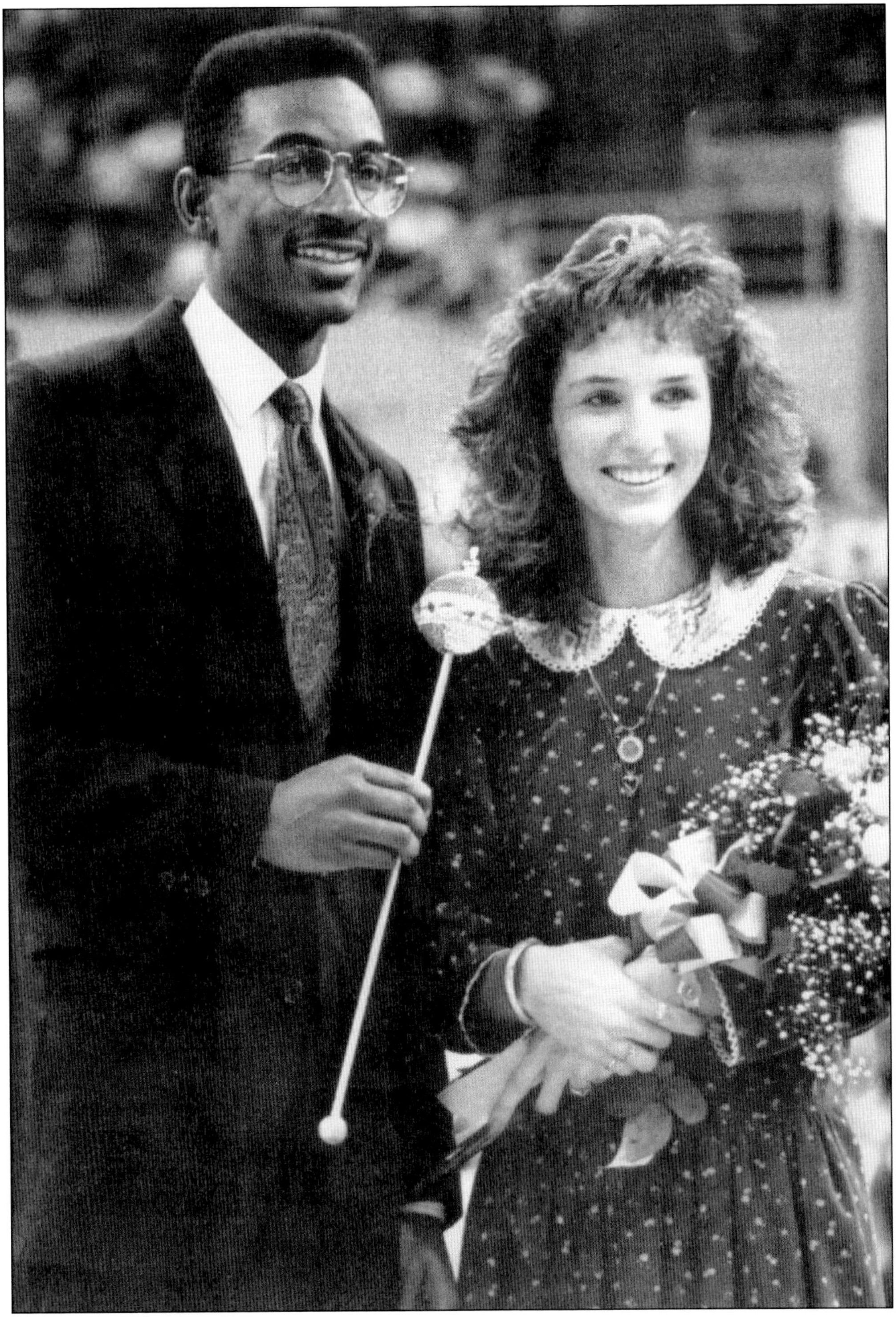

Derek Triplett, left, is depicted reigning as the 1989 Homecoming King during the homecoming basketball game.

Five

RACISM, MULTICULTURALISM, AND DIVERSITY

AFRICAN AMERICANS AT BRADLEY IN THE 1990S AND BEYOND

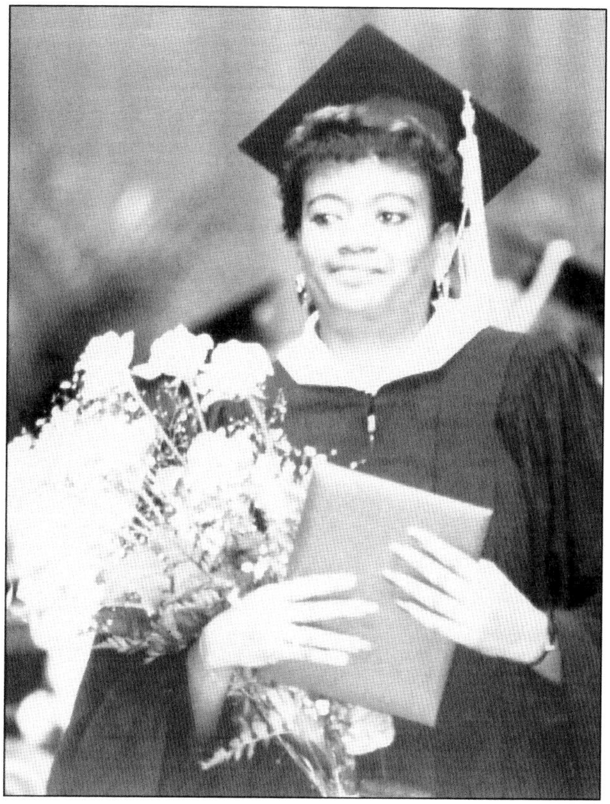

As this 1990 photo shows, African-American students continued to come to Bradley for the same reason they did nearly a century earlier—for a first rate education. As this unidentified student probably realized at Bradley's December graduation, her life journey was just beginning rather than coming to an end.

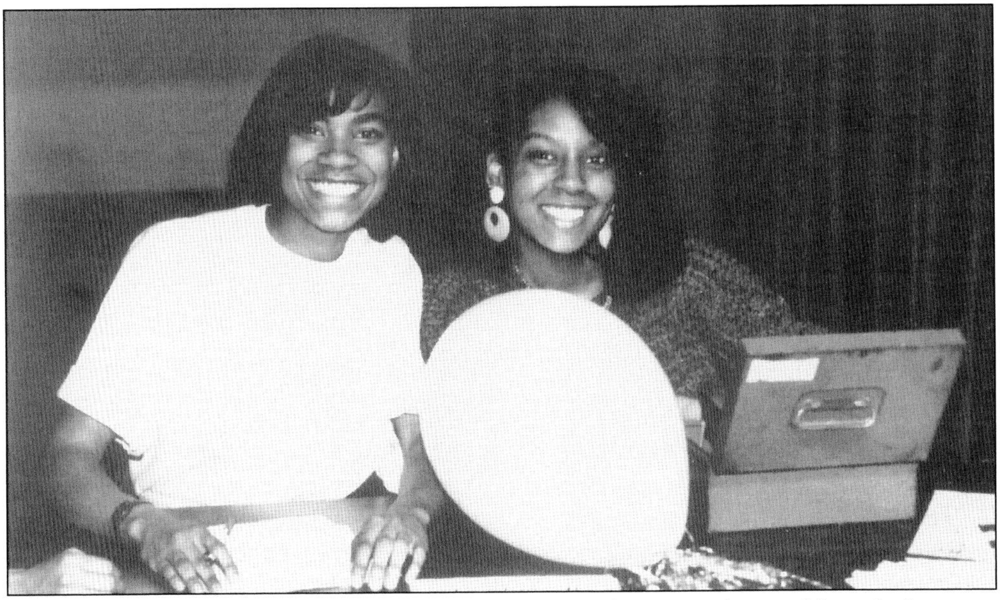

As these unidentified young students demonstrate in this 1990 photo, although there are struggles at any university, there are many opportunities to develop lifetime friendships and to enjoy what Bradley has to offer.

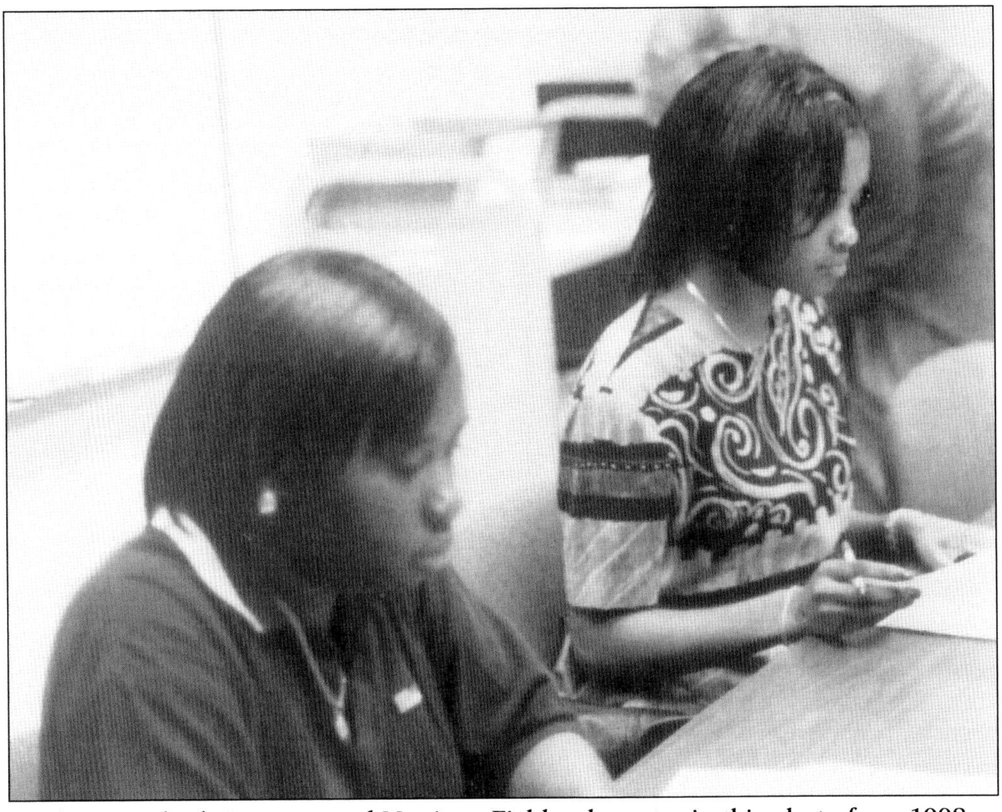

Freshmen Melinda Peterson and Monique Fields take notes in this photo from 1998.

Melvin Flowers, pictured here, was a 1990 graduate who has been active in Bradley's National Alumni Association, serving on its Board of Directors from 1997–1999. Flowers has also been active in raising money for the Dr. Barbara S. Penelton Scholarship and the Black Alumni Scholarship, which were established in 1993. Through his work and that of alumni such as Benjamin Ghess, class of '76, and president of the Black Alumni Scholarship Committee, and Robin L. Kelly, class of '78 and '82, and a member of Sigma Gamma Rho, many African Americans who left Bradley after having a negative experience have given money specifically for African-American students to keep them from experiencing the hardships, financial and otherwise, that they endured while at Bradley.

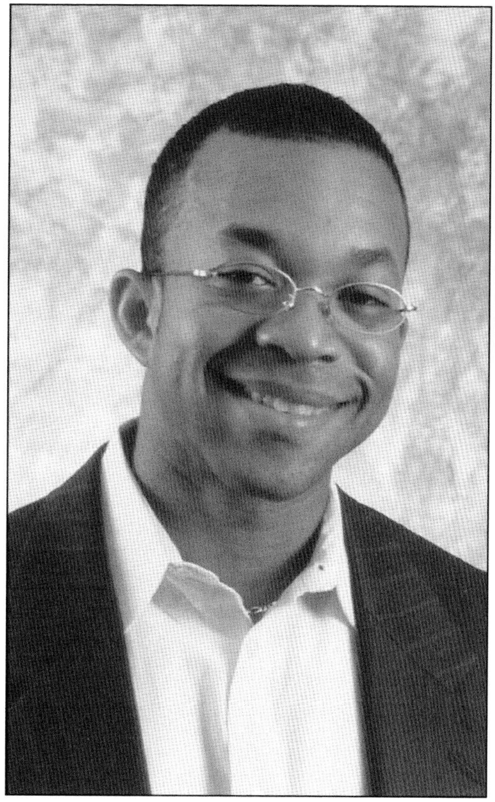

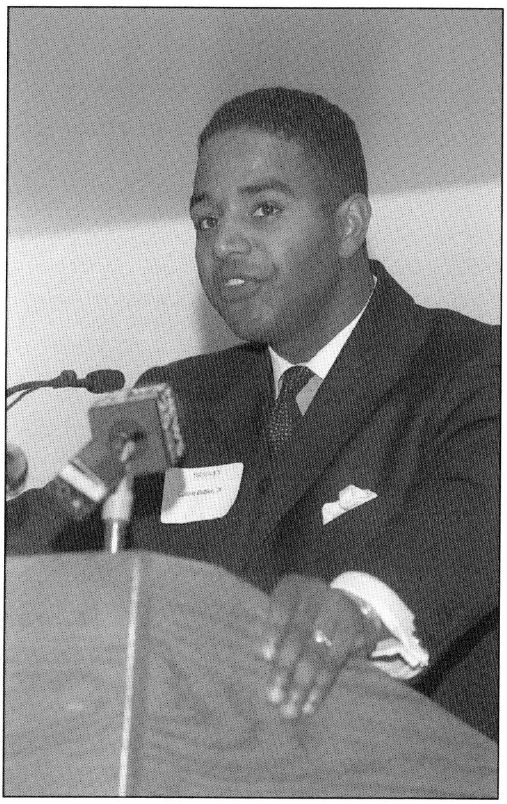

Calvin Butler, a 1991 graduate of Bradley, is famous for becoming Student Body President and for confronting the White supremacist Matthew Hale and racism on campus. He is depicted in this 2000 photograph as president of the National Alumni Association addressing the Founder's Day crowd.

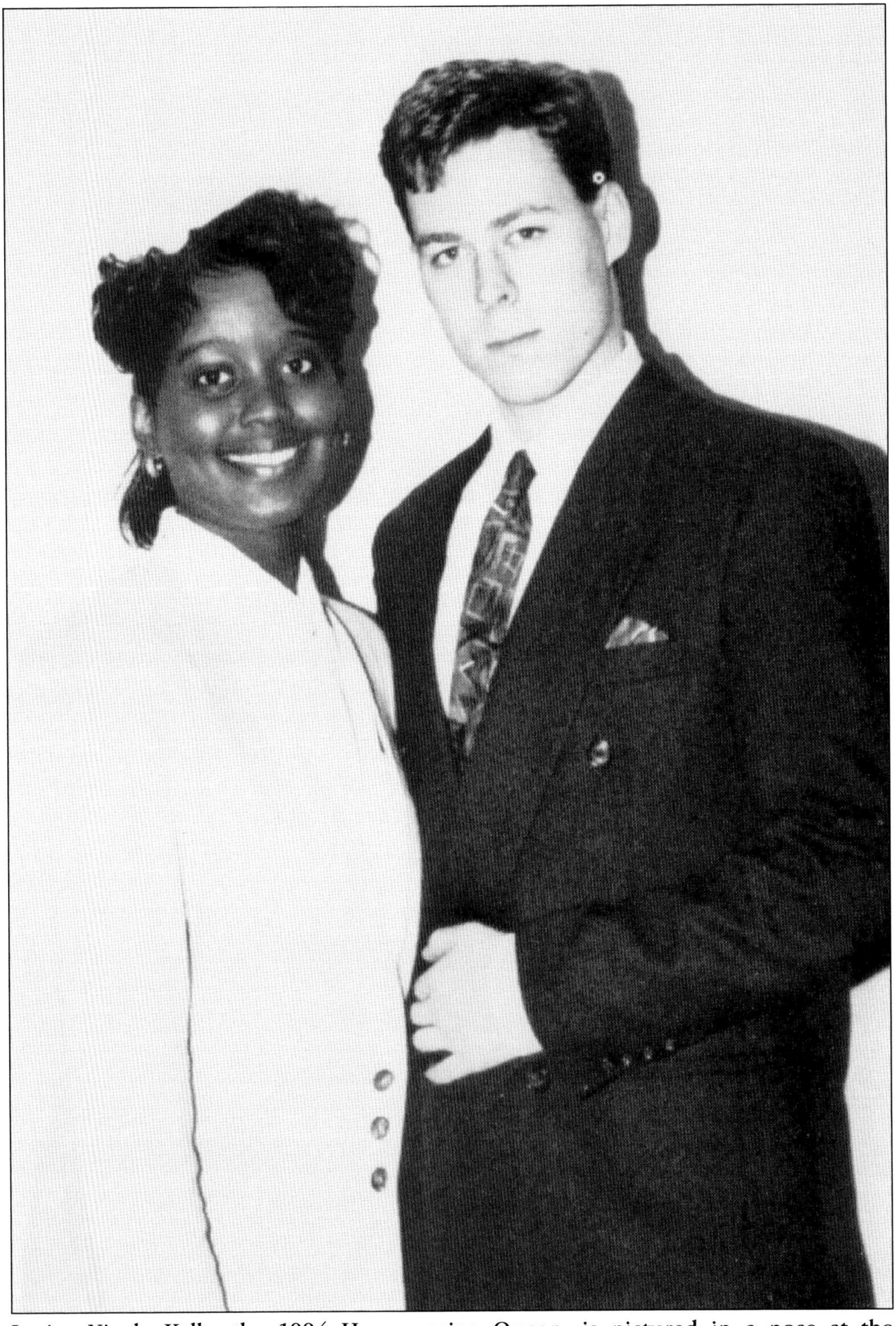

Junior Nicole Kelly, the 1994 Homecoming Queen, is pictured in a pose at the homecoming dance.

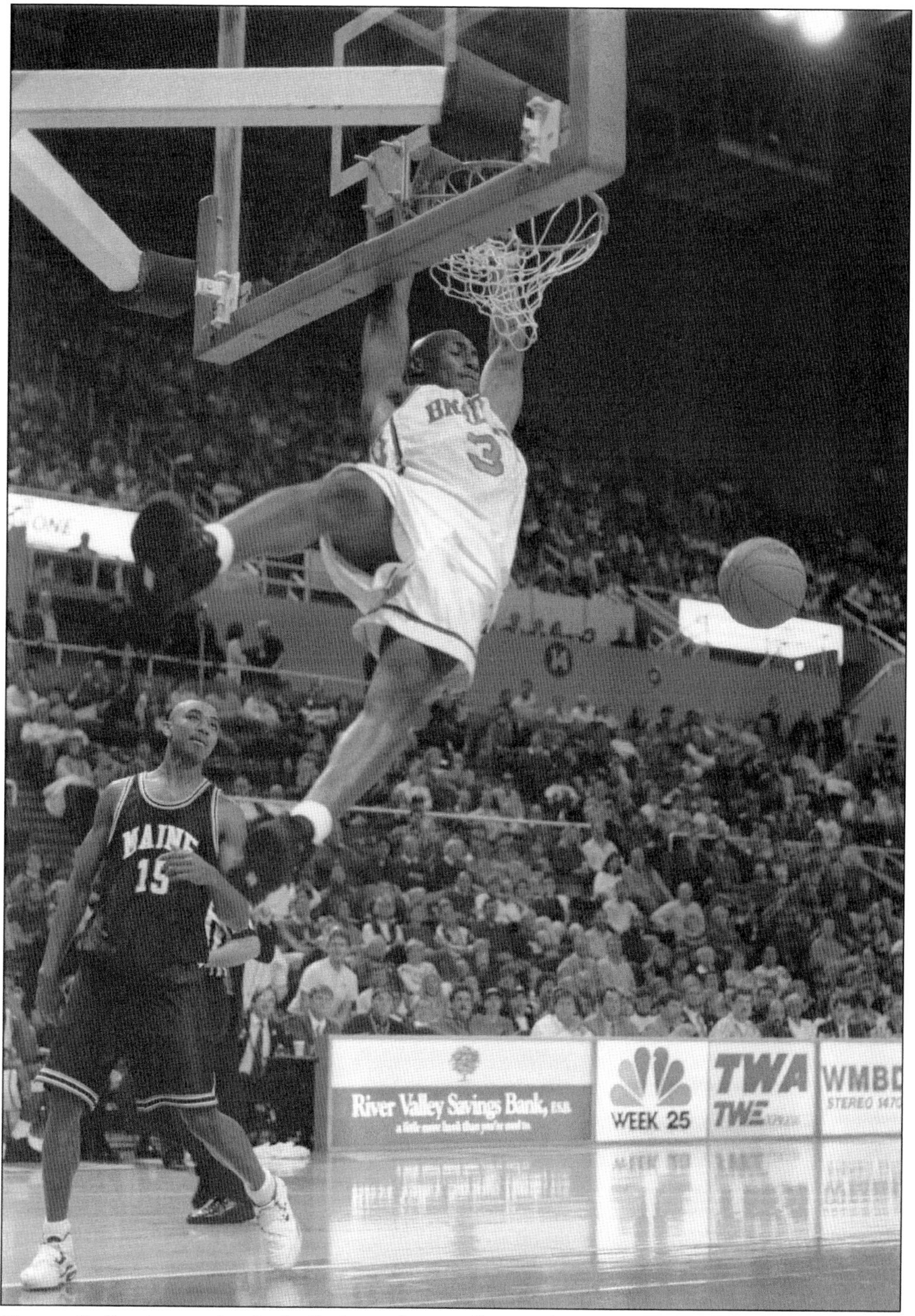

Marcus Pollard, a star basketball player for Bradley, is shown in this 1994 game converting a slam dunk. Pollard is now a professional football player with the Indianapolis Colts.

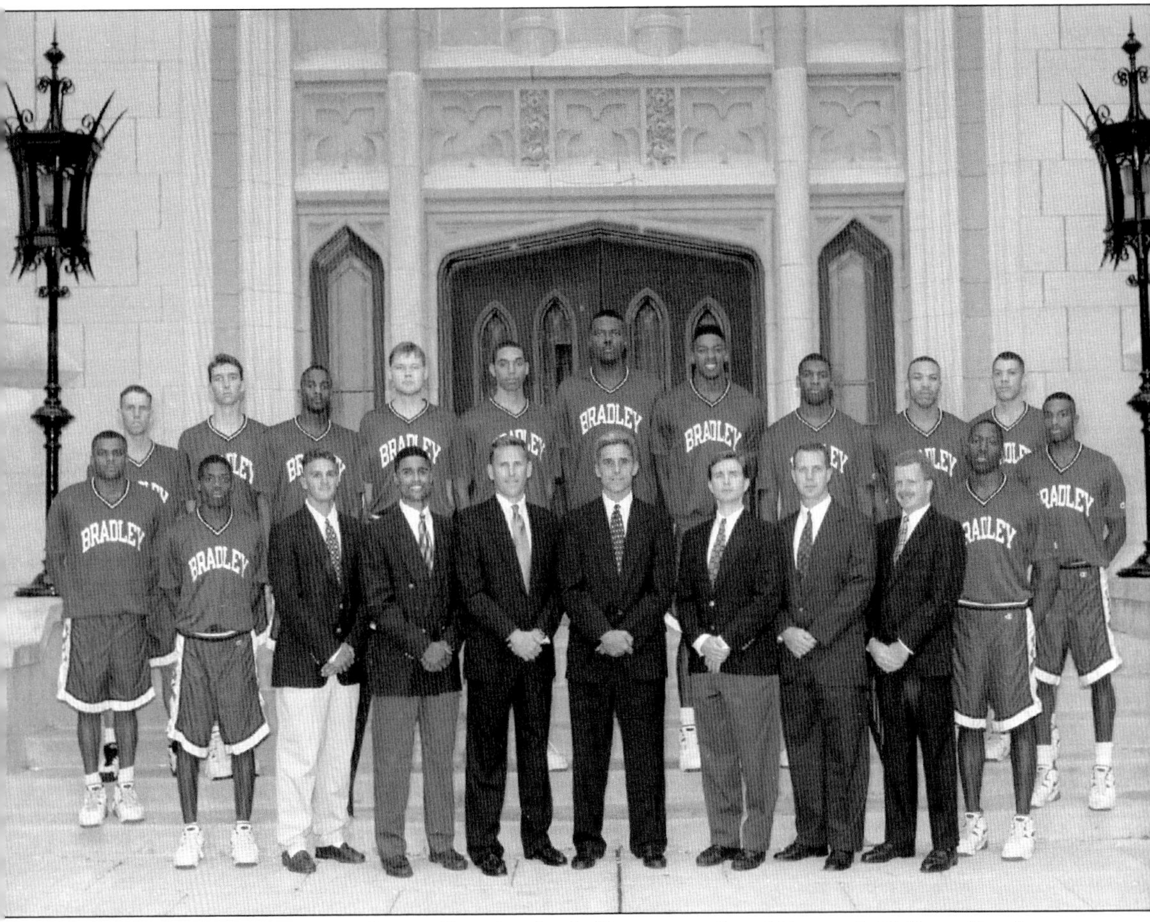

Members of the 1996 Bradley basketball team, the Missouri Valley Conference Champions, are pictured above. The team was also known for its star player Anthony Parker, pictured on the far right in the last row.

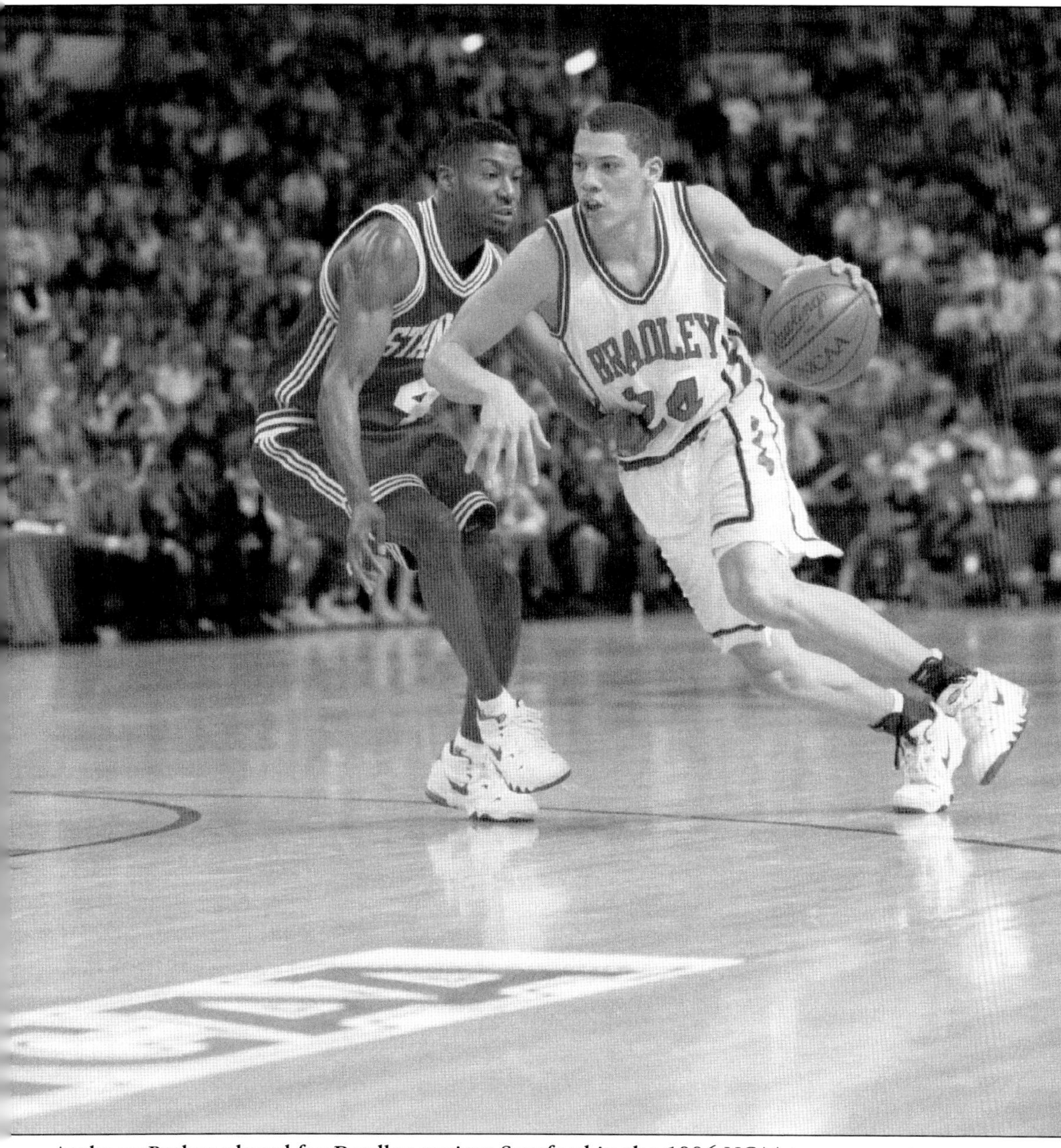

Anthony Parker played for Bradley against Stanford in the 1996 NCAA tournament.

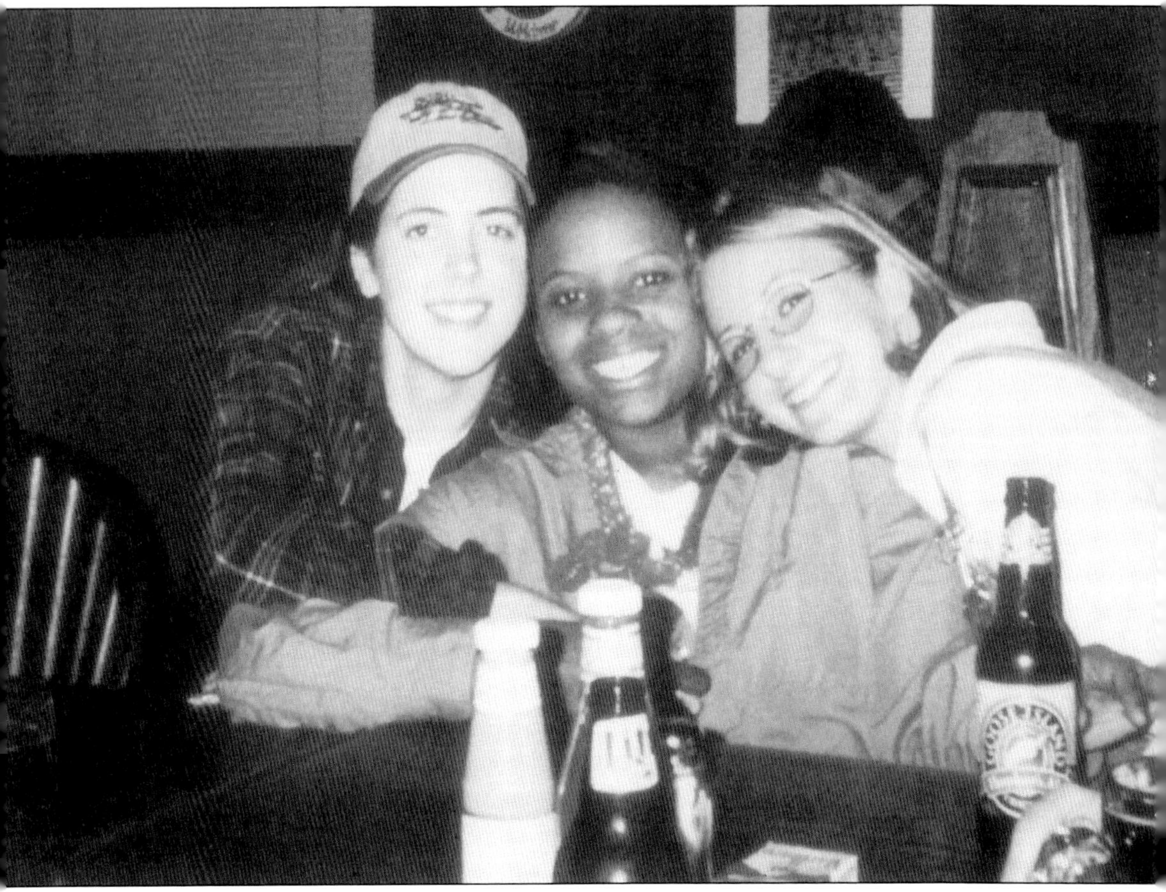

In this 1997 photo, senior Shandell Johnson and two unidentified friends are taking the famous "Senior Walk" in which students spend a day going from bar to bar drinking to celebrate the completion of their senior year at Bradley. It is, to quote an anonymous source from the psychology department, ". . . not to be forgotten."